As You See the Day Approaching

As You See the Day Approaching

Reformed Perspectives on the Last Things

Edited by
THEODORE G. VAN RAALTE

LUCERNA
CRTS PUBLICATIONS

☙PICKWICK *Publications* · Eugene, Oregon

AS YOU SEE THE DAY APPROACHING
Reformed Perspectives on the Last Things

Copyright © 2016 Wipf and Stock Publishers. All rights reserved. Except for brief quotations in critical publications or reviews, no part of this book may be reproduced in any manner without prior written permission from the publisher. Write: Permissions, Wipf and Stock Publishers, 199 W. 8th Ave., Suite 3, Eugene, OR 97401.

Pickwick Publications
An Imprint of Wipf and Stock Publishers
199 W. 8th Ave., Suite 3
Eugene, OR 97401

www.wipfandstock.com

ISBN: 978-1-4982-3406-1

Cataloguing-in-Publication data:

As you see the day approaching : Reformed perspectives on the last things / edited by Theodore G. Van Raalte.

x + 170 p. ; 23 cm. Includes bibliographical references and index.

ISBN: 978-1-4982-3406-1

1. Theology, Doctrinal. 2. Reformed Church—Eschatology. 3. Eschatology. I. Van Raalte, Theodore G.
II. Title.

BT803 A75 2016

Manufactured in the U.S.A.   01/05/2016

Scripture quotations marked (NIV) are taken from the Holy Bible, New International Version©, NIV©. Copyright © 1973, 1978, 1984, and 2011 by Biblica, Inc.© Used by permission. All rights reserved.

Scripture quotations marked (ESV) are taken from The Holy Bible, English Standard Version© (ESV©), copyright © 2001 by Crossway, a publishing ministry of Good News Publishers. Used by permission. All rights reserved.

Scripture quotations marked (RSV) are taken from the Revised Standard Version of the Bible, copyright © 1946, 1952, and 1971 by the National Council of the Churches of Christ in the United States of America. Used by permission. All rights reserved.

The figures in chapter 3, "Finding Eschatology in the Old Testament: The Psalms as Case in Point," are creations of the author, Jannes Smith.

The image of John Calvin in Figure 2 is in the public domain (Wikimedia Commons, https://commons.wikimedia.org/wiki/File:Calvin_1562.jpg/).

Contents

Acknowledgments | vii
Contributors | ix

1. Eschatology, or Doctrine concerning the End Times: An Introduction | 1
   —*Theodore G. Van Raalte*

2. Adam, Moses, and Christ: Pauline Pneumatology and the Pattern of Argument in 1 Cor 15:42–49 and 2 Cor 3:6–18 | 20
   —*Lane G. Tipton*

3. Finding Eschatology in the Old Testament: The Psalms as Case in Point | 36
   —*Jannes Smith*

4. Working Politically and Socially in Anticipation of Christ's Coming | 54
   —*Cornelis Van Dam*

5. In Between and Intermediate: My Soul in Heaven's Glory | 70
   —*Theodore G. Van Raalte*

6. Is Hell Obsolete? The Place of Eternal Punishment in Preaching Today | 112
   —*Jason Van Vliet*

7. A New Earth? | 134
   —*Gerhard H. Visscher*

8. "Until He Comes": Eschatological Aspects of the Reformed Worship Service | 143
   —*Arjan de Visser*

Subject and Names Index | 159
Scripture Index | 163

Acknowledgments

BOOKS, OF COURSE, DO not produce themselves.

The contents of this volume began to take shape in the Spring of 2014, when the planning committee for the annual conference of the Canadian Reformed Theological Seminary (CRTS) of Hamilton, Ontario, began to discuss with the conference speakers what topics they would address at the next (January 2015) conference. We thank this committee of students, professors, staff, and one minister—Jeremy DeHaan, William DenHollander, Leanne Kuizenga, John Smith, John Van Popta, and Ted Van Raalte—for their careful planning. Once the Senate had approved their proposal regarding the presenters and speech titles, they took care of everything. Thanks to them, the conference ran like a well-oiled machine. Whether it was sound, food, supplies, accompaniment to the singing, moderating, programs, parking, etc., everything was completed in a professional manner and on time. Thank you all most warmly!

The seminary community was very pleased to have Lane Tipton, professor of systematic theology at Westminster Seminary in Philadelphia join us for the conference and give the opening speech. Please come again!

We thank the respondents who helped stimulate discussion at our conference, namely, Karlo Janssen, Bill DeJong, André Schutten, and George Van Popta. They had copies of four of the papers ahead of time, and each man gave a five-minute response. Although, per the plan, we are not publishing these brief responses, we truly appreciate their time and expertise. And to all our attendees, especially those who made comments and asked questions, we express our appreciation. Some of the papers have benefited from further reflection, including reflection upon the discussions at the conference.

The Ebenezer Canadian Reformed Church of Burlington is hereby acknowledged for the use of their most suitable facilities and their wonderful

Acknowledgments

army of volunteers who help in the kitchen. Bruce Hartman gave his time as audio-video technician. Immediately upon the conference's close he provided us with a very good quality set of CD and DVD recordings. These are now hosted at canadianreformedseminary.ca. Martin Jongsma encouraged our singing by his spirited accompaniment on the organ.

This volume is now the second to appear under the *Lucerna: CRTS Publications* logo, a series connected to the Publication Fund of CRTS. We are thankful that this fund can offer assistance where needed, to see the volume to print. We're also pleased to have had the manuscript accepted by Wipf & Stock, and we intend to continue publishing with them.

While I remain responsible for any remaining oversights and errors, I am most indebted to Bill Helder for his meticulous attention to detail and his relentless consistency in copy editing each of the essays. Thank-you!

The faculty of CRTS prays that this volume will increase the fervency and the clarity of the church's prayer: Come, Lord Jesus!

On behalf of the faculty of CRTS,

Ted Van Raalte

Contributors

Dr. Lane G. Tipton, PhD, is the Charles W. Krahe Professor of Systematic Theology at Westminster Theological Seminary in Philadelphia, Pennsylvania.

Dr. Jannes Smith, PhD, is the Professor of Old Testament at the Canadian Reformed Theological Seminary in Hamilton, Ontario.

Dr. Cornelis Van Dam, ThD, is the Emeritus Professor of Old Testament at the Canadian Reformed Theological Seminary in Hamilton, Ontario.

Dr. Theodore G. Van Raalte, PhD, is the Professor of Ecclesiology at the Canadian Reformed Theological Seminary in Hamilton, Ontario.

Dr. Jason P. Van Vliet, ThD, is the Professor of Dogmatics at the Canadian Reformed Theological Seminary in Hamilton, Ontario.

Dr. Gerhard H. Visscher, PhD, is the Professor of New Testament at the Canadian Reformed Theological Seminary in Hamilton, Ontario.

Dr. Arjan de Visser, ThD, is the Professor of Diaconiology at the Canadian Reformed Theological Seminary in Hamilton, Ontario.

1

Eschatology, or Doctrine concerning the End Times

An Introduction

Theodore G. Van Raalte

IN 1841 A NEW word entered the English language. Both that year and the next saw the dawn of "eschatology" as a translation of an almost equally new word in another language: the German *Eschatologie*.[1] The word was explained as "doctrine concerning the last things."[2] As such, in both the German and English, it came straight out of Greek, *logos* meaning "study of" or "doctrine of," and *eschatos* meaning "last," "farthest," or "final" (in the New Testament *ta eschata* means "the last things").[3] Nevertheless, prior to

---

1. Neander, *History of the Christian Religion*, xlviii (1841; German edition, 1827, xxv); Tholuck, *Epistle to the Hebrews*, vol. 1, 93 (1842; German edition, 1840, 91). It is possible that there are earlier instances, but I have not found any. According to the *Digitale Wörterbuch der deutschen Sprache*, the word first appeared in German in the nineteenth century, based on the Greek, *ta eschata*, "the last things." See http://www.dwds.de/?qu=eschatologie. Accessed August 19, 2015. See also Mühling, *Handbook of Eschatology*, 3–4.

2. The German was "Lehre von den leßten Dingen."

3. "Eschatology," though etymologically rooted in Greek, first emerged in Latin as *eschatologia*, then appeared in German, then in English. Literature on the topic often notes

about 1900 an "eschaton" in English was a small interval in music and had nothing to do with theology.

In contrast, since about 1900, theologians have frequently used "eschaton" as a word in English for the end-time period itself, and they casually bandy about the term "eschatology" as if everyone knows what the words mean. Some teach that Christians are already in the eschaton; others that it will commence with Christ's return. *The Concise Oxford English Dictionary* (2004) lists "eschatology" as a noun meaning "the part of theology concerned with death, judgment, and destiny." For the most part, the present volume uses the word in this traditional sense. However, more needs to be said.

Analysis suggests that there are three distinct ways in which the word "eschatology" is being used by theologians today. First, there is the most traditional usage, noted above. Although the word itself was coined later, it represents a topic in theology that reaches back to the medieval era and treats of the "last things."[4] Second, there is a more philosophical usage that began to develop in the early twentieth century with scholars such as Barth, Bultmann, Moltmann, and Pannenberg. Third, one encounters a more orthodox development that may have actually preceded the more philosophical usage of the term. This development begins especially with Geerhardus Vos, and in many cases "eschatological" is a synonym for the term "redemptive-historical." While it is the first and third usages that interest us most, we will also review the second.

THE TWENTIETH CENTURY AND ESCHATOLOGY

David Fergusson introduces a series of essays on Christian eschatology as follows: "One of the distinctive features of twentieth-century theology has been the recovery of interest and confidence in eschatology."[5] Carl Braaten and Robert Jenson agree, writing, "The twentieth century will be remembered in the history of theology for its rediscovery of the centrality

---

the first Latin uses as found in a few early seventeenth-century Lutheran theologians. For example, see Sauter, "Concept of Eschatology," 499, and Betz, *Encyclopedia*, 4: 544.

4. Latin works of theology commonly called this locus *novissima, de novissimis,* or *de extremis*. See also note 3.

5. Fergusson, "Introduction," in *Future as God's Gift*, 1. Pannenberg and others speak of the "eschatological turn." See, for instance, Pannenberg, *Systematic Theology*, vol. 3, 84–88.

of eschatology in the message of Jesus and early Christianity." But they add an equally interesting comment, "But it reached no consensus on the shape and meaning of that eschatology."[6] The three usages traced above help explain why this was the case.

Indeed, the renewed emphasis on eschatology did not mean a focus on the end-times and the traditional topics of our death, Christ's return, judgment, heaven, hell, and the new creation. To explain these new emphases, we will first note the effects of the Enlightenment and of Hegelian philosophy, then review several Reformed theologians who were at the fringes of Reformed orthodoxy (Barth, Pannenberg, and others). This will flesh out the more philosophical usage. To introduce the redemptive-historical usage of the term, I will present several theologians (Vos, Ridderbos, Gaffin) whose views were and are in agreement with the confessional Reformed orthodoxy espoused by the contributors to the current volume. Reviewing these distinct usages will help set the stage for the contribution this volume of essays wishes to make. Readers with minimal background knowledge of philosophy and liberal theology could profitably skip the following paragraphs and resume reading where I begin to deal with Geerhardus Vos, but because of the significant role played, still today, by Barth and Pannenberg, some analysis of their contributions must be included.

LIBERAL ENLIGHTENMENT THEOLOGY

First, throughout the nineteenth century, influences of Enlightenment thinking among European philosophers and theologians cast doubt upon the biblical claims of miracles and prophecy. These doubts extended to the biblical teachings about life after death, so that liberal theologians began to focus only on the here and now, spinning out a Christianity that was all about the ethics of imitating Jesus and had little to say about an afterlife. Around 1900, New Testament theologians such as Albert Schweitzer (1875–1965) agreed that Jesus himself and early Christians had expectations that the coming of God's kingdom was imminent, but he concluded that unfortunately Jesus had been mistaken.[7] According to Schweitzer, Jesus himself was not even raised from the dead.

At the same time German theologians had been developing a stronger appreciation for history, in line with the prestige of Hegelian philosophy.

---

6. Braaten and Jenson, "Preface," in *The Last Things*, vii.
7. Runia, "Eschatology," 105–106.

Development and progress became important motifs in philosophy and theology. These motifs played into an organic, evolutionary, and optimistic eschatology, but not a biblical eschatology wherein the resurrection of Christ powerfully opens the way into a new creation. Rather, humanity would just continue to self-improve until the utopian future was reached. In this case both the secular and the Christian views coalesced in a postmillennial optimism.[8] The practice of an ethic of love in the present was the way into this higher and better future, and the signs of reaching this were apparently ubiquitous.

KARL BARTH (1886–1968)

After the First World War, the optimism just noted had been crushed. The great Karl Barth (1886–1968) declared God's judgment on such self-assured views, for they omitted attention to God's awesome righteousness, man's utter sinfulness, and God's intervening sovereign grace in Jesus Christ as the only hope for anything new.

Barth argued that everyone needs to account for the always-present divine judgment that creates a situation of crisis and tension for every person. Crisis, not progress, became his byword: "The eschaton is 'the existential crisis of man living constantly at the brink of God's eternity.'" In his view, every person is faced with the choice for or against Christ and will only find him in the midst of one's own existential crisis in the encounter with the Word. As a result, "If Christianity be not *altogether thoroughgoing eschatology*, there remains in it no relationship with Christ."[9] Barth's view thus represented a radical shift from the liberal theologians who preceded him and from the traditional topics of eschatology as found in Reformed theology (resurrection, judgment, heaven, hell, new creation). The latter he called a "short and perfectly harmless chapter at the end of dogmatics."[10] What Barth meant by eschatology is not easily explained, given his peculiar mix of theology and philosophy.[11] But clearly eschatology became much

---

8. Mühling, *Handbook of Eschatology*, 229–35.
9. As quoted in Runia, "Eschatology," 107 (emphasis added).
10. Ibid., 106.
11. Barth's theology advances dialectically and he develops his own unique metaphysics of time, eternity, existential crisis, and actualism in such a way that it is difficult to explain one part without explaining the whole package. The central point is the "event of the word," by which divine revelation occurs, and Barth has directly tied this

Eschatology, or Doctrine concerning the End Times

more than just a topic within theology—Christianity was to be "thoroughgoing eschatology" that, unlike Schweitzer and the liberals, took divine judgment seriously. Eschatology became a window into all of theology, a vista from which to get the right perspective on everything.

While we could review the ways in which other theologians, such as Rudolf Bultmann (1884–1976) and Jürgen Moltmann (1926–), used the term "eschatology," we will focus momentarily on Wolfhart Pannenberg (1928–2014), one of the most prolific and important theologians of the late twentieth century.[12] He spoke of eschatology probably much more than Barth, though what he meant by the term is not always clear or coherent.

WOLFHART PANNENBERG (1928–2014)

Pannenberg gave the "future" a kind of present reality, as if it exists now, though not fully. He then made this future determinative of all our present knowledge of God and of our task in this world. He took the position that God will be fully revealed only when history reaches its end. Orthodox Reformed believers can agree with the latter statement as such, but before we agree with what Pannenberg means by it, we need to understand why he emphasized this and what he meant by it.

Pannenberg was looking for a new foundation for our talk about God (that is, our theology). He did not want to say that God revealed himself by his past deeds as recorded in Scripture and that he continues to reveal himself through the scriptural record. This would root theology in the past and present, both of which are incomplete as revelations of God. In fact, even *God himself* will only become fully actual or real at the end, the eschaton. Christiaan Mostert summarizes, "Indeed, I call Pannenberg's doctrine of God *eschatological*."[13] Similarly, humans are said to exist "only in anticipation of that which they will be in the light of their final future, the advent of God."[14] Therefore, the future exists now as a kind of power or thing more real than the past or present because the future is more "full"

---

to "eschatology."

12. For an excellent overview of noteworthy theologians from c. 1950 to 2000 on this topic, see Runia, "Eschatology," 105–35.

13. Mostert, *God and the Future*, 2. That is to say, Pannenberg's explanation of the nature of God himself is thoroughly eschatological.

14. Cooper, *Panentheism*, 277.

of being. Existence and being are then rooted in the future because that is where God and humanity will be fully reconciled.

In philosophical terms, Pannenberg espoused a kind of reverse causality, where the future causes the present and past. Pannenberg wrote, "We see the present as an effect of the future, in contrast to the conventional assumption that past and present are the cause of the future."[15] Various authors have called this notion counterintuitive. Cooper asks, "How can anything not yet actual have positive power? . . . In my view, [Pannenberg's] ontology of the future is counterintuitive and philosophically unconvincing."[16] The incoherence only increases when Pannenberg insists that the path from here to the future is not determined in its course; there is freedom for reality to develop one way or another. If this is the case, what future is actually exerting its power in the present? Not only is the future not yet actual, but its final shape is not yet determined. This has led some critics to associate his views with process theology, though this may be incorrect.[17]

What's at least obvious is that for Pannenberg eschatology became the foundation and driving force of all of theology and of the Christian life, even for all existence. What is here and now derives its reality from the future; eschatology is underneath everything. Eschatology became a catchword for an entire philosophical approach, a metaphysics as such.

Unfortunately, although Pannenberg was of Reformed persuasion, his view of the nature of the reconciliation of the divine and human was not within the pale of Christian orthodoxy. John Cooper argues convincingly that Pannenberg put the world's existence inside God, "within the Triune life of God, which he thinks of as an infinite, all-inclusive force field."[18] This puts Pannenberg in the circle of panentheists rather than theists. He failed to maintain a clear demarcation line between the Creator and his creation/creatures.

---

15. As quoted in Zehnder, "Pannenberg's Eschatology," 125.

16. Cooper, *Panentheism*, 281. Zehnder states that Pannenberg's system strains the limits of "logical coherence," and demands "a counterintuitive notion of reality based on quite novel interpretations of Jesus' message and the utopian philosophy of Ernst Bloch." Zehnder, "Pannenberg's Eschatology," 126–27. Mostert also uses the word "counterintuitive." Mostert, *God and the Future*, 238.

17. See a Pannenberg's response to a question about this in an interview. http://thomasjayoord.com/index.php/blog/archives/pannenberg_dies_an_interview. Accessed August 17, 2015.

18. Cooper, *Panentheism*, 260; compare 276–77.

Eschatology, or Doctrine concerning the End Times

In conclusion, although Pannenberg's way of describing Christ as the one in whom this future has already been fully realized is (as will be pointed out in the following pages) quite capable of orthodox understanding, his wider framework of thought elicits significant concerns from Reformed theologians.[19]

OTHER EUROPEAN REFORMED THEOLOGIANS

Similar ideas, by which eschatology was made determinative for all of theology, were voiced by Arnold A. van Ruler (1908–1972), professor of theology at Utrecht.[20] Hendrikus Berkhof (1914–1995) and Gerrit C. Berkhouwer (1903–1996), two other twentieth-century Dutch professors, also paid much more attention to eschatology than had their predecessors.[21] Klaas Schilder (1890–1952) maintained a much more intuitive view of eschatology than Pannenberg later would, for Schilder considered the beginning of history, with the good creation and the subsequent fall into sin, as determinative of the history that followed. Schilder's theology witnesses to an abiding emphasis on eschatology in terms of God's progressive revelation of himself in real human history. His important monographs on the nature of heaven and hell and on the Book of Revelation represented deep explorations in eschatology.[22]

REFORMED INSIGHTS I:
GEERHARDUS VOS (1862–1949)

There are elements of truth in the approaches that make eschatology hegemonic for all of theology, or at least, for soteriology. It is true that in Christ the beginning of the new creation already exists, for he has been glorified in body and soul. One could say that in Christ the end or eschaton is here. Believers today do live with an anticipatory "already" of who we are in Christ

---

19. According to Runia's interpretation of Pannenberg, even Christ's resurrection "is no more than an anticipation and has a provisional quality." Runia, "Eschatology," 113. For another critique of Pannenberg, see Walsh, "Futurity and Creation," 104–13.

20. Runia, "Eschatology," 115.

21. Ibid., 117–21.

22. Ibid., 121. See Schilder, *De openbaring*, Schilder, *Wat is de hemel?*; and Schilder, *Wat is de hel?* For a study of *Wat is de hemel*, see Kamphuis, "Schilder on Heaven," 101–12. Kamphuis characterizes Schilder's theology as "the theology of expectation." Ibid., 106.

combined with the frustrating "not-yet" of our present experience of sin. But these truths need to be rooted firmly in Scripture, the principle external source for our knowledge of Christ, salvation, and the future. In this regard the orthodox Reformed theologian Geerhardus Vos, professor of biblical theology at Princeton from 1893 to 1932, blessed the church with some wonderful insights. With Vos we now come to the third of our three ways in which the term "eschatology" is used—in which "eschatological" often functions as a synonym for "redemptive-historical."

Gaffin summarizes the relationship of Vos's usage to the traditional usage very helpfully in his foreword to the republication of Vos's *The Pauline Eschatology* (1979; originally published in 1930). He writes,

> The title of this volume can be misleading. The reader who understands "eschatology" in its conventional, still popular sense will expect a specialized study limited to those "last things" associated with the second coming of Christ. The author, however, intends something more. *His basic thesis is that to unfold Paul's eschatology is to set forth his theology as a whole, not just his teaching on Christ's return.*
>
> Few developments in biblical studies over the past century are of such far-reaching importance as the increasing recognition of the New Testament writers' broadened understanding of eschatology. Christ's coming, culminating in his death and resurrection, takes place "in the fullness of time (s)" (Gal 4:4; Eph 1:10), in "these last days" (Heb 1:2), at "the end of the ages" (Heb 9:26), in the fully eschatological sense. The present experience of those united by faith to Christ in his suffering and exaltation (Gal 2:20; Eph 2:5, 6; Col 3:1), not only their future, is essentially eschatological; the Christian life is an eschatological life.
>
> Vos was a pioneer in calling attention to this fundamental datum of New Testament teaching—*what can be termed its eschatological, redemptive-historical orientation.* His brief but perceptive volume, *The Kingdom and the Church* (1903), pointed out the eschatological nature of the kingdom proclaimed by Jesus as not only future but present in his person and work. It is also worth noting that *The Pauline Eschatology* first appeared in the same year (1930) as the German original of Albert Schweitzer's *The Mysticism of Paul the Apostle* ... Vos's treatment, however, is much more balanced and true to Paul, faithfully capturing the controlling eschatological motif of his teaching.[23]

---

23. Gaffin, "Foreword," in Vos, *The Pauline Eschatology*, i–ii (emphasis added).

Eschatology, or Doctrine concerning the End Times

Vos calls the apostle Paul "the father of Christian eschatology." He considers Paul under divine inspiration to have taken the various strands of eschatological teaching already present in the Scriptures, gathered them together, and woven them "into a compact, well-rounded system, so coherent, that, speaking after the manner of man, it became next to impossible for any of the precious texture henceforth to be lost."[24]

He notices that believers in the New Testament were conscious of being in the last days or at least of living very close to them. According to the New Testament, the "fullness of the times" refers to the designated time for the Messiah's appearing; he is the last Adam (in Greek: the *eschatos* Adam) with whom the "end of the ages" has come upon believers.[25] This affects the way believers think about their fundamental identity, victory over sin, presence of the Holy Spirit, and guarantee of fully enjoying all that has been promised. All the teachings about Christ, us, and our living are affected by what has happened in Christ in these last days.

Vos explains this by noting that a mere temporal scheme in which the present age is distinct in time from the age to come is insufficient. Instead, he proposes that with the resurrection of Christ the world-to-come has been realized in principle. Believers are not merely moving forward in time towards the end, but they have in principle been moved upwards into the heavenly realms, into a new kind of existence, and it is in this existence that they are now moving forward. God truly did something fundamentally *new* in the sending of his Son, and particularly in the *resurrection*.[26] Thus, Paul writes, "And God raised us up with Christ and seated us with him in the heavenly realms in Christ Jesus" (Eph 2:6). This blessing had already filled Paul with praise at the beginning of the same letter: "Praise be to the God and Father of our Lord Jesus Christ, who has blessed us in the heavenly realms with every spiritual blessing in Christ" (Eph 1:3). Believers "have been raised with Christ" and their lives "are now hidden with Christ in God" (Col 3:1–3).

These sorts of exegetical observations led Vos to write, "Not only the Christology but also the Soteriology of the Apostle's teaching is so closely interwoven with the Eschatology, that, were the question put, which of the strands is more central, which more peripheral, the eschatology would have

---

24. Vos, "Preface," in *The Pauline Eschatology*, v.
25. Vos, *The Pauline Eschatology*, 8, 10, 26.
26. Ibid., 38–39. See Vos's diagram on p. 38, n. 45.

as good a claim to the central place as the others."[27] The New Testament presents the work of Christ in such lofty terms as to make all that came before him seem but shadowy and ephemeral.[28] Some of the most powerful expressions of positive emotion in the New Testament are tied to the Christian's hope, because the reality of the unseen hope has, in Christ, become so real.[29]

One could write much more about Vos, but we can at least appreciate that Vos prescribes an eschatological perspective for much, if not all, of our theology because he sees the progress of God's work of redemption in Christ as central to the gospel.

REFORMED INSIGHTS II: HERMAN RIDDERBOS (1909–2007)

Herman Ridderbos was a Reformed Dutch theologian who also highlighted eschatology. Some of his key works have been translated into English. He studied in great detail all that Jesus preached regarding the coming of the kingdom, and emphasized, in contrast to the nineteenth-century liberals and others, that Jesus' kingdom had both arrived and was yet coming in fullness.[30] He also cultivated a redemptive-historical approach to the New Testament teachings regarding the identity of believers in Christ. Thus he writes, "The great change of which Paul's preaching bears testimony is not in the first place the reversal in his mind with regard to the *ordo salutis*, but first and foremost with regard to the *historia salutis* in the objective sense of the word."[31] In other words (to give a sympathetic interpretation), believers in the Old and New Testaments were all saved in the same way: by grace through faith in the Messiah, but in the New the great change is the huge leap forward that God has made in history concerning the gift of salvation/redemption through the work of Christ. That leap is rightly termed

---

27. Ibid., 29.
28. See the essay by Tipton in the present collection.
29. Vos, *The Pauline Eschatology*, 31–35.
30. Ridderbos, *The Coming of the Kingdom*, 61–184.
31. Ridderbos, *When the Time Had Fully Come*, 48. *Historia salutis* is Latin for "history of salvation" and, according to Gaffin, was coined by Ridderbos as a contrast to the more common term, *ordo salutis*. The latter refers to a logical or causal order of the application of salvation benefits to the believer, whereas the former refers to the history of the work of God accomplishing salvation in the sending of the Messiah. See Gaffin, *By Faith*, 21; and Gaffin, "Biblical Theology," 167–68.

Eschatology, or Doctrine concerning the End Times

"eschatological" because in Christ God has truly brought the church into the last days, the eschaton. Ridderbos relates these teachings of Paul to Christ as follows: "Paul does nothing but explain the eschatological reality which in Christ's teachings is called the Kingdom."[32]

Ridderbos, however, was criticized for his repeated attacks upon Reformed theology's attention to the *ordo salutis*. One sympathetic critic included Richard Gaffin, to whom we turn next.[33]

REFORMED INSIGHTS III: RICHARD GAFFIN (1936–)

For Richard (Dick) Gaffin, the centrality of the resurrection of Christ stands out as the great inaugural event of the eschaton. I might put it this way: If we put our feet in the shoes of members of the early church, it quickly becomes clear to us that the most amazing historical event for them was not the crucifixion but the resurrection. Crucifixion, after all, was a well-known Roman method suffered by many slaves, a torturous death that served as a warning for others. Of course, the results of the Messiah's crucifixion and his divine-human personhood are one-of-a-kind, and these points are much proclaimed in the Scriptures. But the resurrection was a first-ever in every sense, both as historical event and in terms of results. It was that unknown and impossible thing which the philosophers at Athens scoffed about. But the church held on to the resurrection as the new and wondrous act that God had accomplished at the end of history, so that the Spirit could go out finally to gather God's elect from all the nations. Christ had indeed risen, never again to suffer and die.[34]

Precisely because Gaffin understands the resurrection of Christ to play a central role in Paul's soteriology, he also makes eschatology central, for the resurrection of Christ as the firstfruits and the firstborn (1 Cor 15:12–20; Col 1:18, etc.) is the beginning of the new creation and therefore a matter of eschatology.[35] Gaffin argues that "whatever treatment Paul gives

---

32. Ridderbos, *When the Time Had Fully Come*, 48–49.

33. For examples of Gaffin's criticism, see Gaffin, *Resurrection and Redemption*, 42, 56; and Gaffin, "Biblical Theology," 167. For a wider discussion, see Fesko, *Beyond Calvin*, 59–70.

34. Other persons whose resurrections from the dead are recorded in Scripture, died again. Christ rose never to die again.

35. Gaffin, *Resurrection and Redemption*, 35–41.

to the application of salvation to the individual believer is controlled by his redemptive-historical outlook."[36] That is, the events of the cross, resurrection, ascension, and pouring out of the Spirit are the most central works of God, and only out of them flow union of the believer with Christ, and thus the benefits of adoption, justification, sanctification, and glorification.[37]

Gaffin, together with Ridderbos and Vos, has not been without critics, particularly as regards the characterization of the Reformed orthodox and their views on union with Christ and justification.[38] But Gaffin's statements on these points have always been tentative and open to correction. Also, other historians have come to Gaffin's defense.[39] The present work does not delve into this debate or take a stand on it, but clearly the essay by Tipton builds upon Gaffin's and Vos's detailed attention to 1 Corinthians 15 and its teachings about the resurrection.[40]

The present volume approaches eschatology with the big-picture insights of Vos and Gaffin, while also treating various sub-topics of the traditional locus of theology called "eschatology." We do not work with the second of the three usages that have just been explained.

WHAT ABOUT PRE-, A-, AND POSTMILLENNIALISM?

Some readers' contact with eschatology may be primarily through questions regarding the thousand-year reign of Christ, the "millennium" (see Revelation 20). Specifically, will he return before his millennial reign (premillennialism), after it (postmillennialism), or is there actually no *literal* one-thousand-year period of his reign (amillennialism)? As the conference committee worked with the conference speakers to decide on topics, it became clear that in the interests of time and energy this topic had to be left aside. Not that no one is interested. Particularly the postmillennial option and its associated question of preterism has a robust place in Reformed theology. Further, premillennialism continues to have a large following in North America (think of the *Left Behind* series).

---

36. Ibid., 29.
37. Gaffin, *By Faith*, 23–30, 49–59, 123–25.
38. For example, Fesko, *Beyond Calvin*, 17–24, 63–70.
39. For example, Jones, "Foreword," in Gaffin, *By Faith, Not by Sight*, 2nd ed., vii–xiv.
40. Although I have not mentioned Gregory K. Beale in this introductory essay, his exegetical work also builds upon the insights of Vos et al.

Eschatology, or Doctrine concerning the End Times

The committee also considered that our North American culture, awash in luxury and self-indulgence, requires attention to more basic points than the nature or timing of the millennium. Answers to such questions as: Is there a heaven? Is hell really eternal? Do we have souls? and other basic teachings cannot be taken for granted in our multicultural and increasingly secular society.

In James K. A. Smith's analysis, going to the mall turns out to be one of the most common "cultural liturgies."[41] Smith's insights about the worshipful character of shopping at the mall also pertain to the topic of this collection of end-times essays. For it is precisely in a culture of opulence and self-indulgence that concern for one's long-term future falls away. Everything is about the present: neither history nor prophecy receive a prominent voice. Today, speaking of divine judgment is politically incorrect, if not embarrassing.

The North American church, affected by this popular culture, awash in material riches, and seeking academic respectability, wants to be comfortable here, in this world. To many people today, our citizenship on earth means more than our citizenship in "heaven," that is, in the new creation that has begun in Christ. This cultural reality thus challenges us to a re-examination of what Scripture teaches about the end-times. What should we believe and how should we live with a view to the coming of Christ?

The resulting line-up of essays in this book seeks to help Christians answer these questions on the basis of the written Word of God.

OVERVIEW OF THE ESSAYS

Lane Tipton, who teaches systematic theology at Westminster Theological Seminary in Philadelphia, opened our conference with a powerful combination of exegetical insights and spiritual applications that brought out the superior place of the New Testament believer vis-à-vis not only Moses, but even Adam before the fall into sin. This remarkable conclusion flows from the New Testament teaching that believers on earth today already live in the last days, indwelt by the Spirit of Christ, who is the guarantee of their

---

41. Smith, *Desiring the Kingdom*, 19–25, 46–62, etc. Smith's account seeks to analyze the formation of belief patterns as rising from repeated patterns of worship instead of the other way around—a kind of behavioralism. I think his account is one-sided and plays into the hands of physicalists (see chapter 6 of the present volume), but he nevertheless offers some perceptive insights and his remarks about the shopping mall are helpful.

glory. Everything about the believer's life today should be understood from the perspective of the end times: we are in them now, and this makes our time more crowning than any before us in redemptive history. The present days *are* the last day.

Tipton's perspective obviously builds on that of Vos and Gaffin, and this was precisely why we sought his participation in our conference. Interestingly, what he taught, though perhaps forgotten and overlooked—it certainly took many participants by surprise—is not new. One can find it not only in the biblical theology of Geerhardus Vos but also in the dogmatics of Herman Bavinck (1854–1921). According to Jacob Kamphuis, Klaas Schilder's views fully aligned with this also, and Kamphuis offers the following line from Bavinck as the very kind of thing Schilder is saying in *Wat is de hemel?*: "Thus Adam stood not at the end, but at the beginning of the road; his situation was temporary and temporal, it could not remain as it was, and had to go on either to a higher glory or a fall into sin and death."[42] In his *Reformed Dogmatics*, Bavinck added that the Reformed consciously differed from the Lutherans in this regard, and that it was the covenant of works that included this "beautiful thought":

> The covenant of works, accordingly, includes still another beautiful thought. It not only realizes the true and full idea of religion; it also gives expression to the fact that humanity before the fall, though created in God's image, did not yet possess the highest possible blessing. On this point Reformed theology has a primary difference with Lutheran theologians [who taught that] . . . Adam did not have to become anything; he only had to remain what he was . . . That is why in the works of Lutheran theologians . . . the original state of man was frequently pictured in a very exaggerated manner . . . For the Reformed, who walked in the footsteps of Augustine, things were different. According to them, Adam did not possess the highest kind of life. The highest kind of life is the material freedom consisting of not being able to err, sin, or die. It consists in being elevated absolutely above all fear and dread, above every possibility of falling. This highest life is immediately bestowed by grace through Christ upon believers . . . Hence, Christ does not [merely] restore his own to the state of Adam before the fall. He acquired and bestows much more, namely, that which Adam would have received had he not fallen.[43]

---

42. Kamphuis, "Schilder on Heaven," 103–104. See Bavinck, *Reformed Dogmatics*, 2:564 for a later translation of the same passage.

43. Bavinck, *Reformed Dogmatics*, 2:572–3. Readers should consult this whole

Eschatology, or Doctrine concerning the End Times

Hopefully these quotations whet your appetite to turn to the exegesis advanced by Tipton. Having his carefully crafted arguments in print will ensure a wider dissemination of these insights and allow others to reflect carefully upon them. Those who are accustomed to saying that before the fall into sin Adam had everything already and did not need to attain to any higher state will need to consider the scriptural arguments raised by Tipton (and Vos and Bavinck). Further, although Bavinck did not use the term "eschatology" in the quotation above, his statement about "the highest life being immediately bestowed by grace through Christ upon believers" is exactly the sort of thing that Vos and company would call eschatological. Believers have in principle crossed over from death to life (John 5:24).

The next essay, by Jannes Smith, examines the Psalter—so beloved by the church—in order to ascertain the degree of teaching contained within it about the end of one's life and the end of the age. Smith is careful about how teachings are to be derived from the sometimes cryptic expressions of the Psalms. He also gives careful attention to the history of revelation and history of redemption, to avoid reading back the fullness of the New Testament into the text of the Psalms as such. This leads him to distinguish three levels or ways of deriving teachings from the Psalms, namely, explication, implication, and application. Readers will appreciate his careful conclusions, word and concept studies, and warnings against leap-frogging across redemptive history on pogo sticks.

As with Tipton's essay, here, too, a strong connection to the historic Reformed positions obtains, for Smith's distinction between explication and implication, though not exactly like the Westminster Confession's distinction between teachings expressly stated and teachings implied, is similar. The Confession states, "The whole counsel of God concerning all things necessary for his own glory, man's salvation, faith and life, is either expressly set down in Scripture, or by good and necessary consequence may be deduced from Scripture" (WCF, 1.6). Smith considers explication to refer more to the use of Psalm texts as sources for the dogmatic locus of eschatology, while implication refers more to "the redemptive-historical lines and the thrust of the book as a whole, its place in the canon, and its fulfillment in the New Testament age." We encounter here an employment of "eschatology" akin to the Vos–Gaffin usage.

Cornelis Van Dam's topic encourages Christians to work for political and social good within the tension of the already/not-yet situation. Although

---

section. See similar remarks ibid., 3:577.

Christians are considered pilgrims in this world, with a citizenship in the heavenly realms, they are still to seek the well-being of the places where God establishes them. If we are to pray for those in authority over us as per 1 Timothy 2, we cannot fail to act in accordance with our prayers, helping them in every possible way. Van Dam draws instruction from Scripture's accounts of the exiles in Babylon, of Daniel in particular, as well as John the Baptist's and the apostle Paul's ways of relating to the civil authorities. He also engages the two-kingdom views of David Van Drunen, asserting that Christ's rule at God's right hand—surely an eschatological reality, if ever there was one!—gives believers every reason to apply biblical norms to *all* of life. Christians are to work in anticipation of Christ's coming.

One of the strengths of Van Dam's essay is the good balance of encouragement and realism. He realizes that positive change will only happen slowly and cautions us against Kuyperian triumphalism. But he also reminds us that every testimony from Reformed believers seeps into society and affects it like leaven to dough. Citizens of the eschatological kingdom of God belong to the side of the Victor! We suffer, but in order that we may also share in his glory. All our work seeks to partake of, and contribute to, the great "coming of the kingdom" and anticipates the return of our Messiah.

The next three essays were presented in close succession and followed by a panel discussion and question-and-answer period involving all three presenters. The topics covered were hell, the intermediate state, and the new creation. Both Van Vliet and Van Raalte presented truncated versions of their essays; herewith the full text is provided.

Jason Van Vliet took on the difficult doctrine of everlasting punishment in hell. His essay engages varieties of the view that the traditional doctrine of hell should be replaced with some version of annihilationism or universalism. These have been gaining ground via a number of evangelical theologians of the past several decades. Van Vliet helps us understand what the Scriptures mean when they speak of God "destroying" body and soul in hell, or when they speak of the wicked "gnashing their teeth." He also examines passages that speak about God's desiring the salvation of "all." Further, he explains why a finite number of our sins are actually deserving of an infinite punishment. This essay closes with a list of four implications for preaching about hell—very helpful, as our focus is kept on Christ.

Theodore Van Raalte took the backdrop of evolution's materialism and the denial that humans have souls as the impetus for a re-examination of the intermediate state. Is it really true that human souls get separated from their bodies upon death and that personal existence continues, albeit in a reduced state, in the soul? Or are those evangelicals correct who support theistic evolution and who recognize the implication of that in denying the reality of souls? Basing his view on Scripture, and coupling it with a number of theological and philosophical arguments, he vindicates the traditional doctrine. He also suggests that an Aristotelian-Thomistic account of the body-soul relation is more suited to the biblical message than the Platonic-Cartesian version.

Gerhard Visscher takes on the popular talk about "going to heaven." His essay looks beyond the intermediate state, and even beyond the return of Christ, to ask what everlasting blessedness in the new heavens and the new earth will be like. Visscher defends the view that the new creation will be physical. We will enjoy it with our physical bodies and with its plants and trees and mountains. He argues that just as the Flood did not annihilate the earth but purged it, so the fire that Peter speaks of in 2 Peter 3 will purge and refine the earth. The "new" creation should be understood as a "renewed" or renovated creation, not a brand new one, created out of nothing or purely spiritual. In particular, he addresses a crux of interpretation from 2 Pet 3:10, "the earth and the works in it will be found."

Finally, Arjan de Visser closes the present collection—as he brought our conference to its completion—with a study of the eschatological motifs in Reformed liturgy. He examines the ways in which Reformed worship helps believers realize the "already" of what is fully ours in the resurrected and ascended Christ. We are taught to draw upon this reality in order to help us through the "not yet" of suffering in this life. From the moment that we are called to "lift up our hearts to the Lord," to the closing blessing, believers today worship in the era of the "last days." De Visser points out that the ascension of Christ changed worship in both heaven and earth: We are drawn into the holy places of heaven; we join the angels; we are fully accepted because of Christ. Yet we are only tasting the beginning of this: the eschatological already/not-yet tension is well expressed in Reformed worship.

Sermons should have an eschatological urgency; prayers should pray for Christ's coming; baptism looks forward to the moment when we are presented without blemish among the assembly of God's elect in life eternal; the Lord's Supper reminds us to proclaim the Lord's death until he comes, etc. Reformed believers are truly blessed with a forward-looking perspective that is grounded in the riches of who we already are in Christ. When we hold onto these things in faith, we will truly look forward to the return of Christ, with an eschatology that is rooted in love.

The summaries just given show that both the first and third usages of the word "eschatology" function within this collection: sometimes the word is treated as a title for all the teachings about the end-times, but at the same time it can also refer to the wonder of what has happened in Christ's resurrection and ascension, so that we are now in the last days. The far-reaching effects of this truth need to be appreciated.

The contributors pray that these essays will strengthen the faith of God's people as we wait in eager expectation for the fullness of what is already ours in Christ.

BIBLIOGRAPHY

Bavinck, Herman. *Reformed Dogmatics*. 4 vols. Translated by John Vriend. Edited by John Bolt. Grand Rapids: Baker Academic, 2008.

Betz, Hans Dieter, ed. *Religion Past and Present: Encyclopedia of Theology and Religion*. 4th ed. 14 vols. Leiden: Brill, 2007–2013.

Braaten, Carl E., and Robert W. Jenson, eds. *The Last Things: Biblical and Theological Perspectives on Eschatology*. Grand Rapids: Eerdmans, 2002.

Fergusson, David, and Marcel Sarot, eds. *Future as God's Gift: Explorations in Christian Eschatology*. Edinburgh: T&T Clark, 2000.

Fesko, John V. *Beyond Calvin: Union with Christ and Justification in Early Modern Reformed Theology (1517–1700)*. Göttingen: Vandenhoek & Ruprecht, 2012.

Gaffin Jr., Richard B. "Biblical Theology and the Westminster Standards." *Westminster Theological Journal* 65 (2003) 165–79.

———. *By Faith, Not By Sight: Paul and the Order of Salvation*, 2nd ed. Phillipsburg, NJ: Presbyterian & Reformed, 2013. [1st ed., 2006].

———. *Resurrection and Redemption: A Study in Paul's Soteriology*. Phillipsburg, NJ: Presbyterian & Reformed, 1978.

Kamphuis, J. "Schilder on Heaven." In *Always Obedient: Essays on the Teachings of Dr. Klaas Schilder*, edited by J. Geertsema, 101–12. Phillipsburg, NJ: Presbyterian & Reformed, 1995.

Mostert, Christiaan. *God and the Future: Wolfhart Pannenberg's Eschatological Doctrine of God*. London: T&T Clark, 2002.

Mühling, Marcus. *T&T Clark Handbook of Christian Eschatology*. Translated by Jennifer Adams-Massmann and David Andrew Gilland. London: Bloomsbury T&T Clark, 2015.

Neander, August. *The History of the Christian Religion and the Church During the Three First Centuries*. Vol. 2. Translated by Henry John Rose. London: Rivington, 1841.

Pannenberg, Wolfhart. *Systematic Theology*. 3 vols. Translated by Geoffrey W. Bromiley. Grand Rapids: Eerdmans, 2009.

Eschatology, or Doctrine concerning the End Times

Ridderbos, Herman. *The Coming of the Kingdom*. Translated by H. de Jongste. Edited by Raymond O. Zorn. Phillipsburg, NJ: Presbyterian & Reformed, 1962.

———. *When the Time Had Fully Come: Studies in New Testament Theology*. Jordan Station, ON: Paideia, 1982.

Runia, Klaas. "Eschatology in the Second Half of the Twentieth Century." *Calvin Theological Journal* 32 (1997) 105–35.

Sauter, Gerhard. "The Concept and Task of Eschatology—Theological and Philosophical Reflections." *Scottish Journal of Theology* 41 (1988) 499–515.

Schilder, Klaas. *De openbaring van Johannes en het sociale leven*. Delft: Meinema, 1924.

———. *Wat is de hel?* Kampen: Kok, 1932. [earlier editions 1919 & 1920].

———. *Wat is de hemel?* Kampen: Kok, 1935.

Smith, James K. A. *Desiring the Kingdom: Worship, Worldview, and Cultural Formation*. Grand Rapids: Baker Academic, 2009.

Tholuck, August. *A Commentary on the Epistle to the Hebrews*. Vol. 1. Translated by James Hamilton. Edinburgh: T. Clark, 1842.

Vos, Geerhardus. *The Pauline Eschatology*. Phillipsburg: Presbyterian & Reformed, 1991.

Walsh, Brian John. "Futurity and Creation: Explorations in the Eschatological Theology of Wolfart Pannenberg." M.Ph. thesis, Institute for Christian Studies, 1979.

Zehnder, David J. "The Origins and Limitations of Pannenberg's Eschatology." *Journal of the Evangelical Theological Society* 53 (2010) 117–31.

2

Adam, Moses, and Christ
Pauline Pneumatology and the Pattern of Argument in 1 Cor 15:42–49 and 2 Cor 3:6–18

Lane G. Tipton

GEERHARDUS VOS, IN A seminal essay entitled "The Eschatological Aspect of the Pauline Conception of the Spirit,"[1] remarks that the core of Paul's eschatology lies in the sphere—the personal agency—of the Holy Spirit. It is more specifically the Holy Spirit, given to the resurrected and ascended Christ, who inaugurates the eschatological age of the world to come. The presence of the Holy Spirit, given to the resurrected Son of God, marks the realization of the eschatological purpose of God, and those who are united to Christ experience in that Spirit-forged union nothing less than the climax of redemption.

Following the trajectory of Vos, this essay will maintain that Paul characteristically argues from the eschatological fullness that comes in Christ's possession of the Spirit at Pentecost to the relative impotency of everything that preceded, whether that brings into view the prelapsarian

---

1. Vos, "Eschatological Aspect," 91–125.

life of Adam or the redemptive life of the letter mediated though Moses (as a type of Christ).

Given the eschatological fullness of resurrection life that dawns in Christ by the Spirit, everything that preceded it pales by comparison, and this generates in Paul's theology a pattern of theological argument. He compares previous instances of life—Adam's life in the Garden of Eden and redemptive life under the Mosaic covenant—to the fullness of life in Christ by the Spirit and reasons that all forms of life prior to Pentecost seem by comparison death-like. Life, whether before the fall in the covenant of works or after the fall in the Mosaic covenant of grace, is more like death when compared to the eschatological fullness of life in the resurrected Christ, who possesses and conveys the Spirit of life and righteousness.

I want to focus on two texts that advance this point and note the similar pattern of reasoning resident within them. First Corinthians 15:42–49 and 2 Cor 3:6–18, when taken together, argue that neither the mode of life Adam possessed prior to the fall (1 Cor 15:45), nor the forgiveness and stay of life secured through Moses as intercessor (2 Cor 3:6–18 in light of Exodus 32–34), supplies the super-abounding righteousness and life found in Christ, who is the Spirit.

Paul makes this point by using a rhetorical device. He correlates the Adamic and Mosaic epochs with death, even though both supplied life, in order to show how far short each falls of the fullness of life that dawns in Christ, who is raised by the Spirit, and communicates resurrection life in the Spirit to his church. The core of the argument advanced below, then, is that Paul contrasts two forms of sub-eschatological life (Adamic and Mosaic) with the eschatological life in Christ (by the Spirit), rhetorically making a relative contrast in what appear on the surface to be absolute terms. It is Pentecost—Christ raised and endowed with the Spirit—that anchors Paul's point of departure for the relative contrasts he develops in both texts.

FIRST CORINTHIANS 15:42–49[2]

The Natural Body and the Spiritual Body (v. 42–45b)

In the context leading up to verses 42–49, and in light of the question asked in 35b, Paul seeks to clarify that nature of the resurrection body, which is

---

2. This essay will not treat verses 46–49, in order to maintain focus on the comparisons between 1 Corinthians 15 and 2 Corinthians 3, although extending the exegesis

presently realized only in Christ. He makes it clear that different bodies have distinguishing characteristics and different degrees of glory:

> 39 For not all flesh is the same, but there is one kind for humans, another for animals, another for birds, and another for fish. 40 There are heavenly bodies and earthly bodies, but the glory of the heavenly is of one kind, and the glory of the earthly is of another. 41 There is one glory of the sun, and another glory of the moon, and another glory of the stars; for star differs from star in glory. (1 Cor 15:39–41)

The glory of the earthly is of one kind and the glory of the earthly is of another (v. 40). Within the created order different modes of glory exist. In verse 42, he qualifies in a similar way the resurrection body (found only in Christ presently as firstfruits, cf. vv. 20–23) and the dead body of the believer.

In 42–44a, Paul's comparisons and contrasts are crafted in terms of tight antithetical parallelism. The natural body, the body of death, is sown in dishonor, weakness, and perishability. In antithetical contrast, the resurrected body, which dawns in Christ as firstfruits (v. 20), is raised in glory, power, and imperishability. The former is a natural body; the latter is a spiritual body.

However, Paul makes a transition in his argument in verse 44b, so that the focus is no longer the dead body of the believer in comparison to the resurrection body of Christ, but the pre-fall body of Adam.

We know this from two considerations. First, verse 44b ends the list of contrasts and begins a new argument. It has the if/then structure of an argument, and therefore marks a transition from the contrasts in verses 42–44a between the dead body and the resurrection body. Second, in verse 45, Paul offers proof of argument begun in verse 44b by an appeal to the nature of Adam's existence *before the fall:* Gen 2:7. "And so it is written, 'The first man Adam (*'o prōos anthrōpos Adam*) became a living being.' The last Adam (*'o eschatos Adam*) *became* a life-giving Spirit."

In support of the argument that if there is a natural body (*sōma psychikon*), then there is a spiritual body (*sōma pneumatikon*), Paul appeals to Genesis 2:7 and the creation of the first Adam, by which he became a living being. Paul refers to the constitutive activity of the Holy Spirit who formed

---

from 46–49 would only serve to strengthen the argument, since 46–49 presents the Adamic aeon in a manner that could further be correlated with the sub-eschatological aeon of what Paul calls "the letter" in 2 Cor 3:6.

Adam, Moses, and Christ

Adam from inanimate dust from the ground so that he became a "living being."

The transition in the argument forces us to deal with a highly perplexing formulation in the transition from 44a to 44b–45. Paul denotes both the dead body of the believer and the pre-fall body of Adam as a natural body (*sōma psychikon*). Given the fact that the dead body of the believer is such as the wages of sin (Rom 6:23), what possible sense can we make of Adam by using identical phraseology to denote sinless Adam?

Regardless of what more we can say, we must at least note this much: Adam as *sōma psychikon* cannot be understood as the wages of sin, as in the dead body of the believer. Adam as *sōma psychikon* must be understood in terms of the integrity of the prelapsarian order (i.e., Adam as without sin). In other words, Adam's bodily mode of existence is presented as historically real, yet less than glorified. His bodily mode of existence, while free from sin, is not the highest (eschatological) mode of existence.

Put a bit differently, while created very good and without sin, Adam was not good in a consummate sense. He was not clothed in the full perfection of righteousness and holiness, confirmed in glory and immortality. Adam's pre-fall body existed in the estate of innocency, not glory.

So far we have dealt with the connotation of "natural body" in 44b. We need to make a further comment about the protasis (*ei estin sōma psychikon*) and apodosis (*estin kai pneumatikon*), the if/then structure of the argument in light of Gen 2:7. The point is made well by Vos:

> The Apostle was intent on showing that in the plan of God from the outset provision was made for a higher kind of body . . . The abnormal body of sin and the eschatological body are not so logically correlated that the one can be postulated from the other. But the world of creation and the world to come are thus correlated, the one pointing forward to the other.[3]

Eschatological advancement from the natural to the spiritual is implicit in the nature of Adam's historical existence under the covenant of works. From the outset Adam was destined to a higher, spiritual mode of existence—a higher bodily form of glorified and imperishable existence. This means that the ultimate and permanent eschatological order—the Spiritual—was anticipated in the original created order.

The verses 42–44a, in conjunction with 44b–45, then, require us to say that the dead body of the believer, on the one hand, and Adam's pre-fall

---

3. Vos, *Pauline Eschatology*, 169, n. 19.

body, on the other hand, represent distinct species of a sub-eschatological genus. Neither attains the fullness of what dawns in Christ's resurrection by the Spirit.

The Last Adam: Life-Giving Spirit (v. 45c)

However, we must also appreciate a radical discontinuity between the first Adam and the last Adam, which turns not on the mode of life received at the time-point of creation (in the case of the first Adam) or resurrection (in the case of the last Adam) but on the fact that the last Adam both receives and gives resurrection life in the Spirit.

First Corinthians 15:45c will now occupy our attention: *'o eschatos Adam eis pneuma zōopoioun*. What we need to appreciate, from the outset, is the commentary this verse provides on Gen 2:7, "Then the Lord God formed man of dust from the ground, and breathed into his nostrils the breath of life; and man became a living" (Hebrew: *lnepeš khayyah*; LXX: *eis psychēn zōsan*). In the original context of Gen 2:7, note the order of the production of life. The Spirit who hovers over the primal waters, the Lord, engages in the following activity. He forms Adam (*eplasen*) from the dust of the ground and breathes (*enephysēsen*) the breath of life into his nostrils. And given this two-fold action of the breathing of the Spirit of the Lord, Adam becomes *lnepeš khayyah* or *psychēn zōsan*.

The forming and in-breathing are two distinct but inseparable aspects of the one creative work of God. The constitutive, animating activity of the Lord in forming Adam is a work of the Spirit. The Spirit of the Lord "breathes" the breath of life into Adam, and he becomes a living being. It is the agency of the Spirit that comes into view here.

The same language of breathing is associated with the Spirit of the Lord in Ezekiel 37, which is itself a reflection back on Gen 2:7 and the formation of Adam from the dust and a prophetic look forward to a future work of the Spirit raising a people from the dust of death (cf. Ezek 37:9, 14 LXX). This breathing activity, on the one hand, has as its background, its antecedent, the forming of Adam (2:7). The Spirit of the Lord will impart life to those who have returned to the dust, just as the Spirit of the Lord has imparted life to Adam, the first man, who became a living being. This pneumatic activity, with the future verbs, also has a prospective activity in view—the Spirit of the Lord breathing on the whole house of Israel and imparting life. But the point remains that the breathing activity is associated

Adam, Moses, and Christ

with the Spirit of the Lord. As M. G. Kline notes, it is the Glory-Spirit who produces a creaturely replica of the uncreated glory of God as he forms Adam from the dust of the ground and breathes the breath of life into him.[4]

Additionally, and critical for our purposes here, note that Adam is not himself the animating source of the life he receives, but is only a recipient. The economy of creation brings into view a constitutive, pneumatic activity of the Lord, who is the Spirit, granting Adam protological life from the dust of the ground.[5] It is the Lord who by the Spirit breathes life into Adam. The order: Spirit—> breath—> life. This is the background and context for 1 Cor 15:45, with reference to the first Adam.

What, then, do we make of the movement into 45c: *'o eschatos Adam eis pneuma zōopoioun*? First, we need to note that the premised rationale for this quotation is to adduce proof for the appearance of the "spiritual body" in 44b. Christ has been raised with reference to his human nature with a spiritual body, in contrast to Adam, who was created with a natural body. The resurrection of Christ comprises an event that brings to his humanity a permanent transformation that results in glory, power, and imperishability. From this vantage point, then, the natural body, associated with the first Adam at the time point of creation, is superseded by the spiritual body of the last Adam at the time point of somatic resurrection. The resurrection of Christ introduces not a species of a natural body, but inaugurates the genus of a spiritual body. Christ's bodily resurrection as last Adam is the *de facto* advancement of human nature beyond the protological stage of Edenic probation and is the eschatological fulfillment of the natural body of creation.

---

4. Kline, *Images of the Spirit*, 13–25.

5. M. G. Kline helpfully observes that the ground for the functional identification of the Son and Spirit in resurrection is rooted in the antecedent functional identification of the Son and Spirit in creation. He says, "There was a specific divine archetypal referent for the sonship aspect of God's image in man. The eternal, firstborn Son furnished a pattern for man as a royal glory-image of the Father. *It was in his creative action as the Son, present in the Glory-Spirit,* making man in his own son-image that the Logos revealed himself as the One in whom was the life that is the light of men. *Not first as incarnate Word breathing on men the Spirit and re-creating them in his heavenly image, but at the very beginning he was [a] quickening Spirit, creating man after his image and glory*" (*Images of the Spirit*, 24 [italics added]). Kline has in view texts such as Col 1:15–16 and John 1:4 to support his observation. The functional identification of the Son and Spirit in redemption is grounded in the functional identification of the Son and Spirit in creation. We need not speculate, then, regarding the theological grounding of Paul's statement in 1 Cor 15:45c that the Last Adam in his resurrection became "life-giving Spirit."

Second, and bringing into view a staggering disjunction between the first and last Adam figures, the last Adam becomes *"life-giving Spirit"* (45c). The first Adam is only receptive of the life that is given by the Spirit. The last Adam is not only receptive of that life, but he is the constitutive source of that life. With the first Adam, there is only reception of protological life—a purely passive receptivity of the mutable life that the Spirit supplies. But in stark contrast to this situation with the first Adam, with the last Adam there is *both* a reception of eschatological life *and* a communication of eschatological life—eschatological life that brings within its compass imperishable life and everlasting glory.

What this sort of formulation demands, it seems, is that there is a complex uniqueness to the person of the last Adam that is missing in the person of the first Adam. Paul understands the last Adam to be both the recipient of life and the communicator of life in a way that sets him off qualitatively from the first Adam. Put in language that brings into view the person of the Mediator, the last Adam not only receives life, but gives life. The Spirit, distinct from Adam as living being, is the productive agent, the animating source of protological life. When the Son, by resurrection, becomes life-giving Spirit, there is an identification with the Giver of life—the Spirit (cf. Rom 8:9–11). *The Spirit, who is ontologically distinguished from the first Adam as the creative source of protological life, is functionally identified with the resurrected last Adam as the creative source of eschatological life.*[6]

When we view all of this in light of the unity of the person of Christ, we can say Christ both receives a spiritual body and becomes the life-giving Spirit. Put with greater precision, it is in the one act of resurrection and in terms of the unity of his theanthropic person that Christ both receives an eschatologically suited spiritual body and becomes the giver of resurrection life in the Spirit.

It is precisely in this resurrection event that we find the eschatological fulfillment of Ezekiel 37 with regard to human and divine aspects of Christ's person. Christ can rise, with regard to his humanity, as the Israel of God. In his humanity, he rises as the first among the valley of dry bones, as it were. He enters into death, and he rises in possession of resurrection life. Yet, at the same time, with reference to the uniqueness of his person, he is

---

6. See Richard Gaffin's excellent discussion of the functional, but not ontological, identification of Christ and the Spirit in *Resurrection and Redemption*, 78–91.

the creative, spiritual source of resurrection life given to the true Israel, of which he is the firstborn and head.

Therefore, the situation must be presented in light of the redemptive historical movement associated with the complex of events associated with Pentecost (e.g., resurrection, ascension/session, Spirit endowment, outpouring of the Spirit). To relate this to 1 Cor 15:45c, we can say that it is at the time point of Christ's bodily resurrection, and with a view toward Pentecost, that he is identified with the Spirit in such a way that where Christ is, there this Spirt of Christ resides in all of his life-giving fullness, which itself is nothing less than the eschatological fullness *that was yet future to upright Adam in Eden.*

Christ becomes the possessor and conveyor of resurrection life in the Spirit, so that he might embrace his church by the Spirit and unite the church to himself by the Spirit through faith (cf. John 16:14–14; 14:2–3; 20:17–18; Eph 1:13). It is this reality—Christ as life-giving Spirit—that marks the eschatological realization of the covenant of grace. Peter reinforces that point toward the close of his essentially Christ-centered Pentecost sermon. He says,

> This Jesus God raised up, and of that we all are witnesses. Being therefore exalted at the right hand of God, and having received from the Father the promise of the Holy Spirit, he has poured out this that you yourselves are seeing and hearing. (Acts 2:32–33)

Acts 2:32–33 conjoins in sequence the following events: resurrection—> ascension—> reception of the Spirit—> outpouring of the Spirit. The last in sequence, which is Pentecost, is coordinated with the other events as the capstone or climactic expression of those events. Pentecost is no more capable of being a repeatable event than the other events.[7]

From the perspective of covenant history, Christ's resurrection, ascension, session, and Pentecost are consecutive events in calendar time. However, while they are temporally consecutive, they form a unified complex of events—a once-for-all, redemptive-historical unity.

This means that although the events can be distinguished in chronological sequence, they are inseparable in their redemptive efficacy—the one does not exist apart from the others. With this we have come full circle—back, in effect, to 1 Cor 15:45. This reality, then, sequentially depicted by Peter and telescopically portrayed by Paul, supplies the redemptive core

---

7. I am indebted to Richard B. Gaffin's excellent work, "Pentecost: Before and After," 3–24, for clarity on this issue.

of realized eschatology in the *historia salutis* (the accomplishment of redemption) as well as the basic frame of reference for the *ordo salutis* (the application of redemption).

All of these considerations provide the frame of reference for Paul to correlate the dead body of the believer and the prelapsarian body of Adam (with the careful qualifications noted above), since neither possesses the eschatological fullness of what dawns in Christ's resurrection body by virtue of Christ's own pneumatic activity. *Adamic life is therefore death-like*[8] *when compared to the super-abounding life in the Spirit that is eschatologically realized in Christ's bodily resurrection as life-giving Spirit, which is then poured out on the church in Spirit-forged union with the ascended Christ at Pentecost.*

The pneumatological pattern of argument in 1 Cor 15:42–49 is extended to the Mosaic covenant of grace in the companion passage of 2 Cor 3:6–18.

SECOND CORINTHIANS 3:6–18

Paul applies the same sort of logic in 2 Cor 3:6–18, but it is not applied to Adam but Moses—not to the Adamic covenant of works but the Mosaic covenant of grace. The comparison and contrast here turns on different epochs in redemptive history—Mosaic and New, respectively. The framing statement in 2 Cor 3:6 is a programmatic summary of the letter and the Spirit: "For the letter kills, but the Spirit gives life." The letter represents the Old Mosaic Covenant, and the Spirit represents the New Covenant. The comparison and contrast is therefore between covenantal orders in redemptive history.

What comes into view as the point of comparison is the letter and Moses' *fading glory*, on the one hand, and the Spirit and the Lord's *abiding glory*, on the other hand. Paul correlates the letter and Moses' fading glory (vv. 7, 13), on the one hand, and the Spirit and an unfading glory, on the

---

8. By "death-like" I mean that the protological life in Eden had not yet attained the confirmed and irrevocable life constitutive of the future estate of glory. That is, protological life is susceptible to terminating in death, whereas eschatological life is not. Given this fact, Paul, by denoting both the dead body of the believer and the pre-fall body of Adam as "natural body," understands the two as species of a sub-eschatological genus. This observation appreciates the categorical distinction between pre-fall and post-fall bodies, yet recognizes their sub-eschatological commonality.

other hand (vv. 10, 17). And the contrasts drawn from verses 6–11 will bring those realities into concrete comparison.

What are we to make of the distinction between the letter killing and the Spirit giving life? An interpretive key for understanding the contrasts that Paul draws in 2 Cor 3:6–11 rests in the fact that he is making a *relative contrast* in *absolute terms*. Paul is not talking about an unqualified contrast. He is instead talking about a qualified contrast.

The Fading Glory of Moses' Face (Exodus 32–34)

What we need to appreciate in the context of 2 Corinthians 3 is the theological significance of the person and face of Moses as a symbol of life under the letter (v. 13). Responsible interpretation of this text must appreciate that the reference to the glory on Moses' face alludes to Exodus 32–34, where the Lord, through Moses' mediation, *graciously forgives sin and grants a temporary stay of life to his wilderness people.*

To summarize that narrative, remember that while Moses is on Mount Sinai with the Lord, the Israelites sin against God by worshiping a golden calf. God, who is holy and righteous, is poised to judge his people in his wrath. However, Moses intercedes before the Lord as a type of Christ. He tells the people that he will inquire of the Lord to "make atonement for your sin" (Exod 32:30) and pleads with the Lord to "forgive their sin" (Exod 32:32). He does this so that the Lord might continue to dwell in a redemptive communion bond with his covenant people (Exod 33:3, 14). The Lord relents, forgives sin, extends a temporary stay of life to his people and continues to abide in a redemptive communion bond with them *en route* to Canaan.

Moses comes down from the mountain with the glory-presence of God on his countenance. The Shekinah Glory on Moses' face is a symbol of the forgiveness and life that is secured through Moses' mediation on behalf of the wilderness generation. The glory of Moses' countenance is a typical sign of the forgiveness of sin and continuation of life in communion with the Lord that is granted through Moses' mediation.

These observations from Exodus 32–34 suggest, then, that the letter, the Old Covenant, is not in an absolute sense a ministry of death. The precise sense in which Paul speaks of the letter is bound up with the mediation of Moses and the consequent transformation of his countenance. Wrath does not break out against Israel, because Moses, as a type of the Messiah, intercedes on behalf of the people of God, and the Lord knows Moses, acknowledges Moses, and relents/forgives through Moses' intercession.

But here is the question: how will this communion bond—this presence of God—continue with God's people if it is secured through Moses, *and Moses' glory is fading*? This is the problem viewed from within the Old Testament itself. Through Moses' intercession, which is typical of Christ, God will abide *for a time* with his wilderness people, forgiving their iniquities and granting them a temporary stay of life.

The ad-hoc forgiveness and the temporary stay of life points in the direction of something that is not eschatological in character. Moses was concerned to secure pardon and life for the generation that was with him in the wilderness. His intercession brought that particular group into view and did not extend beyond them. Accordingly, the fading glory of Moses illustrates the provisional and ad-hoc character of the redemptive provision secured through his mediation. In a word, what transpires with Moses is *sub-eschatological*.

As goes Moses' glory, so goes God's presence with his wilderness people under the letter. This means, among other things, that Moses' glory is not only typological; it is a prophetic sign that demands a greater glory, a glory that secures for God's people an eternal communion bond with God. When the surpassing glory of Christ, who is the Spirit, arrives in the New Covenant, what came through Moses becomes, by contrast, death and condemnation.

This point emerges forcefully in verse 10: "What once had glory, now has come to have no glory, because of the glory that surpasses it." The glory associated with Moses and his mediation now has come to have no glory, because the glory of the Spirit of Christ eschatologically supersedes that former glory.

It is in terms of this pattern of reasoning that we can make sense of verses 7–11.

> 7 Now if the ministry of death, carved in letters on stone, came with such glory that the Israelites could not gaze at Moses' face because of its glory, which was being brought to an end, 8 will not the ministry of the Spirit have even more glory? 9 For if there was glory in the ministry of condemnation, the ministry of righteousness must far exceed it in glory. 10 Indeed, in this case, what once had glory has come to have no glory at all, because of the glory that surpasses it. 11 For if what was being brought to an end came with glory, much more will what is permanent have glory.

Adam, Moses, and Christ

We can encapsulate the major concern here by noting the way that "glory" qualifies the apparently absolute contrasts drawn within this section.

First, notice that the contrast in 7–8 between the ministry of death and the ministry of the Spirit turns on the difference in *glory*. If the ministry of the letter, the ministry of death, came in *glory* (*en doxē*) that was fading (v. 7), how much more *glory* (*mallon . . . en doxē*) appears in the ministry of the Spirit (v. 8).

Second, notice that if glory (*doxa*) attended the ministry of condemnation, then how much more glory (*pollō mallon . . . doxē*) abounds in the ministry of righteousness (v. 9). The ministries of condemnation and glory, however else they differ, are united in that both are accompanied by glory.

These observations are encapsulated in a terse way in verse 10: "What once had glory has lost its glory, because of the surpassing glory (*heineken tēs hyperballousēs doxēs*)." Here *heineken* with a genitive supplies the reason for what precedes, and the point is that the Old, which had glory and supplied forgiveness of sin and an extension of life for the wilderness generation, now has no glory, in light of the surpassing glory that has appeared in the ministry of the Spirit, who gives life.

Paul appeals to Moses' shining face serving as a microcosm of the Mosaic economy as a whole. Moses' glory become a synecdoche for the letter as a whole, and his mediation for the wilderness generation as representative of the typical indicative (i.e., as a type) under the letter. The typical indicative under the letter has been climactically fulfilled and superseded by the eschatological indicative in the Lord, who is the Spirit.

Union with Christ, then, means that believers are being transformed from glory unto glory (v. 18), and a veil remains anytime someone assumes that the redemptive life conveyed by God through Moses is ultimate. A veil remains anytime someone mistakes the provisional for the permanent—the letter for the Spirit—but that veil is removed whenever someone turns to the Lord. The letter is only a provisional instance of the glory that is surpassed in Christ, who is the Spirit.

To return, then, to 2 Cor 3:6, the fact that the letter kills but the Spirit gives life should not be understood in an absolute sense, as though there was no saving reality communicated in the Old Covenant. The contrast more specifically is between Moses' fading glory (vv. 7, 11), on the one hand, and the abiding glory of the Lord, who is the Spirit, on the other hand (cf. 6, 11, 17). Paul draws a relative contrast between the letter, represented by Moses' fading glory, and the Spirit, functionally identical to the Lord, and argues in verse 11 that "if what was being brought to an end came with glory, much more will what is permanent have glory."

Let us now turn to both texts in order to observe the pattern of argument that emerges from the Pauline pneumatology.

THE PATTERN OF REASONING IN 1 CORINTHIANS 15 AND 2 CORINTHIANS 3

Notice the book-ending function of the Spirit in verses 6 (*pneuma zōopoiei* [the Spirit gives life]) and 17 (*ho de kurios to pneuma estin* [The Lord, who is the Spirit]). What brackets the comparisons and contrasts between the letter and the Spirit is the functional identification of Christ and the Spirit, which is *precisely* what comes into view in 1 Corinthians 15:45c (*ho eschatos Adam eis pneuma zōopoioun*). The righteousness/forgiveness and temporary stay of life through Moses, on the one hand, and the provisional character of Adam's prelapsarian life, on the other hand, are death-like when each is compared and contrasted to "the Lord, who is the Spirit" (2 Cor 3:17) and "the life-giving Spirit" (1 Cor 15:45).

Adam and Moses were concrete embodiments of orders within covenant history. Whether it is the prelapsarian life of Adam or the redemptive life given by God through Moses' mediation, each falls short of the eschatological fullness realized in Christ's resurrection, by which he becomes the life-giving Spirit. By contrast, then, Adamic life in the Garden of Eden or redemptive life under Moses becomes death-like in direct comparison to the eschatological age of the Spirit inaugurated by Christ's exaltation. The following table maps out the pneumatologically regulated pattern of reasoning.

1 Cor 15: 42–49	2 Cor 3:6–18
Pneumatological Center	**Pneumatological Center**
The last Adam is a life-giving Spirit (45c)	The Spirit gives life (6) The Lord, who is the Spirit (17)
Contrasts	**Contrasts**
(2) Adam's natural body (44b, 45)	(2) Moses' fading glory (7,11, 13)
(3) The natural body lacks glory; the spiritual body is raised in glory (43)	(3) Moses/letter came with glory; the Spirit surpasses that glory (10)
(4) Adam's life was provisional; resurrection in the Spirit is imperishable (42–44)	(4) Moses' glory was being brought to an end; Christ's glory is permanent (11)
Conclusion: Adam's life is like death when compared to the resurrection life in Christ, the life-giving Spirit.	**Conclusion**: Moses' redemptive mediation is like death and condemnation when compared to the Lord, who is the Spirit.

Adam and Moses are microcosms of the orders they represent. Both modes of life are death-like compared to the super-abounding eschatological plenitude that dawns in Christ, who is the Spirit. Life, for Paul, means eschatologically robust communion with God through Christ by the Spirit (Eph 2:18, 22). Thus, the righteousness and life that God gave to Adam prior to the fall and through Moses after the fall, when compared to the righteousness and life in Christ who is raised as the life-giving Spirit, is as good as death and condemnation. Both are sub-eschatological species of life and cannot deliver the eschatological purpose of God that dawns only in Christ, the life-giving Spirit.

The images that Paul wants etched in our minds are Adam, susceptible to a return to dust, and Moses' fading glory. Neither Adam's life before the fall, nor the forgiveness and stay of life secured by Moses as a type of Christ bring eschatological life and righteousness. For that, we must look to Christ, who, through the Spirit, has been raised as "life-giving Spirit" and through whom we receive righteousness and life that endures forever. Here, in broad strokes, lies the path we are to walk if we wish to understand the interface of pneumatology and eschatology, grasp the nature of the contrasts in 1 Cor 15: 42–49 and 2 Cor 3:6–18, and develop our theology along the concrete lines of covenant historical revelation.

CONCLUDING ADDENDUM: THE PATTERN EXTENDED

A final brief and suggestive addendum that addresses the possibility of extending this insight to another difficult text in Paul's corpus seems to be in order.

Paul in Gal 3:14 speaks of the fulfillment of the Abrahamic covenant in terms of the giving of the Spirit. He speaks of Israel under the law as being "enslaved to the elementary spirits of the world" (Gal 4:3). He then presents the coordinated events of sending the Son (v. 4) and giving the Spirit (v. 6)[9] as the eschatological realities that fulfill the Abrahamic promises and effect the transition out of the elemental principles of the world and into the age to come (1:4; 3:14; 4:3).

It is precisely within the matrix of the Pauline pneumatology—and specifically the coordination of the Son and the Spirit (vv. 4–6), which as a unity brings the adoption and freedom of the sons of God (v. 5)—that he draws the contrasts between the Jerusalem that is below (v. 25) and the Jerusalem that is above (v. 26)—the latter being the fulfillment of the Abrahamic promise, which is realized in the presence of the eschatological Spirit. He even goes so far as to apply the rhetorical tool of an absolute contrast in relative terms that he calls Sinai (Old Covenant) and Zion (New Covenant) "two covenants" (v. 24). All of this is to convince those who want to be under the law (v. 21) that is it the sending of the Son and gifting of the Spirit that fulfills the Abrahamic promise—not the law itself. The contrasts between the law and the Spirit, between the Jerusalem below and the Jerusalem above, turn on the way that it is only in the latter that we have the Spirit in his eschatological fullness. The former is associated with the flesh; the latter with the Spirit (v. 29).

If these observations are on the mark, it seems that Paul does with Sinai—the Jerusalem that is from below—what he does with prelapsarian life in the covenant of works (1 Cor 15:45) and typologically mediated redemptive life associated with Moses and the letter (2 Cor 3:6, 18). The point, as brief and undeveloped as it may be, is that the eschatological fullness of the Spirit of Christ supplies a central hermeneutical and theological category

---

9. It is preferable to take verse 4 as a reference to the earthly ministry of Christ in his humiliation and verse 6 as a reference to Christ's heavenly ministry in the Spirit, given his exaltation and identification with the Spirit. In this way Paul sets the earthly and heavenly ministry of Christ, who is the Spirit, over against the law, and argues that only the latter realizes the Abrahamic covenant.

that offers extensive explanatory power when it comes to sorting out the contrasts drawn within Pauline covenant theology.

BIBLIOGRAPHY

Gaffin, Richard. "Pentecost: Before and After." *Kerux* 10.2 (1995) 3–24.
———. *Resurrection and Redemption: A Study in Paul's Theology*. Phillipsburg, NJ: Presbyterian & Reformed, 1987.
Kline, Meredith G. *Images of the Spirit*. Grand Rapids: Baker, 1980.
Vos, Geerhardus. "The Eschatological Aspect of the Pauline Conception of the Spirit." In *Redemptive History and Biblical Interpretation: The Shorter Writings of Geerhardus Vos*, edited by Richard B. Gaffin Jr., 91–125. Phillipsburg, NJ: Presbyterian & Reformed, 2001.
———. *The Pauline Eschatology*. Grand Rapids: Eerdmans, 1953.

3

Finding Eschatology in the Old Testament

The Psalms as Case in Point

Jannes Smith

CHRISTIANS OFTEN TURN TO the book of Psalms for comfort in times of crisis. Some of their favorite passages are those that speak of a future beyond the grave. The way we use the book assumes that it is eschatological to some degree. To *what* degree? Just how eschatological is the Psalter? That is the question which this essay addresses.[1]

TWO PRELIMINARY QUESTIONS

To answer it, we need to be clear on two preliminary questions. First, what are we looking for? What is the *eschaton*? That depends on one's vantage point. If one studies eschatology from the vantage point of an Old Testament believer,

---

1. The breadth of the topic and the parameters of the article prevent me from quoting biblical texts at length or explaining them in detail. Biblical references outside of Psalms are seldom provided, and the wealth of extra-biblical Jewish literature relevant for eschatology must be left out all together, as well as the eschatology of the daughter versions (i.e., the ancient translations of the Hebrew text) and the Qumran material.

Finding Eschatology in the Old Testament

then the *eschaton* is the end that he envisions; it is the future hope of Israel, aspects of which may already be past from our perspective.[2] But if one is looking for eschatology as understood by the field of Christian dogmatics, then the focus is on events surrounding the second coming of Christ and on that which is still largely future for us today. I would like to sidestep the dilemma by making two brief observations. The first is that I will address the eschatology of Psalms both from the vantage point of the Old Testament authors and readers and from that of New Testament and contemporary readers. The second is that, as I understand it, eschatology addresses two issues, namely, what happens at the end of one's life, and what happens at the end of the age.[3] Those two issues are constants regardless of one's vantage point. So that addresses the first preliminary question: What are we looking for?

The second preliminary question is: How do we find it? I will argue that the amount of eschatology one finds will depend on one's criteria and one's methodology. In terms of criteria, we might consider three options (see *Figure 1*): one might choose to restrict oneself to those passages that contain explicit teaching about the end or that provide evidence of a pervading eschatological theme; or one might broaden the criteria to include passages that have more or less clear eschatological implications; or, more broadly still, one might include passages that are not overtly eschatological but from which one can draw eschatological trajectories or make direct applications to personal, social, or global circumstances.

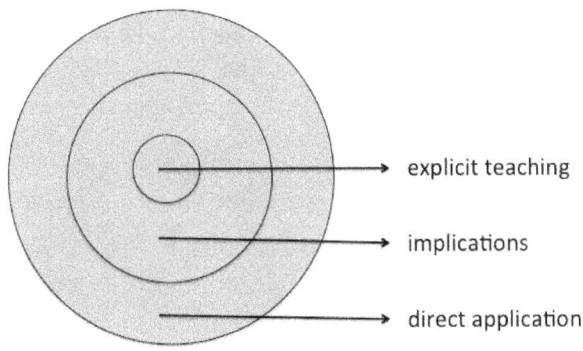

Figure 1

---

2. See, e.g., *qiṣṣî* "my end" in Ps 39:4, *'aḥărîtām* "their end" (LXX *ta eschata autōn*) in 73:17, and *'al mût* "to the end" in 48:15 (LXX has *eis tous aiōnas*, perhaps by orthographic error, though the ESV has adopted the variant).

3. The first is commonly referred to as individual eschatology and the second as general eschatology. See, e.g., Berkhof, *Systematic Theology*, 668, 695; Hill, "Lord," 10.

Depending on one's criteria, then, the sorts of data one finds will span a spectrum ranging from proof texts and a full-fledged eschatological program to redemptive-historical lines and typologies, to homiletical trajectories, links to global and social phenomena in today's world, or even a personal identification with the psalmist on the part of the Christian reader. In short, the broader one's criteria, the more data of an eschatological nature one will find, and vice versa. To be clear, my point is not that some data are more legitimate than others, but that they are of different kinds and that they will be either admitted or refused as evidence of eschatology depending on how broad or restrictive one's criteria for admission are. That may help to explain why some people find eschatology only here and there while others seem to find it everywhere.

In terms of methodology, those who use the strictest criteria, looking only for explicit passages that speak directly to the end of life or the end of time, will focus on the sorts of passages that might function as proof texts for the *locus* of eschatology and will study such passages especially in the immediate context of the particular psalm or as they contribute to a theme of the book as a whole. I call this approach *explication*. Those who look for an eschatological program or for redemptive-historical lines are more concerned with the thrust of the book as a whole, its place in the canon and its fulfillment in the New Testament age. I call this approach *implication*. Thirdly, those concerned to make direct links to the situation of the Christian reader today will study texts with little concern for the lengthy and circuitous route by which we have received the Bible or the cultural and historical divide between it and us. That is to say, they will simply read themselves or their context into the Psalms. This approach I call *application*.

Finding Eschatology in the Old Testament

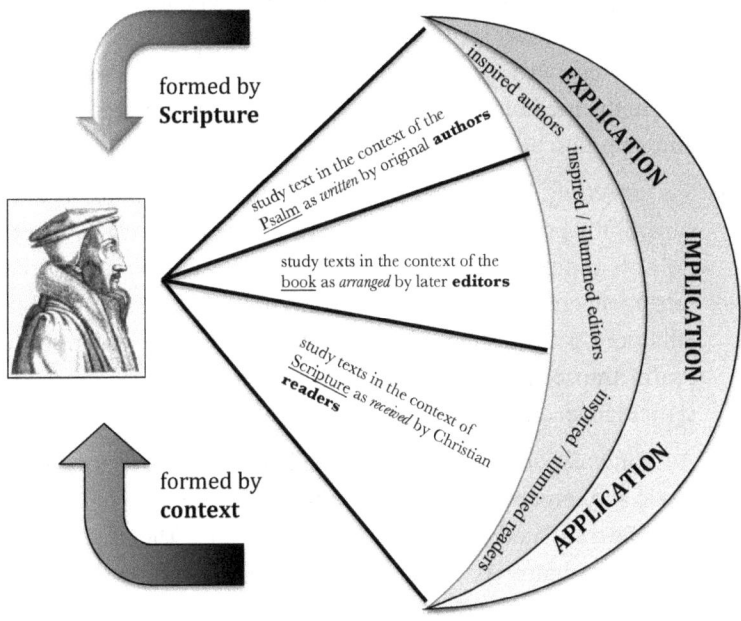

Figure 2

To be sure, no interpreter can use one method to the exclusion of another. Indeed, some will hopelessly muddle the three without even realizing it—which is why *Figure 2* has a picture of a *respectable* exegete. More to the point—looking at the arrows in *Figure 2*—even the most rigorous exegete is formed by his or her context (the bottom arrow), while the Christian who reads the Psalms for direct comfort in an hour of trial is a Christian formed by Scripture (the top arrow). My intention, then, is not to endorse one method or to disparage another but simply to distinguish the three and to outline some of the fruits of each. This answers the second preliminary question, namely, how we find eschatology in an Old Testament book.

EXPLICATION

Let us turn now to eschatology by *explication*. There are at least five challenges facing the interpreter who wishes to extract end-times doctrine from the Psalms. I will summarize them with the acronym P–S–A–L–M.

- P is for *poetry*. The book is replete with imagery, metaphor, hyperbole, and a host of other stylistic features. A plain sense approach to the text might work well for historical narrative, but not so well for poetry, where the medium does not merely convey the message but adorns it and, at times, becomes it.

- S is for *setting*. Doubtless each psalm was written at a particular occasion. Some psalms mention the setting in a superscription, but many do not, and even where they do, the psalm is less specific than the setting: enemies are anonymous, the precise nature of troubles and afflictions is unspecified, and no dates or times are given, so that the psalm transcends its setting and lends itself to a variety of circumstances in space and time.

- A is for *ambiguity*. Besides the lack of historical specificity there is syntactic and semantic ambiguity. Should a Hebrew verb in the imperfect form be translated as present tense or as future? The future tense lends itself to eschatological interpretation, but the present not so much. Does 'ereṣ mean "land" or "earth" (Ps 37:11, 22, 29)? The first is local, the second global. Context is determinative but often not decisive. Is the pronoun "I" intended to refer to the psalmist alone or to include anyone who reads the psalm and identifies with it?[4] Does *nepeš* refer to my "soul" or to my "self"? And where in the world is Sheol?

- L is for *literary unity*. Ordinarily the context of the book as a whole helps to explain the meaning of a particular passage, but to what extent is that true of the Psalter, where the chapters are independent compositions, yet collected and arranged in a particular order? Can one even speak of the eschatology of the Psalter or only of the eschatolog*ies* of individual psalmists or groups of psalms?

- M is for *meditation*. To be sure, the Psalms are divine revelation, but they are largely revelation of the responsive variety—not prophetic oracles but prophetic praise and prayer.[5] In prophetic oracles, it is God who speaks in the first person, but in the Psalms the first person is

---

4. For the use of "I" in Psalms, see De Groot, *Psalmen*, 101–9; Kwakkel, "'I' in Psalms," 48–51.

5. As Geerhardus Vos put it, "As prophecy is objective, being the address of Jehovah to Israel in word and act, so the Psalter is subjective, being the answer of Israel to that divine speech." Vos, "Eschatology of the Psalter," 2.

more often a human.[6] The person who speaks about death and Sheol and about vindication and hope beyond the grave is not the all-knowing Creator but a finite creature with questions, convictions, struggles, and fears. So too, the data one encounters are not *systematic* eschatology but *occasional* eschatology, tied to the occasion of the psalm.

All this is not to suggest that doctrines are irretrievable, much less nonexistent, but that passages in Psalms are often open to more than one interpretation.

End of Life

With these challenges in mind, let me try to summarize the main eschatological doctrines that one encounters in the Psalms. What do the Psalms say about the end of life? First, death comes to all, righteous and wicked alike. Where do the dead go? The Psalter uses at least five words for their destination: nine times it mentions *šaḥat* "corruption";[7] seven times it uses *bôr*, a "pit" or "cistern" into which people fall; three times we find *qeber* "the grave," and one time *'ăbaddôn* "destruction" (Ps 88:11; cf. Rev 9:11). The most common word is *šĕ'ôl* (sixteen times), so I will limit myself to that one.[8] What is *šĕ'ôl*, and who goes there? Let me make three brief comments.

1. It is impossible to find an English equivalent that fits every instance of this word. The ESV follows the RSV and transcribes it as "Sheol," which has the advantage of consistency but the disadvantage of outlandishness. The NIV84 usually opts for "grave," which has the advantage of clarity, but the disadvantage that "grave" makes one think of a burial place, while *šĕ'ôl* is broader, or deeper, than that: a realm of

---

6. That is not to deny the presence of divine speech in Psalms. Using the NIV84 as a convenient indicator, one finds that eighty-five of the 798 occurrences of the pronoun "I" in Psalms, or 10.7%, refer to God (2:6-8, 12:5, 46:10, 50:7-23, 60:6-8, 68:22, 75:2-4, 81:6-16, 82:6, 87:4, 89:3-4, 19-35, 91:14-16, 95:9-11, 105:11, 108:7-9, 110:1, 132:11-18). The point, however, is that the remaining 89.3% refer to man, reflecting its character as responsive revelation. On the revelatory character of Psalms, see also De Groot, *Psalmen*, 130-36, 137-44.

7. Cf. *šĕḥît* in 107:20.

8. For an excellent treatment, see Johnston, *Shades of Sheol*. For Sheol in Psalms, see also Hauge, *Between Sheol and Temple*. Some fifty years ago B. Telder's treatment of Sheol and the afterlife sparked controversy in The Netherlands (Telder, *Sterven . . . en dan?*). For a rebuttal of Telder's views and a transcription of the relevant ecclesiastical decisions made at the time, see Wiskerke, *Léven tussen sterven en opstanding*.

death and decay, an underworld (49:14).[9] Yet the NIV84 is not alone here: the KJV opted for "grave" nine times and "hell" the other seven. The NKJV followed the KJV for the nine instances of "grave," but four times it changed "hell" to "Sheol" (16:10; 18:5; 86:13; 116:3)—understandably, since these four passages deal with the fate of the righteous, while "hell" commonly refers to the final destiny of the wicked. You can see the difficulties of translation, and you can well imagine how translation choices affect theology and vice versa.

2. Although *šĕ'ôl* refers to the realm of the dead, psalmists often spoke of it to describe the depths of their sufferings while still alive.[10] Think especially of Psalm 88. The psalmist has felt *šĕ'ôl* coming close, but has never actually been there (88:3; cf. 116:3), though it would be an exaggeration to say that he does not know Sheol from a hole in the ground. Think, too, of Ps 86:13: "You have delivered my soul from the depths of Sheol" (NKJV, ESV). The psalmist does not mean that he comes back from the realm of the dead, but that he has been spared from death.[11] So why does he speak of his soul? Here it is worth mentioning that the Hebrew word *nepeš* often refers not to the disembodied soul of one who has died but to the living person as a whole—flesh, breath, bones and all (34:20, 22; 35:9, 10).[12]

3. Sheol is always the place where the psalmist does *not* want to go, because it means death and is therefore unprofitable (6:5; 88:10–12; 115:17–18), and because it means joining the wicked in their fate (9:17; 31:17; 49:14; 55:15). Nowhere do we read that the righteous

---

9. The NIV84 has "grave" for fifteen occurrences of *šĕ'ôl*, but "depths" for the sixteenth (139:8), where the contrast is with heaven. That contrast could also have been achieved by using "hell." The NIV84 also uses "grave" for *qeber*, obscuring the distinction between them.

10. Similarly the verb *ḥāyāh* (Piel), often translated as "revive" in the NKJV, can also be rendered "keep alive" and refers to a near-death experience rather than a resurrection. There is very little direct reference to physical resurrection in the Psalms, if any at all.

11. See 18:5; 30:3; 116:3–4. Similarly in Ps 142:7 the NKJV has, "Bring my soul out of prison, that I may praise your name." A naïve reader might think of the "spirits in prison" of 1 Peter 3 and wonder whether the psalm refers to the afterlife. But its title offers a better explanation: the prison is the cave where David was hiding from Saul.

12. Whether by definition or by synecdoche (*pars pro toto*) I am not certain. My first Hebrew professor, Dr. Robert W. Fisher, liked to say that *nepeš* = *rûaḥ* +*bāśār*. To be sure, English "soul" does not always refer to an entity distinct from the body either, as in the expression, "poor soul." For the 144 occurrences of *nepeš* in Psalms, NKJV has "soul" 103 times, ESV has it ninety-seven times, and NIV84 only fifty times.

actually ended up there[13]—perhaps because the Psalms were written by people not yet dead, but more likely because a better destination was in view for them, namely life in the presence of the Lord (Ps 16:11; 17:15; 48:14; 49:14, 15; 73:24; 133:3).[14] Comparing Ps 89:48 with 49:15 we may deduce that Sheol is the destiny of all mankind, but God will redeem the righteous from it and take them to himself.

End of the Age

So much for what happens at the end of life. What about the end of the age? As far as I can tell, most prominent is the belief that God will come to judge the wicked and to vindicate the righteous. Whether the psalmist means judgment in this life or in the one to come, and whether it is a specific act of judgment or a general day of reckoning, is usually left unspecified. The eschatological "Day of the Lord," mentioned so often in the prophets, is virtually absent in the Psalms.[15] Nevertheless, the scope of God's judgment is universal: he judges the world (9:8; 82:8; 94:2; 96:13; 98:9), he judges the nations (7:8; 96:10; 110:6), he judges his own people (50:4), and he judges the psalmist (7:8; 51:4).

When God will come the psalmist does not know (101:2), not even whether it will happen in his lifetime or after his death, but *that* he will come is certain. There will be ultimate glory for the righteous and final destruction for the wicked (1:5–6; 112:9–10; 145:20). This certainty is not based on a full-orbed doctrine of the afterlife, but on faith in God's covenant loyalty (5:5, 6; 107:43) and his mercy towards the oppressed (82:2–6; 146:7–9; 147:2–3), on the belief that a disconnect between a righteous and sovereign Lord on the one hand and an unjust society on the other cannot be permitted to continue interminably (1:5–6; 9:16–18; 11:4; 12:5; 140:10–13), and on the awareness that God keeps time and keeps track of the weal and

---

13. Psalm 16:10 is no exception, since it does not say "in Sheol" but "to Sheol" (*pace* NKJV).

14. Re Ps 48:14, Mitchell argues convincingly that *'al mût* means not "to death" but "over death," i.e., beyond it. Mitchell, "'God Will Redeem My Soul,'" 378.

15. Cf. "the day of his wrath" in 110:5. Psalm 118:24 speaks of "the day the Lord has made," but in all likelihood this expression refers to the occasion for singing this psalm rather than to the eschatological day of the Lord. Vos notes, probably correctly, that references to "morning" (e.g., 49:15) suggest the dawning of a new age. Vos, "Eschatology of the Psalter," 14–15.

woe of his people (56:8; 90:8–12; 139:16). The psalmists long for judgment to come, lacing their prayers with "Why?" (sixteen times), "How long, O Lord?" (seventeen times), and "Arise, O God!" (six times). Three times the Psalms urge the Lord—who never slumbers or sleeps (121:4)—to "Wake up!" (7:6; 35:23; 44:23).[16]

Several passages suggest that it is the Lord's anointed who will execute judgment (2:9–12; 101:5–8; 110:6), and one passage indicates that it will be the privilege of the saints (149:6–9).[17] There does not, however, appear to be a distinction between the first and second comings of Christ. From an Old Testament perspective messianism and eschatology are inextricably linked: when the Lord comes, he comes to establish his kingdom and to judge the nations (145).[18] Finally, the punishment of the wicked and the establishing of righteousness will have an impact on all creation. Psalm 102:25 suggests that creation will pass away,[19] but other passages indicate that it will be set right and rejoice (85:10–13; 93:1, 96:10–13, 98:4–9).

New Testament Perspectives

Many of these eschatological truths are recognizable for us as Christians of the New Testament age. Yet one should not assume them to be static or timeless. Psalms is an Old Testament book expressing truths that the coming Messiah still had to fulfill. The victory of Christ results in a changed perspective on suffering, death, and the afterlife. In Acts 5:41 the apostles rejoiced that they were counted worthy to suffer for the name of Jesus (cf. Matt 5:11; Luke 6:22; Jas 1:2). That perspective of joy in the midst of suffering is hard to find in Psalms (cf. 4:7; 34:2). The psalmist does not say with Paul that "to die is gain" (Phil 1:21). Rather, he says in Ps 30:9: "What gain is there in my destruction, in my going down into the pit? Will the dust praise you? Will it proclaim your faithfulness?" The implied answer is, "No." Or take Ps 88:10–12, where Heman says to the Lord, "Do you show

---

16. The Psalms also share with the New Testament the knowledge that justice must come speedily: compare Ps 12:5 with Luke 18:7–8.

17. This is less likely the point of Ps 122:5.

18. That said, my focus is not on messianism. For a recent treatment, see Fitzmyer, *The One Who Is to Come*. On messianic expectation in the Psalms, see De Groot, *Psalmen*, 145–51.

19. The point of the verse is not eschatological but theological, namely that God is eternal, outlasting even the heavens.

your wonders to the dead? Do those who are dead rise up and praise you? Is your love declared in the grave, your faithfulness in Destruction? Are your wonders known in the place of darkness, or your righteous deeds in the land of oblivion?" Again the implied answer is, "No," but in Christ our answer is also "Yes!" That is to say, on the one hand we share with the psalmist the desire to cling to this life, we do not easily let it go, but on the other we say with Paul, "I desire to depart and be with Christ, which is better by far" (Phil 1:23). *Not* to explain the Psalms redemptive-historically would be to deprive the church of the comfort she has in Christ, who has conquered death.[20] Hence we need also to find eschatology by *implication*.

IMPLICATION

Our Savior said that the Psalms were written about him (Luke 24:44; cf. vs. 27; John 5:39; Acts 2:25, 31).[21] Hence we may read the Psalter christologically, and we should. Before considering its Christology, however, we need to consider its messianism. The two are not the same. Messianism is forward-looking; it is about expecting a future Messiah.[22] Christology is backward-looking; it is about looking at the Old Testament with the benefit of hindsight, knowing that Christ *has* come. I refer you to figure 2 above, the middle triangle, where I suggest that *implication* means to "study texts in the context of the *book* as *arranged* by later *editors*."

Several decades ago, Gerald Wilson, a student of Brevard Childs, launched a veritable revolution in Psalms studies. (I wanted to say the *world* of Psalms studies, but I am willing to admit that it is more like a dwarf planet.) While previous scholars had studied the Psalms in a piecemeal fashion, classifying them into various types with little attention for the arrangement of the whole, Wilson proposed that the final canonical form of the book gives evidence for the work of a purposeful editor, who deployed the Psalms in strategic positions in order to convey a message.[23] Central

---

20. *Heidelberg Catechism*, Lord's Day 1.

21. In Klaas Schilder's words, "The Author Sings His Own Psalms" (Schilder, "Author," 269–86).

22. Scholars who study messianism do not necessarily identify the Messiah as Jesus Christ but treat the topic as a social and literary phenomenon. For an older treatment of messianism as part of the eschatology of Psalms, see Vos, "Eschatology of the Psalter," 29–35. For Vos's treatment of the various references to the Lord's anointed in Psalms, see Vos, *Eschatology of the Old Testament*, 131–40.

23. Wilson, *Editing of the Hebrew Psalter*; Wilson, "King, Messiah, and the Reign of

to the Book of Psalms is the failure of the Davidic monarchy in Psalm 89, followed by a series of psalms that announce that Yahweh is king. Books 1–3, then, highlight the demise of the Davidic kingship, while Books 4 and 5 proclaim the Lord's kingship. Wilson concluded that Psalms is a wisdom book intended to teach the post-exilic community to turn its focus away from the human kingship to the kingship of the Lord. Scholars since Wilson have almost exclusively been preoccupied with the shape and shaping of the book. Time fails me to summarize the hypotheses that have emerged.[24] There is broad agreement that the book is purposive, but disagreement on what its purpose is. For Gerald Wilson it is didactic, pointing to a future without the house of David; for another scholar, David Mitchell, it is eschatological, pointing to a future son of David.[25] It is of course Mitchell's proposal that concerns us here.

Briefly stated, David Mitchell argues that the Book of Psalms was not a collection that grew over time, but one that was edited just once, soon after the return from exile during a time of growing eschatological hope.[26] Further, the purported authors of the Psalms are to be understood as prophets who spoke about the future. The royal psalms refer directly to the coming Messiah, and groups of psalms within the book express an "eschatological programme" that reflects Zech 9–14: in the Psalms of Asaph (50; 73–83) the scattered Israelites are gathered from exile and hostile nations gather against Jerusalem; in Psalm 89 the messianic king is temporarily cut off; in Psalms 90–106 Israel is exiled in the desert, but in Psalm 110 king messiah rescues

---

God," 391–406; Wilson, "Structure of the Psalter," 229–46. On the strength of the alternate sequence of Psalms attested in 11QPsa, Wilson concluded that the collection was still fluid at Qumran and dated the final redaction of the Psalter to the first century BC–first century AD. Mitchell has correctly responded, however, that the Septuagint Psalter, which reflects both the text and sequence of MT, provides evidence that it was already stable by the second century BC at the latest. Mitchell, "Lord, Remember David," 543–47.

24. To cite only monographs in English, see Cole, *Shape and Message of Book III*; Creach, *Yahweh as Refuge*; deClaissé-Walford, *Reading from the Beginning*; Grant, *King as Exemplar*; McCann, *Theological Introduction*; Wallace, *Narrative Effect of Book IV*. For convenient summaries of the scholarship, see Crutchfield, "Redactional Agenda," 21–47; Murphy, "Is the Psalter a Book?," 283–93.

25. Mitchell, *Message of the Psalter*; Mitchell, "God Will Redeem My Soul," 365–84. For a clarification and defense of his views against criticism from Wilson, see Mitchell, "Lord, Remember David," 526–48.

26. Mitchell, *Message of the Psalter*, 76–78; "Lord, Remember David," 532. His theory of a single redaction seems unlikely, given the clusters of Psalms within the whole as well as the colophon to Psalm 72, a psalm attributed to Solomon: "This concludes the prayers of David son of Jesse" (NIV84).

them again; in the *Hallel* Psalms (111–118) the messiah receives a hero's welcome; in the Songs of Ascent we are to understand that Israel, together with all the nations, goes up to Zion to celebrate the Feast of Tabernacles; the Davidic Psalms of Book 5 are not psalms about the historical David but about the future David and his messianic kingdom. In short, the book of Psalms expresses its editor's vision of Israel's eschatological future.

Mitchell's proposal has not been widely accepted. Critics appreciate the evidence for eschatology and messianism in the Psalter but are not convinced that it is as sustained or programmatic as Mitchell makes it out to be.[27] My own concerns are as follows. First, in his concern to see the book as prophetic, Mitchell releases it from its historical moorings: historical allusions within a psalm are reread as ideological.[28] Second, he makes the text of the original authors subservient to the subtext of the editor. Third, he turns a book which presents itself as an anthology of independently written compositions into something more akin to acts in a play, scenes in a pageant, or floats in a parade.

More recently, scholars have attempted to negotiate the competing claims of Wilson, Mitchell, and others by suggesting that the Psalter is not *either* didactic *or* eschatological but *both*.[29] I believe that this is a good development. Think only of Psalm 1, which is now widely understood as an introduction to the book.[30] It contrasts the man who follows the right way with those who follow the wrong—that is didactic. But a way leads somewhere: the way of the righteous to happiness with the Lord and the way of the wicked to judgment and death—that is eschatological.

The scholarly work of Wilson, Mitchell, and others has produced an abundance of evidence for the interconnectedness of the Psalms, such that it is no longer responsible to treat psalms as isolated units with no relation

---

27. Crutchfield, "Redactional Agenda," 42–43.

28. As Vos lamented (against different opponents, of course), "All the concrete, plastic, lifelike self-portrayal by which the figure of David stands before our eyes as the most real of realities, and which plays such a role in the New Testament, is at one stroke swept aside, and figures like Asaph and Ethan likewise lose for us their value as sources of individual comfort and delight." Vos, "Eschatology of the Psalter," 6.

29. See, e.g., Gillingham, "Zion Tradition," 313. Crutchfield adds a third trajectory, namely Brueggemann's suggestion that the theme of the Psalter is "the transformation of lament into praise of God." Crutchfield, "Redactional Agenda," 43–47, citing Brueggemann, "Bounded by Obedience and Praise," 63–92.

30. For an excellent recent treatment, see Seow, "An Exquisitely Poetic Introduction," 275–93.

to the whole; it is an ordered collection.[31] At the same time, scholars have not been able to agree upon a thoroughgoing editorial program.[32] Perhaps we simply do not know enough about the editors' role. Did they merely collect and arrange the psalms, or did they rework them? Did they commission or compose psalms to fill the gaps? It is hard to say. Given that the text gives more evidence for the work of individual authors than for the work of a general editor, it seems better to relegate editorial concerns to secondary status and give interpretive priority to the internal context of a psalm rather than to its function within the book. There are exceptions, however. As mentioned, Psalm 1 is now widely understood to introduce the book, and many scholars add Psalm 2, making it a twofold introduction.[33] Hence the eschatological themes found there—of preservation for the righteous and destruction for the wicked, and of a king at God's right hand who metes out judgment upon those who refuse to submit to him—those themes may be understood as the eschatology of the whole book. From a methodological perspective, when we seek to understand the eschatological implications of a particular psalm, we should interpret it within the context of the eschatological themes of the book before interpreting it in light of its New Testament fulfillment.

With that we return, very briefly, to Christology. An interpreter who has understood Psalm 1 (or Psalm 2, or any other psalm, for that matter)

---

31. I wonder, incidentally, what liturgical implications there might be. We Canadian Reformed (and other Reformed and Presbyterian denominations as well) are Psalm-singing folk. What benefit, eschatological or otherwise, might we gain from singing the Psalms *sequentially*, be it at home, church, or school?

32. Some have expressed doubts that the book is as structured as scholars have claimed. See, e.g., Whybray, *Reading the Psalms*. Further, as an anthology of independent compositions, the Book of Psalms lends itself easily to segmentation and alternate arrangements, such as those found at Qumran, which changes both the context of individual psalms and the perceived message of the whole. See most recently Pajunen, "Perspectives," 139–63, for incisive analysis and helpful statistics on the Qumran material. That said, the consistent order of Psalms in LXX manuscripts and its well-documented unity as the work of a single translator attest to the antiquity of the sequence found in MT, such that it remains legitimate, *pace* Pajunen, to speak of an "authoritative book of Psalms in the late Second Temple period," and to discuss its editorial concerns.

33. See, e.g., Whiting, "Psalms 1 and 2," 246–62; Taylor, "Psalms 1 and 2," 47–62; Miller, "Beginning of the Psalter," 83–92. Note that Psalm 1 begins, and Psalm 2 ends, with *'ašrê*. As Seow observes, "According to Codex Bezae, Acts 13:33 refers to a citation from Ps 2:7 as 'in the first Psalm,'" though, as he rightly notes, the two psalms were not "composed as a single piece" (Seow, "An Exquisitely Poetic Introduction," 292; see the additional evidence he cites there).

in its original context and in the context of the book cannot leave it there but must explore its fulfillment in the Christ who has come and will come again. The interpreter should discipline himself, however, to remain true to the psalm's intent, drawing redemptive-historical lines as specifically and precisely as possible. To give just one example, Psalm 8 speaks to the role that God has given man over creation, inviting lines to Christ as the second Adam and ultimately to a restored creation with a renewed humanity. It is not, however, a psalm in which man groans and asks, "Why is there so much suffering and injustice, Lord? When will you come? How long will it be?" Other psalms do ask such questions, but this one has a different tone, one of amazement: "What is man that you are mindful of him, the son of man that you care for him?" The implications of the psalm must be true to its explication.

APPLICATION

We turn, finally to *application*, by which I mean, "studying texts in the context of *Scripture* as *received* by Christian *readers*." That is to say, readers of Scripture make more or less direct links from the text to their own situation. The New Testament authors already did so, under inspiration of the Holy Spirit. Peter said on Pentecost Day that Psalm 16 was not about David, who was long dead, but about Christ, whom God raised from the dead (Acts 2:25–35). Paul made a direct link from the righteous man of Psalm 112, who "scatters abroad his gifts to the poor," to the generosity that the Corinthians ought to show (2 Cor 9:6–11). Still today, Christians illumined by the Holy Spirit identify with the struggles and joys of the godly psalmist and apply the psalms directly to their own situation. It is legitimate to do so: the deliberately ambiguous language of the Psalter makes it readily applicable for the church of all times and places. Multivalent constructs, such as salvation, house of God, Jerusalem, and the Lord's cup, allow interpreters to make grand typological jumps, leapfrogging merrily across great swaths of redemptive history to infinity and beyond.

I get nervous, however, when interpreters start bouncing uncontrollably, like Tigger on a pogo stick. I am worried they might break something, even though "the Scriptures cannot be broken" (John 10:35). Hence I would like to present three artifacts that illustrate the limits of eschatological application.

As You See the Day Approaching

My first artifact is the use of the future tense. In my introduction I mentioned the challenge of syntactic ambiguity. I wrote, "Should a Hebrew verb in the imperfect form be translated as present tense or as future? The future tense lends itself to eschatological interpretation, but the present not so much." It is interesting to compare the frequency of the future tense in a number of different translations of Psalms. The KJV uses the future tense 981 times, the NKJV 886 times, the NIV84 698 times, and the ESV 628 times.[34] In other words, the Psalter is decidedly more future-oriented in the KJV and NKJV than in the NIV or the ESV. That is in part due to the fact that the translators of the KJV had an older understanding of Hebrew grammar, namely that tense is embedded in the form of the verb, so they defaulted much more quickly to the future tense, while linguists now understand tense to be a matter of grammatical context. The interpreter should not assume the future tense to be correct but should at least ask whether the present fits better.[35]

My second artifact is the word "salvation." The verb "to save" is fairly general, and several different nouns are associated with it. In modern English parlance the noun "safety" makes one think in more practical terms of being saved from danger or from enemies, while the noun "salvation" makes one think in more theological terms of being saved from sin or Satan. Saving is virtually always an act of God in the Psalms, often from enemies or from dangerous circumstances. Interestingly enough, the KJV uses the word "salvation" sixty-three times in Psalms, while the NKJV has it sixty-four times, the ESV seventy-two times, and the NIV84 only forty-four times.[36] When the reference is to immediate rescue, the NIV84 uses a variety of words such as "deliverance" and "victory." My concern is that translations which use the word "salvation" in contexts of rescue from present danger will bias readers to think of salvation in the ultimate sense rather than of safety in the immediate sense. They will tend to think of God—and perhaps lead congregations to think of God—as someone who saves them particularly in the theological and ultimate sense, but not enough of him as someone who *keeps* them *safe* in all kinds of daily and practical situations. Then they make the Psalter more eschatological than they should. A pas-

---

34. I suspect that the low count for the ESV is a residue of the RSV, from which it was revised, but have not been able to generate statistics to confirm this.

35. Old habits die hard, e.g., "The Lord is my shepherd; I *shall* not want." Grammatical context makes clear that the present tense is meant, i.e., "I do not want," or "I lack nothing," as the NET Bible has it.

36. The NET Bible has "salvation" only twice.

sage about rescue from danger may very well have broader soteriological *implications*, but immediate context should take precedence.

My third and final artifact is the word "forever." The Psalms brim over with hyperbolic expressions such as "everlasting" and "forever." It should be noted, however, that the presence of such words does not automatically make a passage eschatological. It often is not. In context "forever" often does not mean "for eternity" but "for always," "all my life," "all the time."[37] That is to say, it often refers to that which is true for the *foreseeable* future, for as long as the *present* age continues, not to that which happens after this age or after this life.

CONCLUSION

In this essay I have attempted to describe the eschatology of an Old Testament book. Just how eschatological is the Psalter? Much in every way. By way of *explication*, we have seen that key components of Christian eschatology are largely present in the Psalms already. Yet the book lacks something of the perspective of joy in the face of suffering and death that only comes with the victory of Christ, and that lack should be kept in mind when we use the Psalms in our preaching and our pastoral care. By way of *implication*, we have seen that individual psalms ought to be studied within the context of the book, since the arrangement of the whole gives evidence for a messianic-eschatological thrust, though not an eschatological program. By way of *application*, we have seen that the deliberate ambiguity of the Psalms gives them a timeless, universal, dare I say "catholic," character that invites and encourages personal appropriation, though within limits. As broadly applicable as they might be, the Psalms are and remain Old Testament revelation. Hence the methods of explication and implication provide an essential control to guard against unlimited applicability.

---

37. E.g., Ps 23:6; 30:12; 37:27; 45:2; 48:8; 61:4; 69:23; 74:1; 78:69; 86:12; 89:36–37; 121:8; 131:3. To take just one example, Ps 89:36–37 says that David's dynasty would endure forever "like the sun" and "like the moon," i.e., as long as the created order endures. It does not say that it will continue to endure "when sun and moon shall shine no more," to quote Hymn 80:4 (*Book of Praise*).

BIBLIOGRAPHY

Berkhof, Louis. *Systematic Theology.* Grand Rapids: Eerdmans, 1949.
Book of Praise: Anglo-Genevan Psalter. Winnipeg: Premier, 2014.
Brueggemann, Walter. "Bounded by Obedience and Praise: The Psalms as Canon." *Journal for the Study of the Old Testament* 50 (1991) 63–92.
Cole, Robert L. *The Shape and Message of Book III (Psalms 73–89).* Journal for the Study of the Old Testament Supplement Series 307. Sheffield: Sheffield Academic, 2000.
Creach, Jerome F. D. *Yahweh as Refuge and the Editing of the Hebrew Psalter.* Journal for the Study of the Old Testament Supplement Series 217. Sheffield: Sheffield Academic, 1996.
Crutchfield, John C. "The Redactional Agenda of the Book of Psalms." *Hebrew Union College Annual* 74 (2003) 21–47.
deClaissé-Walford, Nancy. *Reading from the Beginning: The Shaping of the Hebrew Psalter.* Macon, GA: Mercer University Press, 1997.
Gillingham, Susan E. "The Zion Tradition and the Editing of the Hebrew Psalter." In *Temple and Worship in Biblical Israel: Proceedings of the Oxford Old Testament Seminar,* edited by John Day, 308–41. Library of Hebrew Bible/Old Testament Studies 422. London: T & T Clark, 2007.
Grant, Jamie A. *The King as Exemplar: The Function of Deuteronomy's Kingship Law in the Shaping of the Book of Psalms.* SBL Academia Biblica 17. Atlanta: SBL, 2004.
Groot, Joh. de. *De Psalmen: Verstaat gij wat gij leest?* Baarn: Bosch & Keuning, 1941.
Fitzmyer, Joseph A. *The One Who Is to Come.* Grand Rapids: Eerdmans, 2007.
Hauge, Martin R. *Between Sheol and Temple: Motif Structure and Function in the I-Psalms.* Library of Hebrew Bible/Old Testament Studies 178. Sheffield: Sheffield Academic, 1995.
Hill, Edmund. "Lord, When Will You Come? Psalm 101:2." *Journal of Theology for Southern Africa* 16 (Spring 1976) 9–18.
Johnston, Philip S. *Shades of Sheol: Death and Afterlife in the Old Testament.* Downers Grove, IL: IVP Academic, 2002.
Kwakkel, Gert. "'I' in Psalms and Hymns." *Lux Mundi* 28.2 (2009) 48–51.
McCann, J. Clinton. *A Theological Introduction to the Book of Psalms: The Psalms as Torah.* Nashville: Abingdon, 1993.
Miller, Patrick D. "The Beginning of the Psalter." In *The Shape and Shaping of the Psalter,* edited by J. Clinton McCann, 83–92. Journal for the Study of the Old Testament Supplement Series 159. Sheffield: Sheffield Academic, 1993.
Mitchell, David C. "'God Will Redeem My Soul from Sheol': The Psalms of the Sons of Korah." *Journal for the Study of the Old Testament* 30 (2006) 365–84.
———. "Lord, Remember David: G. H. Wilson and the Message of the Psalter." *Vetus Testamentum* 56 (2006) 526–48
———. *The Message of the Psalter: An Eschatological Programme in the Book of Psalms.* Journal for the Study of the Old Testament Supplement Series 252. Sheffield: Sheffield Academic, 1997.
Murphy, S. Jonathan. "Is the Psalter a Book with a Single Message?" *Bibliotheca Sacra* 165 (2008) 283–93.
Pajunen, Mika S. "Perspectives on the Existence of a Particular Authoritative Book of Psalms in the Late Second Temple Period." *Journal for the Study of the Old Testament* 39 (2014) 139–63.

Schilder, Klaas. "The Author Sings His Own Psalms." In *Christ in His Suffering*, 269–86. Translated by Henry Zylstra. Grand Rapids: Eerdmans, 1938.

Seow, C. L. "An Exquisitely Poetic Introduction to the Psalter." *Journal of Biblical Literature* 132 (2013) 275–93.

Taylor, J. Glen. "Psalms 1 and 2: A Gateway into the Psalter and Messianic Images for the Restoration of David's Dynasty." In *Interpreting the Psalms for Teaching and Preaching*, edited by H. W. Bateman and D. B. Sandy, 47–62. St. Louis: Chalice, 2010.

Telder, B. *Sterven . . . en dan? Gaan de kinderen Gods, wanneer zij sterven, naar de hemel?* Kampen: Kok, 1960.

Vos, Geerhardus. *The Eschatology of the Old Testament*. Edited by James T. Dennison Jr. Phillipsburg, NJ: Presbyterian & Reformed, 2001.

———. "Eschatology of the Psalter." *Princeton Theological Review* 18.1 (1920) 1–43.

Wallace, Robert L. *The Narrative Effect of Book IV of the Hebrew Psalter*. Studies in Biblical Literature 112. New York: Lang, 2007.

Whiting, Mark J. "Psalms 1 and 2 as a Hermeneutical Lens for Reading the Psalter." *Evangelical Quarterly* 85 (2013) 246–62.

Whybray, R. Norman. *Reading the Psalms as a Book*. Journal for the Study of the Old Testament Supplement Series 222. Sheffield: Sheffield Academic, 1996.

Wilson, Gerald H. *The Editing of the Hebrew Psalter*. SBL Dissertation Series 76. Chico, CA: Scholars, 1985.

———. "King, Messiah, and the Reign of God: Revisiting the Royal Psalms and the Shape of the Psalter." In *The Book of Psalms: Composition and Reception*, edited by Peter W. Flint and Patrick D. Miller, 391–406. Vetus Testamentum Supplements 99. Leiden: Brill, 2005.

———. "The Structure of the Psalter." In *Interpreting the Psalms: Issues and Approaches*, edited by David Firth and Philip S. Johnston, 229–46. Downers Grove. IL: IVP Academic, 2005.

Wiskerke, J. R. *Léven tussen sterven en opstanding*. Goes: Oosterbaan & Le Cointre, 1963.

4

Working Politically and Socially in Anticipation of Christ's Coming

Cornelis Van Dam

SINCE THE DAY OF Pentecost, we are living in the final age, the age of the Holy Spirit. Christ is coming. He is en route (Rev 1:7), but he is not here yet (Rev 22:7). We live in the tension of the fulfillment of the coming of the Messiah, Jesus Christ, and his anticipated second coming. Many prophecies have been fulfilled, but more need to be realized. How are we to live and work in this tension of the *already* and *not yet*? We live in the last days (Acts 2:17; 2 Tim 3:1), but the last day has not yet come (John 6:39; 12:48).[1]

This tension of the *already* and *not yet* can serve as a tremendous stimulus for Christians to be actively involved in the life of our country. After all, Christ is king already, seated at God's right hand, and he is coming! There is continuity between the present and the future. Both are in Christ's sovereign control, and as Christians we are in his service in this world. It is this world that will be renewed, and it is on this earth that our risen King has given us a task as those anointed by his Spirit. But what exactly is our task politically and socially? What sort of guidance do we get from

---

1. Beale, *Revelation*, 198; for a discussion of the tension between the *already* and *not yet*, see, e.g., Hoekema, *The Bible and the Future*, 13–22, 68–75.

Working Politically and Socially in Anticipation of Christ's Coming

Scripture on this score? Do we in fact have a task? Some would question this and deny that we should get involved in the political scene and culture of our times. After all, our citizenship is in heaven (Phil 3:20), and we are only aliens and strangers here (1 Pet 2:11). Indeed, a theologian such as Stanley Hauerwas argues that precisely for those reasons Christians should not attempt to change secular governments or get too involved in politics and try to change society.[2]

Let us then consider the biblical rationale for getting involved, the norms we should follow, and the expectations we can have. We will conclude with some closing reflections.

BIBLICAL PRECEDENTS FOR GETTING INVOLVED

The Letter to the Exiles

The argument that we are only pilgrims here, with our real citizenship elsewhere, and therefore should not get involved socially and politically sounds compelling. But biblically speaking it is not. Consider Israel in Babylon. In that faraway land they were surely strangers. They certainly were not in the first place citizens of Babylon. They were there against their will. Indeed, they were in a land that had destroyed their country and would destroy their holy city Jerusalem. In short, they must have totally felt out of place.[3]

Now what was their attitude to their new surroundings to be like? Inspired by God's Spirit, Jeremiah sent them a letter, probably shortly after they went into exile,[4] with very specific instructions. In that letter, as recorded in Jer 29:5–7, we read the following:

> Build houses and settle down; plant gardens and eat what they produce. Marry and have sons and daughters; find wives for your sons and give your daughters in marriage, so that they too may have sons and daughters. Increase in number there; do not decrease. Also, seek the peace and prosperity of the city to which

---

2. Hauerwas, *Resident Aliens*. For the historic Anabaptist avoidance of involvement in government affairs and today's changing attitudes, see, e.g., Kyle, "Anabaptist and Reformed Attitudes toward Civil Government," 27–33, and Redekop, *Politics under God*, 55–68.

3. In the context of Jeremiah 29, these thousands of exiles were the first to be deported (in 597). They included King Jehoiachin, members of the royal family, and the leading men (2 Kgs 24:14–16; Jer 29:2; 52:28–30). Wiseman, *1 and 2 Kings*, 309–10.

4. Lundbom, *Jeremiah 21–36*, 360.

I have carried you into exile. Pray to the Lord for it, because if it prospers, you too will prosper.[5]

In other words, they were told to participate in the culture and business of their new place of dwelling. We cannot go into all the detail here, but for our purpose we especially need to note that the letter clearly mentions seeking the peace and prosperity of the city in which they lived. The term used for peace and prosperity is *shalom*, a very comprehensive term covering all of life. It can also be translated as "welfare." Those who were exiled to Babylon were to "seek the welfare of the city" (NASB, RSV). This advice to exiles is without parallel in the Old Testament. Indeed, it contrasts sharply with the imprecations of Psalm 137.[6] These exiles were to seek the welfare of their captors and pray for them. They were not to hate the pagans who would destroy Jerusalem, but to work for the good of their country and their society. Seeking their welfare meant getting involved, culturally and also politically. Furthermore, such involvement would be of benefit to the Judean exiles: "If it prospers, you too will prosper" (Jer 29:7). And so they were to give their best efforts for the well-being of the land of the Babylonians.

And they did have something to give. The heritage of godly wisdom in the Scriptures they had received was something to be shared. Indeed, had God not said to Abraham that his descendants were to be a blessing to the nations (Gen 12:2–3)? Was Israel not to be a light to all peoples on earth (cf., e.g., Isa 42:6; Deut 4:6; Psalm 67)?

It is striking that the Lord made it clear that they were to be exiles for at least three generations. He said: "Marry and have sons and daughters; find wives for your sons and give your daughters in marriage, so that they too may have sons and daughters" (Jer 29:6). They were to be in it for the long haul. At the same time, they had to realize that they would eventually return. For Jeremiah also said: "This is what the Lord says: 'When seventy years are completed for Babylon, I will come to you and fulfill my gracious promise to bring you back to this place,'" i.e., to Jerusalem (Jer 29:10). In other words, their staying in Babylon was ultimately to be temporary. They had to keep that in mind and therefore build not just homes but families,

---

5. Unless indicated otherwise, biblical texts are quoted from the New International Version 1984.

6. Huey, *Jeremiah, Lamentations*, 253; cf. Matt 5:43–48; Rom 12:21; Titus 3:1–2; 1 Pet 2:18. The injunction in Deut 23:6 not to seek the peace of Ammon or Moab has been understood as "not to seek a treaty of friendship with them" (NIV).

Working Politically and Socially in Anticipation of Christ's Coming

not as the Babylonians, but with a view to God's sovereign plan. There is a future for the children of God, and they must increase.

Now we need to step back and consider the principles involved in this part of Scripture. There are a couple of points relevant for our situation today. As believers we are in some ways like the Judean exiles living in Babylon. We are also not of this world, though living in it. We too know that ultimately our sojourn here is temporary, and we too look forward to the promised land of the new world that is coming. And so on one level this world is a hostile place for us, a temporary place, and some would say, "Let us avoid it and be separate. Let us concentrate on our own community and take care of our own needs—they are plentiful enough. Forget about the society around us." That is a response which could have been expected from the Babylonian exiles and which historically is an Anabaptist approach. However, God said otherwise. His children have an obligation towards the society in which they live, even if that society is hostile to their faith and values. That obligation toward society also involves the political sphere. After all, like the Judean exiles, we too have explicit instructions to pray for those in authority over us. As we read in 1 Tim 2:1–2, "I urge, then, first of all, that requests, prayers, intercession and thanksgiving be made for everyone—for kings and all those in authority, that we may live peaceful and quiet lives in all godliness and holiness."

How can we pray for those in authority over us if we do not do what we can to get involved in the affairs of our society and nation? Those in authority over us are not our adversaries but those to whom we owe respect and obedience. They have been placed there by God himself (Rom 13:1–5). We should therefore help them in every possible way and get involved in the political process, working for the welfare and prosperity of our country and society. There are challenges enough. Christians must be the best citizens possible.

There is of course a very striking example of how children of God became involved in political life, namely, the example of Daniel and his friends. Let us briefly consider how Daniel exercised his calling as a believer.

Daniel

Although they were exiles, Daniel and his friends did not object to being part of the political order of the day as long as they did not have to compromise their faith. They served the king, even though he fought their own nation and would destroy the temple and the holy city. But they refused to eat the royal food (Dan 1), probably because, as was customary, part of it would have been offered to idols (cf. 1 Cor 10:20–31). They also refused to worship any other god but the true God, even if it meant being thrown to the lions or into a blazing furnace (Dan 3, 6). But for the rest, they participated in the affairs of state, did not hide their faith, and influenced the affairs of the empire.

Think for a moment of how Daniel addressed the mightiest ruler of the world at that time.[7] Daniel had just interpreted the king's dream and in doing so had told the king that he would be driven from his palace and live like the wild animals. He then said (as recorded in Dan 4:27): "Therefore, O king, be pleased to accept my advice: Renounce your sins by doing what is right, and your wickedness by being kind to the oppressed. It may be that then your prosperity will continue." Notice that Daniel is polite in how he addresses the king: "Be pleased to accept my advice." He is after all speaking to Nebuchadnezzar, in whose hand is the life of every one of his subjects. But he is also firm and gives direction. "Renounce your sins by doing what is right, and your wickedness by being kind to the oppressed." After all, God has just revealed to Nebuchadnezzar the terrible future he must endure until he acknowledges that God is king. Daniel is to the point in charging the king to repent and do right.

Now in our current multicultural context, this is not what you would expect. Rather, you would have expected Daniel to be sensitive to postmodern political correctness and multiculturalism and say something like: "O King Nebuchadnezzar, I am a Jewish prophet, but I would not presume to impose my Jewish moral standards on your Babylonian kingdom. Ask your astronomers and your soothsayers. They will guide you in your own traditions. Then follow your own heart. It would not be my place to speak to you about right and wrong." No, Daniel spoke the truth, politely but boldly. We need to do the same wherever God has placed us and wherever he gives us the opportunity. And, unlike the average Jewish exile, we have many opportunities in a democracy. We are even encouraged to confront government and our elected representatives and we are even blessed with such organizations as the Association for Reformed Political Action, of which we have a representative with us today.[8] As those ultimately set in their high place by God, our leaders can expect input from God's children.

7. What follows is dependent on Grudem, *Politics according to the Bible*, 58–60.
8. At the conference where this essay was first presented, the respondent was Mr.

Working Politically and Socially in Anticipation of Christ's Coming

The results are in God's hand. In Daniel's case, Nebuchadnezzar even ended up praising, exalting, and glorifying the true God (Dan 4:34-37). So too did King Darius after Daniel came out of the lions' den. Daniel's simple act of confessing his faith by praying to God in spite of a Persian law resulted in Darius extolling God (Dan 6:25-27).

New Testament Teaching

As we move on to the New Testament we also find examples of believers confronting their government and using legitimate means to challenge the state with God's demands and thus also to advance the gospel.

Several examples come to mind.[9] Like Daniel, John the Baptist confronted the evil ruler of the day. He had told Herod the tetrach that it was not lawful for him to have as wife the spouse of his brother Phillip (Matt 14:3-4). But he had also admonished him about "all the other evil things he had done" (Luke 3:19). He addressed the government policies of Herod and pointed out the evil he was doing. It cost John the Baptist his freedom and then his life, but he knew his responsibilities before Herod, also his political responsibilities.[10]

In a similar way the apostle Paul confronted the Roman governor Felix while he was a prisoner in Caesarea. He talked to him about "righteousness, self-control and the judgment to come" (Acts 24:25). One can be sure that he also dealt with the moral standards of the day and thus with government policy. On an earlier occasion the apostle Paul facilitated the acceptance of the gospel by a government official, Sergius Paulus, by liberating him from the hand of a Jewish sorcerer and false prophet (Acts 13:6-12).[11]

An example of using government rules to promote the gospel and its spread is seen in Paul's making use of his Roman citizenship to escape from the hands of the Jews and benefit from the opportunity provided by Roman justice to present the gospel to those who would judge his case. Indeed, in the end he even appealed to Caesar to hear his case (Acts 22:22-30; 24-26). This last act guaranteed that the gospel would be heard in Rome, in the

---

André Schutten, LLB, LLM, legal counsel and Ontario director for the Association for Reformed Political Action.

9. For what follows, see Grudem, *Politics according to the Bible*, 60-61.

10. See also Storkey, *Jesus and Politics*, 61-68.

11. For a useful account of the political aspects of the book of Acts, see Van Eck, *Paulus en de koningen*.

heart of imperial power. And this is exactly what God intended (Acts 23:11; 27:24).

One could say: "I am not John the Baptist, or Paul, the apostle. I am just a simple believer." However, the examples just given show that God's Word is relevant for government officials and that those who believe in God are not silent when an opportunity to advance the gospel presents itself. Indeed, Scripture also indicates that we should not be shy about asserting our rights, especially if they are being denied because of our faith. God gives opportunities for us to testify to those whom he has set above us, often in most unexpected ways.

Now that we have seen the biblical precedents for getting involved in the affairs of our nation, the next question is how to proceed. How do we do work in anticipation of Christ's coming? What sort of guidance does Scripture give?[12]

THE NORMS OF OUR INVOLVEMENT

There are a number of areas that could be considered when reflecting on the manner of our involvement. For our present purpose we will focus on one current and basic issue. What norm should we use? Natural law or biblical law? At the moment there is among Calvinists a debate about how Christ and his kingdom relate to our government institutions, society, and culture. We need to pause at this dispute.

On the one hand there are those who say that biblical norms need to be promoted and applied to our society. Nothing is to be excluded from Christ's lordship. As Kuyper famously said: "There is not a square inch in the whole domain of our human existence over which Christ, who is sovereign over *all*, does not cry: 'Mine!'"[13] According to this view Chris-

---

12. Bruce Winter has argued that the New Testament teaches that Christians in the first-century Graeco-Roman world were to "seek the welfare of the city" by adopting and adapting the traditional Roman role of benefactor to help sustain and enhance the life of the cities in which they lived. Winter, *Seek the Welfare of the City*. His main thesis does not appear to have been widely embraced since much hinges on interpreting the "good" in Rom 13:3–4 (ESV) and 1 Pet 2:14–15 (ESV) as public benefaction, which he is unable to prove conclusively. See, e.g., the review by Walters in *Journal of Biblical Literature*, 536–38. His contention that Christians did not withdraw from society is credible, given injunctions such as 1 Pet 2:15 and the Lord Jesus' teaching in Matt 5:14–16 and elsewhere.

13. Kuyper, "Sphere Sovereignty," 488. The emphasis is Kuyper's.

tians therefore have the mandate to assert Christ's claims wherever this is possible. To paraphrase Bavinck, wherever Christians function, whether in one's family, in society, in the affairs of the state, in one's occupation, in art, or in science, a renewing and sanctifying influence must radiate from their lives. "The spiritual life is meant to refashion the natural and moral life in its full depth and scope according to the laws of God."[14] Put differently, grace restores nature.[15] As we seek to refashion life in a manner pleasing to God, Satan pushes back and we experience the antithesis. This is one view of how Christ's lordship should impact our walk as Christians. It is the view that has made possible Christian activism in such areas as education, the arts, and politics.

On the other hand, there are those who assert that there are two separate kingdoms. This view maintains that there is the common kingdom, which God preserves according to his promises given after the Great Flood (Gen 8:20—9:17), and the redemptive kingdom, whose citizens are the redeemed whom God is gathering in the church. Anything not directly related to the rule of Christ with respect to his church is part of the common kingdom where Christians live as exiles. Important implications are drawn from this view. In general, Christians are not to seek an objectively Christian way of pursuing cultural activities. The importance of Christian education is downplayed, for according to this two-kingdoms view, it is questionable whether we can call non-theological fields of learning Christian. Since politics is a matter of the common kingdom, it can be misleading to speak of Christian political activity because Scripture speaks only in a general way of civil government and political responsibilities. As a result the two-kingdoms vision downplays Christian action that is intended to influence the political process.[16]

---

14. Bavinck, *Reformed Dogmatics*, 4:437. David VanDrunen has (unsuccessfully) attempted to use Bavinck in support of his two-kingdom approach. See the discussion in VanDrunen, "The Kingship of Christ is Twofold," 147–64, and Kloosterman, "A Response," 165–76. Kloosterman's essay was later reprinted in McIlhenny, ed., *Kingdoms Apart*, 65–81.

15. It has been argued that grace restoring nature is "the fundamental defining and shaping theme of Bavinck's theology." See John Bolt's introduction in Bavinck, *Reformed Dogmatics*, 4:23.

16. A popular introduction is VanDrunen, *Living in God's Two Kingdoms*. For the issues mentioned, see 15, 26, 168, 179–87, 198. A more scholarly treatment can be found in VanDrunen, *Natural Law and the Two Kingdoms*. For a constructive critique and interaction, McIlhenny, *Kingdoms Apart*. See also the previous footnote. For a brief critique of VanDrunen's confusing treatment of Kuyper, see Dennison, "Review of VanDrunen,"

But there are major problems with this view. It divides God's government of all things into two parts as if he rules creation in two distinct realms. But there is no evidence of such an understanding in Scripture. God is sovereign Ruler over all history and creation. Furthermore, all human beings as created in the image of God are obligated to submit to the will of God as Creator and Redeemer.[17] The two-kingdoms view introduces an unbiblical dualism into the life of a Christian. According to this view, Christians, as citizens of the redemptive kingdom, are to live subjectively according to the Scriptures, but in the common kingdom they are not to seek an objectively unique Christian way of pursuing cultural or political activities. It is said that natural law governs the common kingdom.[18] But Christians will or should always be involved in cultural and political endeavors in ways completely different from those of unbelievers even though some of the outcomes can be similar. Christians will be motivated to act to God's glory and, therefore, according to God's law, for they recognize that God's Word is relevant for all of life, both public and private, ecclesiastical and non-ecclesiastical. Furthermore, the basic principles of the Ten Commandments are known to all men. God has written the requirements of the law on their hearts, and so they are without excuse (Rom 2:15; cf. 1:20–21). The so-called natural law is not natural in that it originates from man but has been given by God.[19] Since natural law can only be fully and correctly known in the light of Scripture, Christians have the obligation to let the light of God's good will be known in all areas of life and to try to subject all areas of life to the criteria of God's Word (cf. 1 Cor 10:31; 2 Cor 10:5; Col 3:17; 1 Pet 4:11). It is in the area of Christian education that the consequences of the two-kingdoms position are especially obvious. The two-kingdoms position denies that there is such a thing as Christian scholarship in non-theological disciplines. With this view there is no incentive to build a Christian school or to bring every thought into subjection to Christ (2 Cor 10:5).[20]

One needs to remember that God demands that all recognize him as the Lord of all of life (cf. Psalms 96; 99). At this very moment Christ rules

---

365–67.

17. Further on this topic, see Venema, "One Kingdom or Two?," 102–3.

18. VanDrunen, *Living in God's Two Kingdoms*, 166–72, 198–203.

19. Ridderbos, *Aan de Romeinen*, 58–59. See also Van Dam, *God and Government*, 87–89.

20. On this issue, see Venema, "One Kingdom or Two?," 124–27. For a defense of keeping one's faith private in the academy, based on the notion of the two kingdoms, see Hart, "Christian Scholars," 383–402; for a strong rebuttal, Davis, "Contra Hart," 187–200.

Working Politically and Socially in Anticipation of Christ's Coming

at God's right hand (1 Pet 3:22). Christians therefore have every reason to apply the biblical norms to all of life, both in the so-called redemptive kingdom as well as in the common kingdom. Society needs to hear from believers what is proper for a correct understanding of the issues of the day, such as marriage, euthanasia, and abortion. General revelation is not sufficient here. Applying biblical norms can be very difficult and mean struggle and estrangement from mainline culture.[21] Christians are indeed pilgrims here, and our citizenship is in heaven (1 Pet 2:11; Phil 3:20). But we have been placed in this world not to separate ourselves from our society but to work for Christ's glory in anticipation of his coming (John 17:15–17; 1 Cor 10:31). This entails getting positively involved in the challenges facing our contemporary culture and society's institutions, including government. It will also mean that, over against the immorality of the present age, we will be profoundly countercultural (1 Pet 2:11).

OUR EXPECTATIONS

What expectations can Christians have as they go about this task? First of all, we need to be biblically realistic. We are after all strangers here, and our sojourn is limited. We cannot expect to see immediate results; indeed, we may see only marginal results, or we may not even see any positive results at all. The Kuyperian triumphalism of the past should indeed belong to the past.[22] For real positive change to occur in our cultural, political, and social life as a nation, the hearts and minds of our country need to be changed.[23] This implies that change will usually come slowly and incrementally. We live in the tension of the *already* and the *not yet* of the coming of Christ.

---

21. On the challenge of discerning divine ordinances and applying biblical norms to current issues as evidenced in the work of Abraham Kuyper, see, e.g., Bacote, *The Spirit in Public Theology*, 57–61.

22. Rightly cautioning against this easy Kuyperian triumphalism is, e.g., Mouw, *Uncommon Decency*, 159–69; also Crouch, *Culture Making*, 189–201, 252.

23. A point also made by Storkey when he writes: "In the end, people changing their hearts, minds, and attitudes is *the only feasible political method*." Storkey, *Jesus and Politics*, 116 (italics in the original). In an interview of Canada's Prime Minister, Stephen Harper, broadcast on CBC on January 17, 2011, the Prime Minister stated that "if you want to diminish the number of abortions, you've got to change hearts and not laws." Harper, however, used this fact to justify refusing to consider legislation on this issue and so shirked the government's responsibility as God's servant to give moral leadership. See http://www.cbc.ca/news/interview-with-stephen-harper-1.1007264.

When our Savior lived on earth, he announced that the kingdom of God had arrived. He cast out demons and so indicated his superior power over Satan (Matt 12:28). He restored creation by healing the sick and so showed that the devil's might had been broken (Luke 13:11–16). Through the proclamation of the gospel, the kingdom had come near and had been given to those who believed (Mark 2:1–12; Mark 10:15). But at the same time the kingdom had not yet arrived in fullness. Christ therefore taught his disciples to pray: "Lead us not into temptation, but deliver us from the evil one" (Matt 6:13). Indeed, even after Christ's coming and victory, Satan, though cast out of heaven, still rages on this earth (Rev 12:12).[24]

This reality makes us realistic as to our expectation with respect to the fruits of our labor. It will be slow and difficult, for we have a powerful adversary, and "at present we do not see everything subject to Christ" (Heb 2:8). Socially changing the culture is a task beyond the ability of any one individual, but with every testimony from Reformed individuals and families the salt and light of the kingdom seeps into society. Every life lived in holiness in an unholy world is a witness to God's work and to the reality of his kingdom in our lives.

It is good to remember that God's kingdom is "like yeast that a woman took and mixed [lit. hid] into a large amount of flour until it worked all through the dough" (Matt 13:33). Children of God are to be like a holy leaven in today's worldly culture and society, which constitute a huge amount of flour. The yeast, representing the citizens of God's kingdom, is, as it were, hidden in this large mass. In the eyes of the world, the kingdom of heaven is as nothing. It is virtually invisible. But, like leaven, it works slowly but surely, and the fermentation will continue until the whole batch has risen. The citizens of the kingdom demand that every sphere of life be subjected to the Lord of the universe, Jesus Christ. God's Word does not promise that all of life will show obedience to Christ before his return (2 Thess 1:7–10; 2:8). But the citizens of God's kingdom know and believe the promise that in God's time this will be the case (Rom 14:11; Phil 2:10–11). The leaven of God's kingdom works slowly and is almost invisible. But by God's grace some of its effects slowly become obvious. Indeed, it could be argued that much of what we enjoy, such as democracy, the rule of law, and the many freedoms we cherish, can be traced to historic biblical influences on our society. With our society turning away from the biblical moorings

---

24. For an excellent study on this topic, see Ridderbos, *Coming of the Kingdom*. For a popular study of Revelation 12, see D. A. Carson, "This Present Evil Age."

Working Politically and Socially in Anticipation of Christ's Coming

that have benefited our culture, it is a real challenge to make the leaven of the kingdom effective. However, every Christian who lives his faith inside and outside the home is a cultural force.[25]

The image of the slow working of leaven reminds us that when it comes to politics and passing laws we may need to seek change incrementally. It will not always be possible to get everything one desires in a single step. We may need to exercise some tolerance and compromise by accepting the less than ideal in the short term while keeping the desired goal in focus.[26] In all our activity to seek social, cultural, and political change, we also need to be biblically realistic and realize that ultimately Christ's kingdom is not of this world (John 18:36). Christ resisted any attempt to make him an earthly king (John 6:15). His kingdom will one day come in perfection on this earth, but in the meantime he gives us our duty here. For even if we cannot effect the kind of meaningful social and political change that we would like, Christ has nevertheless given his people a task and calling in this world. We are to be witnesses to God's claim on his creation and to his will for a world lost in sin.

Scripture and history are very sober on this point of being a witness. Many have given their lives while testifying to God and his kingdom. The two witnesses in Revelation 11 also end up being killed. But they were where they had to be, out in the public square, on the streets of the great city figuratively called Sodom, giving their prophetic testimony. And God is sovereign: Satan could kill these witnesses only after they had finished their testimony (Rev 11:3–10). This is in a nutshell a picture of the believers, the community of faith, in the last days before the final coming of the kingdom of God in fullness and perfection. Christians give their testimony in public, and their testimony is rejected, rendering the world of sin guilty and ready for the final judgment. In Revelation 11 the beast, representing the forces of evil, kills the witnesses. But God restores them, his church, to life (Rev 11:11–19).[27] This emphasizes the continuum we are on. This present world will transition to the renewed creation.[28] The victory is Christ's!

---

25. For the above, see Hendriksen, *Matthew*, 567–68; Van Dam, *God and Government*, 3–17; Schilder, *Christ and Culture*, 81–86.

26. Van Dam, *God and Government*, 246–51, cf. 66–76, and, e.g., Penninga, "Saving Some is *Not* a Compromise," 10–18.

27. For a brief and a fuller exposition of Revelation 11, see Hendriksen, *More Than Conquerors*, 129–32, and Beale, *Revelation*, 572–620, respectively.

28. On this topic, see Bavinck, *Reformed Dogmatics*, 715–20; in relation to the two-kingdoms idea, Venema, "One Kingdom or Two?" 114–21.

We need to keep this glorious end in mind in order to maintain a proper perspective. God is sovereign, and his kingdom will triumph.

At the same time, suffering comes with the identity of being a Christian. Preaching the good news, Paul and Barnabas also said: "We must go through many hardships to enter the kingdom of God" (Acts 14:22). It is good to keep in mind that Scripture regards suffering for the cause of Christ as a blessing and a privilege. Christ said: "Blessed are those who are persecuted because of righteousness, for theirs is the kingdom of heaven" (Matt 5:10). As Christians we live and work here in holy communion with Christ. That includes sharing in his suffering (1 Pet 4:12–13) so that we may share in his glory (Rom 8:17).[29] After the apostles were flogged by the Sanhedrin, they left "rejoicing because they had been counted worthy of suffering disgrace for the Name" (Acts 5:41). Such suffering occurs in the context of the close communion Christians have with Christ. When Saul persecuted the believers, Christ asked, "Why are you persecuting *me*?" (Acts 9:4).

Our relationship as Christians to Christ is so close that we also share in his anointing. Also here there is the continuity between this age and the one to come; between this world of sin and the glory to be revealed on a new earth. In our sharing in Christ's anointing we may exercise our calling as prophets, to confess his name; as priests, to present ourselves as living sacrifices; and as kings and queens, to fight with a free and good conscience against sin and the devil in this life, and hereafter to reign with him eternally over all creatures. One will recognize in these words Lord's Day 12 of the Heidelberg Catechism. Our calling is closely connected to Christ. It involves all of life and anticipates the coming of his Great Day.[30]

Indeed, as we also confess in the Heidelberg Catechism, we have in this life a beginning of the new obedience (QA 114) and experience now already the beginning of the eternal joy (QA 58). This continuity of our present life with the future glory is also evident in our being transformed into Christ's likeness with every-increasing glory (2 Cor 3:18).

So, in spite of a fittingly sober realism there is also the joy of faith. And that joy allows us to be optimistic in a biblical sense. We can work hard for change in our society, nation, and government with the knowledge that

---

29. This sharing has nothing to do with contributing to Christ's suffering for our redemption. Rather, it is a suffering with Christ because of our close identity with him. It is a suffering for his sake (cf. Gal 6:17). Further see Ridderbos, *Aan de Romeinen*, 183–84; Lenski, *Romans*, 527–28.

30. In this context, see also Venema, "One Kingdom or Two?," 122–24.

as we witness to Christ and the biblical norms, we are planting seeds. As Christ said, "The kingdom of heaven is like a mustard seed, which a man took and planted in his field. Though it is the smallest of all your seeds, yet when it grows, it is the largest of garden plants and becomes a tree, so that the birds of the air come and perch in its branches" (Matt 13:31–32). In other words, the coming of the kingdom in all its glory has very small beginnings, insignificant in the eyes of the world, but in the end the kingdom of heaven will surpass all others.[31] As Christians we can plant that seed in our families and homes, for the home is an institution of critical importance for God's work. That seed of the kingdom is also planted through the preaching of the Word, through Christian education, and through a Christian walk and talk as we oppose the culture of narcissistic self-interest, of abortion, and euthanasia. Through it all, the church has the indispensable duty to preach the pure gospel and in this way equip faithful confessors of Christ for all of life.[32]

We do need to exercise much patience but we are engaged in a project that is ultimately guaranteed to succeed in a glorious completion. And so, as Christians, we may joyfully and with godly zeal be involved in the cultural, social, and political affairs of our country. We do have something to give: the true light in a world of darkness (Matt 5:13–16; Eph 5:8). And we have the promise that our labor in the Lord is not in vain (1 Cor 15:58). We even have the promise that those who die in the Lord "will rest from their labor, for their deeds will follow them" (Rev 14:13). What we do as Christians in this life has significance for the renewed world to come. "There is continuity, in other words, between what is done for Christ now and what we shall enjoy in the hereafter—a continuity expressed in the New Testament in terms of reward or joy (cf. 1 Cor 3:14; Matt 25:21, 23)."[33]

Yes, we can work expectantly in great anticipation of Christ's coming, for already he rules at the Father's right hand, and it is this world which will be renewed. And remember: "No eye has seen, no ear has heard, no mind has conceived what God has prepared for those who love him" (1 Cor 2:9).

---

31. Ridderbos, *The Coming of the Kingdom*, 144–45; Hendriksen, *Matthew*, 565–67.

32. For the task of the church and its relationship to the state, see Van Dam, *God and Government*, 47–77; Van Dam, "The Church and Public Policy," 274–76.

33. Hoekema, *The Bible and the Future*, 74. The rest from our labors should, however, not be conceived of as inactivity. We will function as prophets, priests, and kings on earth forever (Rev 5:10; 22:5). See Bavinck, *Reformed Dogmatics*, 4:727–28.

BIBLIOGRAPHY

Bacote, Vincent E. *The Spirit in Public Theology.* Grand Rapids: Baker Academic, 2005.
Bavinck, Herman. *Reformed Dogmatics.* 4 vols. Edited by John Bolt. Translated by John Vriend. Grand Rapids: Baker Academic, 2003–2008.
Beale, Gregory K. *The Book of Revelation: A Commentary on the Greek Text.* The New International Greek Testament Commentary. Grand Rapids: Eerdmans, 1999.
Carson, D. A. "This Present Evil Age." In *These Last Days: A Christian View of History*, edited by Richard D. Phillips and Gabriel N. E. Fluhrer, 17–37. Phillipsburg, NJ: Presbyterian & Reformed, 2011.
Crouch, Andy. *Culture Making: Rediscovering Our Creative Calling.* Downers Grove, IL: InterVarsity, 2008.
Davis, William C. "Contra Hart: Christian Scholars Should Not Throw in the Towel." *Christian Scholar's Review* 34 (2004–2005) 187–200.
Dennison, William D. "Review of VanDrunen's *Natural Law and the Two Kingdoms*." *Westminster Theological Journal* 75 (2013) 349–70.
Eck, J. van. *Paulus en de koningen.* Franeker: Van Wijnen, 1989.
Grudem, Wayne. *Politics according to the Bible.* Grand Rapids: Zondervan, 2010.
Hart, Darryl G. "Christian Scholars, Secular Universities, and the Problem of the Antithesis." *Christian Scholar's Review* 30 (2000–2001) 383–402.
Hauerwas, Stanley. *Resident Aliens: Life in the Christian Colony.* Nashville: Abington, 1989.
Hendriksen, William. *Exposition of the Gospel according to Matthew.* New Testament Commentary. Grand Rapids: Baker, 1973.
———. *More Than Conquerors: An Interpretation of the Book of Revelation.* 1940. Reprinted, Grand Rapids: Baker, 1982.
Hoekema, Anthony A. *The Bible and the Future.* 1979. Grand Rapids: Eerdmans, 1994.
Huey, F. B. *Jeremiah, Lamentations.* New American Bible Commentary. Nashville: Broadman & Homan, 1993.
Kloosterman, Nelson D. "A Response to '"The Kingdom of God is Twofold': Natural Law and the Two Kingdoms in the Thought of Herman Bavinck' by David VanDrunen." *Calvin Theological Journal* 45 (2010) 165–76.
Kuyper, Abraham. "Sphere Sovereignty." In *Abraham Kuyper: A Centennial Reader*, edited by James D. Bratt, 461–90. Grand Rapids: Eerdmans, 1998.
Kyle, Richard. "Anabaptist and Reformed Attitudes toward Civil Government: A Factor in Political Involvement." *Direction* 14.1 (1985) 27–33.
Lenski, R. C. H. *The Interpretation of St. Paul's Epistle to the Romans.* Columbus, OH: Lutheran Book Concern, 1936.
Lundbom, Jack R. *Jeremiah 21–36.* Anchor Bible 21B. New York: Doubleday, 2004.
McIlhenny, Ryan C., ed. *Kingdoms Apart: Engaging the Two Kingdoms Perspective.* Phillipsburg, NJ: Presbyterian & Reformed, 2012.
Mouw, Richard J. *Uncommon Decency: Christian Civility in an Uncivil World.* Rev. and exp. ed. Downers Grove, IL: InterVarsity, 2010.
Penninga, Mark. "Saving Some is *Not* a Compromise: The Case for Advancing Abortion Legislation in Canada One Step at a Time." *Reformed Perspective* 30.12 (2011) 10–18.
Redekop, John H. *Politics under God.* With a foreword by John A. Lapp. Scottdale, PA: Herald, 2007.
Ridderbos, Herman. *Aan de Romeinen.* Commentaar op het Nieuwe Testament. Kampen: Kok, 1959.

———. *The Coming of the Kingdom.* Edited by Raymond O. Zorn. Translated by H. de Jongste. Philadelphia: Presbyterian & Reformed, 1962.

Schilder, K. *Christ and Culture.* Translated by G. van Rongen and W. Helder. Winnipeg: Premier, 1977.

Storkey, Alan. *Jesus and Politics: Confronting the Powers.* Grand Rapids: Baker Academic, 2005.

Van Dam, Cornelis. "The Church and Public Policy." *Clarion* 58 (2009) 274–76.

———. *God and Government. Biblical Principles for Today: An Introduction and Resource.* Eugene, OR: Wipf & Stock, 2011.

VanDrunen, David. *Living in God's Two Kingdoms.* Wheaton, IL: Crossway, 2010.

———. *Natural Law and the Two Kingdoms: A Study in the Development of Reformed Social Thought.* Emory University Studies in Law and Religion. Grand Rapids: Eerdmans, 2010.

———. "'The Kingship of Christ is Twofold': Natural Law and the Two Kingdoms in the Thought of Herman Bavinck." *Calvin Theological Journal* 45 (2010) 147–64.

Venema, Cornelis P. "One Kingdom or Two? An Evaluation of the 'Two Kingdoms' Doctrine as an Alternative to Neo-Calvinism." *Mid-America Journal of Theology* 23 (2012) 77–129.

Walters, James C. Review of Bruce Winter, *Seek the Welfare of the City: Christians as Benefactors and Citizens.* In *Journal of Biblical Literature* 115 (1996) 536–38.

Winter, Bruce. *Seek the Welfare of the City: Christians as Benefactors and Citizens. First-Century Christians in the Graeco-Roman World.* Grand Rapids: Eerdmans, 1994.

Wiseman, Donald J. *1 and 2 Kings.* Tyndale Old Testament Commentaries. Downers Grove, IL: InterVarsity, 1993.

5

In Between and Intermediate
My Soul in Heaven's Glory

Theodore G. Van Raalte

INTRODUCTION TO THE INTERMEDIATE STATE[1]

"She's in a better place." The details of what happens to persons at death may be studiously avoided in polite conversation, but popular sentiment has not let go of the fuzzy hope that departed loved ones are in some better place. For centuries the church has advanced a fairly straightforward biblical account: human beings are a unity of body and soul, but upon death the soul separates from the body, leaving the body lifeless until the resurrection. The souls of believers go to be with God in glory; the souls of unbelievers enter a preliminary state of suffering in hell. During this time—called the intermediate state—these persons-as-souls await the resurrection of their own bodies, the final judgment, and the eternity that will follow. The hearts

---

1. Scripture quotations in this essay are taken from the New International Version (1984), unless otherwise specified. I would also like to acknowledge the clarity on this topic gained from a course taken with Dr. John Cooper some years ago, as well as from his remarkable book, *Body, Soul, and Life Everlasting* (2nd ed., 2000).

In Between and Intermediate

of Reformed believers resonate deeply with the confession, "I am not my own, but belong, with body and soul, both in life and in death, to my faithful Saviour Jesus Christ."[2]

The foregoing traditional position is nicely summarized in the Westminster Confession, chapter 32.

> The bodies of men, after death, return to dust, and see corruption: but their souls, which neither die nor sleep, having an immortal subsistence, immediately return to God who gave them: the souls of the righteous, being then made perfect in holiness, are received into the highest heavens, where they behold the face of God, in light and glory, waiting for the full redemption of their bodies. And the souls of the wicked are cast into hell, where they remain in torments and utter darkness, reserved to the judgment of the great day. Besides these two places, for souls separated from their bodies, the Scripture acknowledgeth none.[3]

THE CHALLENGE OF PHYSICALISM

However, this deeply comforting account seems no longer to be regarded as tenable. One of the fundamental reasons has more to do with the doctrine of the first things (protology) than the last things (eschatology). A foundational shift has been occurring in thinking about origins that, when consistently followed, requires a seismic change in beliefs about the soul and the intermediate state. Whereas in the 1960s our own Reformed churches in The Netherlands had to deal with the error of soul sleep, at least its proponent agreed that there is a human soul of some kind.[4] He also tried, unsuccessfully, to root his views in Scripture.[5]

---

2. Heidelberg Catechism, Answer 1, *Book of Praise*, 517.

3. *Confession of Faith*, 147–48.

4. Bartus Telder's monograph of 1960 argued that persons, body and soul, "sleep" in the intermediate state. See Telder, *Sterven . . . en dan?* He followed this with Telder, *Sterven . . . waarom?* in 1963. Telder emphasizes that the whole man is dust, the whole man dies, the soul is in the blood, etc., and thus de-emphasizes as much as possible any kind of dualistic nature of man. He regards the body-and-soul distinction to be tainted with Aristotelian and scholastic influences (see *Sterven . . . en dan?* 47, 105, 142). For a limited discussion in English, see Van Genderen and Velema, *Concise Reformed Dogmatics*, 828–29.

5. Telder's views were condemned by the ecclesiastical assemblies and refuted in a learned monograph by Wiskerke, *Léven tussen sterven en opstanding*. Many readers will also know that John Calvin's first book, *Psychopannychia* (1534, first published 1542),

But lately the intermediate state has been facing a more aggressive attack. (In answering it, we can consider ourselves to have also answered the lesser error of soul sleep.) Some prominent evangelical scholars have for two decades been advancing the argument that humans do not have souls. One might consult, for example, various publications from the theologian Joel Green at Fuller Seminary and the philosophers Nancey Murphy, Kevin Corcoran, and Trenton Merricks at Fuller Seminary, Calvin College, and the University of Virginia, respectively.

Murphy relates how in 1996, when Dolly the sheep had been cloned successfully, a reporter was trying to obtain Murphy's response. She had no concern about the matter, and the reporter kept trying to provoke a negative response from her. She relates that a "light dawned" for her.

> I asked him, "Do you read a lot of science fiction?" "Well, some." "Are you imagining that if we try to clone a human we'll clone a body but it won't have a soul? It will be like the zombies in science fiction?" "Yes, something like that." "Well," I said, "Don't worry. None of us has a soul and we get along perfectly well."[6]

When one investigates the origins of this new conception of human persons, one will typically either arrive in the laboratory of a neuroscientist or become entwined in an evolutionary biologist's study of DNA. The neuroscientist argues that all of our thinking, feeling, desiring, choosing, loving, and hating—the whole world of the mind—is merely chemical and electrical brain activity.[7] The biologist argues that we are just a higher form of the animals, sharing most of our DNA with chimpanzees, and thus not beings of a different order.[8] Going further, many biologists insist that humans are just as much an assemblage of parts as a machine, a "particular collection of material phenomena."[9] Soul is reduced to mind, and mind is reduced to brain. Persons are merely physical; there is no soul. This position is called "physicalism."

---

was a critique of soul sleep.

6. Murphy, "Nonreductive Physicalism," 95.

7. Preston et al., "Neuroscience and the Soul," 31–37; Murphy, *Bodies, Souls*, ch. 2, e.g., 56.

8. Murphy, *Bodies, Souls*, ch. 2. See also the literature and arguments reviewed in Carroll, "Does a Biologist Need a Soul?" 17–23. Carroll argues that biologists who deny the soul are committing themselves to a pre-theoretical philosophical reductionist position that is not based on research or empirical evidence. In the same vein, see Beauregard, *Spiritual Brain*, xi–xiv.

9. Carroll, "Does a Biologist Need a Soul?," 18.

In Between and Intermediate

PHYSICALISM: SUPPORT FROM BIOLOGOS

One of the leading Christian forums that investigates and promotes toleration of forms of physicalism is BioLogos, an organization that in the last few years has received about nine million dollars from the Templeton Foundation, particularly to promote theistic evolution among Christians.[10] BioLogos's statement of faith includes the following:

> We believe that the diversity and interrelation of all life on earth are best explained by the God-ordained process of evolution with common descent. Thus, evolution is not in opposition to God, but a means by which God providentially achieves his purposes... We believe that God created humans in biological continuity with all life on earth, but also as spiritual beings.[11]

This is the organization's way of stating that humans have biological ancestry (whether apes, chimps, Neanderthals, etc.) but also are elevated above other creatures and enabled to have a special relationship with God. But such a position does not necessarily mean that these humans who are "spiritual beings" actually have a spiritual soul.

Correctly or not, many Christians have linked the human soul with the "image of God" in humans. In contrast, one series of BioLogos articles advanced the view that the image of God in man is really about God graciously choosing *Homo sapiens* over other animals and hominids and *not* about any uniquely human capacities or characteristics beyond those of "other" animals. The scriptural emphasis, it was argued, "lies on the commonality that exists between the humans and the rest of the animal creation."[12] Further, Adam and Eve, "as the primal human pair, are chosen and called to be a species of priests to the other hominids and to non-human animals."[13] Those who portray humans as unique because they have a soul, and who therefore reject Darwin, are part of a "reaction" that "has more to do with secular French Enlightenment notions of the 'dignity of man' and Italian

---

10. Devine, "Interpretive Dance," para. 2. Fuller Theological Seminary, Calvin College, and Trinity Western University have each received several grants from Biologos's Templeton funds. Funding is also being provided to translate important works that support theistic evolution. See BioLogos, "Evolution and Christian Faith Grant Program."
11. BioLogos, "What We Believe," points 9 & 10.
12. Moritz, "Chosen by God," Part 1, para. 7.
13. Ibid., Part 2, para. 10.

Renaissance ideas of 'man as the measure of all things' than with anything that is taught in the Christian Bible."[14] In conclusion,

> *Apart from God's choosing and blessing* there was no fundamental difference between Abraham's lineage and the other families of the Earth; likewise, there was no fundamental distinction between humans and other animals *apart from God's choosing and blessing* . . . Indeed, one is hard-pressed to name a single distinctive characteristic of humankind that does not *also* suggest our continuity with other animals.

As in all articles on its website, BioLogos states that these are not necessarily its own views, but those of the author. However, it is obvious that the organization wants the views of authors such as Moritz to be considered *permissible* for Christians.[15]

Moritz's study says absolutely nothing about how God "formed the man from the dust," as if with his hand. It omits any mention of the next event, that "God breathed into his nostrils the breath of life." Also missing is any mention of the special deliberation of God in Gen 1:26 when he said, "Let us make man in our image, in our likeness." Neither the hortative "let us" nor the use of the verb "make" (rather than "choose") receives any attention. No indication at all of man's superiority over the animals is included, especially no metaphysical grounds for such superiority.[16] Particularly this last omission is hardly within the pale of historic Christian orthodoxy.

Other authors may be more willing to speak of human superiority and stewardship, but still argue against regarding a human soul as a distinct

---

14. Ibid., Part 3, para. 3.

15. Another author in a series of interchanges on the topic wrote, "BioLogos seems to lean toward the image being produced through evolution, but is ultimately non-committal on the possibility of divine intervention." Hammett, "Southern Baptist Voices," para. 2. Further, BioLogos editors introduce the discussion to which Moritz contributes by writing in part: "Both views of the image of God ("spiritual capacity" and "commission") are compatible with the scientific evidence for evolution." Finally, among the suggestions for "further reading" about this topic, BioLogos includes only one author out of six in support of an immaterial soul. See https://biologos.org/common-questions/human-origins/image-of-god.

16. In this essay I will not study the *Imago Dei* except to say that while "let them rule" (Gen 1:26) surely refers to function (as representatives of God) rather than essence and while "in our image, in our likeness" may likewise refer to function, one would still rightly ask what qualities God gave to humans in order to equip them to function in this way. The New Testament certainly relates the image of God in man to such qualities as truth (true knowledge), righteousness, and holiness. See Rom 8:29; Eph 4:24; and Col 3:10.

In Between and Intermediate

entity. N. T. Wright, another contributor to BioLogos, introduces what he calls a "differentiated unity" as the description of human nature, eschewing any real distinction between body and soul. He writes, "To insist that we 'possess' an 'immortal part' (call it 'soul' or whatever) which cannot be touched by death might look suspiciously like the ontological equivalent of work-righteousness in its old-fashioned sense: something we possess which enables us to establish a claim on God, in this case a claim to 'survive.'"[17]

PHYSICALISM: EFFECTS IN BIBLICAL COMMENTARIES

The effects of such a position regarding origins obviously require a major re-thinking of one's eschatology. Joel Green, already mentioned, has written commentaries on both Luke and First Peter.[18] One rightly wonders what comment he would provide on Jesus' words in Luke 23:46, "Father, into your hands I commit my spirit," or 23:43, "Today you will be with me in Paradise," or Jesus' parable about Lazarus and the rich man (Luke 16:19–31). No mention is made of the body-soul distinction. Instead, at Luke 23:46 the reader encounters this curious footnote:

> Jesus' entrusting his "spirit" need not be read as a reference to the separation of his body and spirit in death. Such a reading owes more to a Cartesian anthropology than to that shared by Luke's contemporaries (cf. D. B. Martin, *Corinthian Body*, 3–37). *pneuma* [spirit] refers to "life (in its totality)."[19]

If one follows the physicalist position, what is described in this essay's title will ever occur. No one will ever live in a state that is "In Between and Intermediate" nor have any reason to speak about "My Soul in Heaven's Glory." If believers cease to exist at death and then are created anew or reconstituted at the resurrection, they will simply go from one earth to another, from the old earth to the renewed earth. Then nothing happens

---

17. Wright, "Mind, Spirit, Soul and Body." Unfortunately Wright's arguments frequently counter straw men. He also provides no documentation. When compared to some of his earlier writings, Wright appears to be confused. Cogent responses have been advanced by Rickabaugh, "Responding to NT Wright" (cited with permission), and by Goetz, "Is N. T. Wright Right?"

18. Green, *Luke*; Green, *First Peter*.

19. Green, *Luke*, 826, n. 57. John Cooper, in his chapter on views of the afterlife in the intertestamental period, has thoroughly disproven Green's assertion about Luke's contemporaries lacking any notion of a body and soul distinction. Cooper, *Body, Soul*, 73–93.

for them between death and resurrection.[20] There will be no intermediate stage wherein one's soul goes to Christ, one's Head, immediately upon one's death.[21] There just is no soul.

Instead of focusing on the salvation of their souls, so physicalists argue, Christians need to be more concerned about this life on this earth, about ecological issues of pollution, deforestation, and global warming, about the flourishing of other animals besides ourselves, and about the likelihood of extra-terrestrial life. After all, in their view humans are not so special or unique, nor are they the center of, or stewards of, creation.[22]

RESPONSE: THESIS AND STRUCTURE

Against this position regarding the soul, I wish not just to reassert the Reformed confessional position, but to do this while also noting the deep exegetical, theological, and philosophical complications that physicalism imports into the Christian faith, and for that matter, into our understanding of reality as such. What I hope readers will appreciate most of all is the immense comfort enjoyed by believers who hold to God's revealed truth. We can relate to the God who is spirit (John 4:24), because his Spirit testifies in our spirits that we are children of God (Rom 8:16). We do belong to a new creation already now (2 Cor 5:17), by virtue of the new life that is given when we, in our souls, are born again (John 3:3–8). We can reflect on who we are, also before God, because God has given us the gift of self-consciousness in our souls and hearts (Ps 42–43). Our God is a God of love, deep and abiding love. He is with us always, also in the intermediate state, just as he promised. And the intermediate state will be such a delight that with Paul we should say, "I desire to depart and be with Christ, which is better by far" (Phil 1:23).

The foregoing does not mean that Scripture teaches us a detailed metaphysics of the soul, or that it uses consistent technical terms for the heart, soul, mind, etc. Nor does it mean that body and soul are entirely distinct, entailing a radical dualism. But there are ways of understanding body and soul in the Christian tradition that do not disagree with what Scripture reveals, accord with experienced reality, and avoid the sorts of problems

---

20. In contrast, note the subtitle of K. Dijk's book, *Over de laatste dingen*. The subtitle is, *Tussen sterven en opstanding* [Between Death and Resurrection].

21. See the Heidelberg Catechism, Q&A 57, *Book of Praise*, 536.

22. See Fergusson, *Creation*, esp. 1, 13–14, 96–110; Murphy, *Bodies and Souls*, 27.

that physicalists bring up when people talk about the soul as distinct from the body. Typically these ways will involve some kind of Thomistic understanding of the body-soul relation, as opposed to the Platonic-Cartesian understanding.

The following sections of this essay will move through selected Old Testament texts that are relevant, then New Testament texts, followed by discussion of what the soul is, biblically speaking. This will open the way for some further points about the theological and philosophical problems created by physicalism before drawing the argument to its conclusion.

Note that in what follows disproportionately greater attention will fall on the Old Testament. This is because it is much easier and more common for physicalists to dismiss evidence of belief in the soul when they restrict themselves to the Old Testament; the New Testament is clearer with respect to the body-and-soul distinction.

SELECTED OLD TESTAMENT SCRIPTURES

Genesis 2:7: the breath of life

Let us now begin with Gen 2:7: "The Lord God formed the man from the dust of the ground and breathed into his nostrils the breath of life, and the man became a living being." For centuries English readers of the Authorized Version (KJV) read in this verse the expression "the man became a living soul," and this wording was used to support the idea of a body formed from the dust and a soul received from God.[23] However, the man did not *become* a soul. We may believe he received a soul, but he did not become one, and the Hebrew word *nepeš*, though rightly translated "soul" in other places, does not mean "soul" as distinct from body in this text.[24] Certainly, God's *rŭaḥ* (spirit) breathed into man's nostrils, to give life, and certainly this is contrasted to forming man's body from the dust. Thus, if we argue that the

---

23. William Shedd, a nineteenth-century traducianist, treats Genesis 2:7 as the indication that God created man one part material from the dust and the other immaterial, by his breath. He translates: "the man became a living soul." Shedd, *Dogmatics*, 430.

24. In Gen 1:24 *nepeš* refers to animals, and is typically translated as "creatures." Shedd notes that whereas the human *nepeš* is breathed by God directly, the animals have (or become) *nepeš* naturally. He therefore concludes that the animal soul is physical, material, and mortal in nature, while the human soul is immaterial, rational, and immortal. Shedd, *Dogmatics*, 430. Note: the distinction of plant, animal, and human souls is as old as Aristotle.

text has something to do with a soul, this would seem to follow from God's act of bestowing life, but not from the word *nepeš*. In fact, this exegetical point was acknowledged long ago already.[25] Also, astute readers will already have noticed that the terms for both soul and spirit have already appeared in this essay. Though the two are not identical, I need to remark at the outset that they are often used interchangeably in Scripture.[26]

At any rate, we cannot hang this discussion of body and soul on one term such as *nepeš*. This word is often better translated as a personal pronoun or as "life" or "being" or "person."[27] It is flexible.

At the same time, one should carefully study the various words that describe aspects of human inner life in Hebrew, and one should not simply flatten out the rich variety of biblical vocabulary, as though *nepeš* (soul), *rŭaḥ* (spirit), and *lēv* (heart) each refer to persons in their totality or as if they are only about relations of persons and not at all about their natures or essences.[28] All of these errors are indulged in by post-modern physicalists. Matthew Levering reflected on this in the case of Nancey Murphy: "Murphy affirms that 'participation in the post-resurrection kingdom' will involve 'personal transformation,' and she notes that 'a great deal of what lasts in the post-resurrection kingdom must be those relationships within the body of Christ that now make us the people we are.'"[29]

Confirmation that Gen 2:7 may indeed be speaking about the origin of more than just "breath" occurs in the description at Zech 12:1, "The Lord, who stretches out the heavens, who lays the foundation of the earth, and who forms the spirit of man within him." Here the same verb as was used for God's "forming" the human body from the dust (Gen 2:7) and "forming" the animals (Gen 2:19) is used for his creation of the human spirit (*yāṣar*). This usage makes the word "spirit" very close to the word "soul," as an entity or thing distinct from the body. After all, one can hardly speak of "forming" wind and breath. This verb, "to form," came to be used

---

25. Vermigli, *Common Places*, 121–22.

26. See, e.g., Berkhof, *Systematic Theology*, 192–95

27. In English we also use "soul" in ways that mean "person." For example, "Oh, the poor soul!" and "What a brave soul!" We also talk about "a town of a hundred souls," and "soul mates." For the semantic range of *nepeš*, see *NIDOTTE*, 3:133 [#5883]. Note that the semantic range of "soul" in English may also vary from the time of the 1611 KJV to the present, but I have not studied that question.

28. Green, *Luke*, 826, n. 57.

29. Levering, *Jesus and Demise of Death*, 106.

to describe all of God's acts of creation (e.g., Pss 65:6; 90:2; 95:5).[30] However we parse this, God made or formed something non-bodily within Adam, the first human.

Deuteronomy 6:5: to love with all one's soul

If there is a text that suggests against flattening out the various psychological or anthropological Hebrew descriptions, it would be Deut 6:5, where three terms occur side by side: "You shall love the Lord your God with all your heart, with all your soul, and with all your strength." From the context, we learn that Yahweh is One: his undivided nature is to be served by us in an undivided and total fashion. But what distinguishes one's soul from one's heart and strength? The rabbis did not explain what these are with elaborate philosophical distinctions, but gave the following helpful comments:

> *With your whole heart* (thereby is meant): with both your inclinations, with the good inclination and the evil inclination.
>
> *With your whole soul* (thereby is meant): even if he takes your soul (i.e., your life).
>
> *With your whole might* (thereby is meant): with your whole property. Another saying: *With your whole might* (is meant): for whatever measure he measures to you, you shall bring to him an overflowing thanksgiving.[31]

For God to take one's soul could mean to take to himself the soul while leaving the body on earth, but this is not the obvious meaning. Another way of expressing what it means to love God with all one's soul was: "till the last ounce of life/soul is squeezed out of you." Thus, the rabbis took "soul" in the Shema to refer to one's life. I think they were correct as to the meaning of the Shema, even if their exegesis is not exhaustive or exclusive.[32]

Yet that does not mean the rabbis and Old Testament believers had no notion of a substantial soul (however they may have conceived of it), for in

---

30. See *NIDOTTE* 2:503–505. The use of *yāṣar* as a retrospective description of God's work of creation in various Scripture texts underlines his personal involvement in the work and his care over that which resulted.

31. Gerhardsson, *Testing of God's Son*, 74. See also 48–53, 71–76.

32. What the rabbis teach about the two inclinations of the heart may be an interesting way of speaking of the old and new nature in a believer, but certainly does not describe the unregenerate, who lack a good inclination.

this text the soul exists in some kind of parallel with the heart and strength, as an identifiable entity. What is it that holds, contains, or governs the life that is enjoyed in the body? Many of the psalmists appear to posit some kind of substantial (subsistent?) entity that particularly relates to God, in distinction from the body.

Psalm 103:1, etc.: O my soul!

Examining the not infrequent occurrence of "O my soul" in the Psalms highlights, first, the important distinction between oneself and one's soul. Secondly, it reveals some of things that the *nepeš* does, in distinction from the body.

Psalm 103 opens with a self-exhortation,

> Praise the Lord, O my soul [*nepeš*]; all my inmost being, praise his holy name. Praise the Lord, O my soul, and forget not all his benefits—who forgives all your sins and heals all your diseases, who redeems your life from the pit and crowns you with love and compassion, who satisfies your desires with good things so that your youth is renewed like the eagle's. (Ps 103:1–5)

Noteworthy—and so obvious that it easily goes unnoticed—is the fact that the author speaks as a unified personality to a faculty or entity within himself. He distinguishes his *nepeš* from himself. His soul is not merely his entire self from another perspective, but something that is "within him." Verse 1 is chiastic, and the synthetic parallelism of verse 1b makes clear the meaning of verse 1a: "Praise the Lord, O my soul, *and all that is within me,* praise his holy name." David regards his soul to be an entity "within him" or the summing up of everything that is within him.

He admonishes his soul not to forget (v. 2). We could say that this simply means that he himself, as a whole person, should not forget. True, but this would also be a simplification of his words, for the way in which he himself will prevent escape from his memory is by having *his soul* remember. He then reminds his soul of God's forgiveness, healing, redemption, and the satisfying of his desires (vv. 3–5). His soul then includes his memory. Never do persons in Scripture admonish their bodies to remember, fear, or praise Yahweh, though they do speak of their bodies being healthy or ill, wasting away, and becoming thin and gaunt (Pss 38:3, 7; 109:24).

The phrase "O my soul" occurs more often in the Psalms. In Ps 31:9 it is used in direct distinction from the body: "Be merciful to me, O Lord, for

In Between and Intermediate

I am in distress; my eyes grow weak with sorrow, my soul and my body with grief." The word rendered as "body" is not a common one; elsewhere it is translated as "womb" or "belly," but here "body" is quite defensible.[33] At any rate, the two terms indicate a suffering that affects everything.

Other Psalms reveal that the soul can grieve and suffer turmoil (Psalms 6; 42–43), live in hope and patience (Ps 62:5), enjoy rest when at peace (Pss 62:1; 116:7), entrust itself to God (Ps 57:1; 86:2), cling to God (Ps 63:8), yearn and faint to be near God (Ps 63:1; 84:2), and be satisfied with God's love as the body would be with the richest of foods (Ps 63:2–5). The activities of the heart (*lēv*) and soul have some overlap; however, the heart has a greater moral aspect to it than the soul—righteousness, holiness, purity, and steadfastness of faith belong to the believer's heart, and the heart can be tested by God (Ps 17:3; 19:14; 26:2; 51:10; 57:7; 108:1). A "wicked heart" would mean "an evil *disposition* of the person," whereas "a wicked soul" would just mean "an evil person."

Also important to compare to the soul is the spirit (*rŭaḥ*). In the Old Testament, the human spirit is given by the Spirit (*rŭaḥ*) of God, as per Gen 2:7 (cf. Job 33:4). The Spirit (or spirit) within a person can motivate or compel him (Job 32:18). "Spirit" in the Scriptures represents life and power (cf. Isa 31:3). One might say that the *rŭaḥ* gives life to the *nepeš*. One dictionary states, "This breath is the essence of life." The same dictionary entry adds that *rŭaḥ* and *nepeš* sometimes serve as synonyms, indicating a person's disposition, attitude, mood, inclination.[34]

In a case of poetic expression even the psalmist's flesh (*bāśār*) "cries out for the living God" (84:2), but this is an unusual statement.[35]

Finally, one's soul can be rescued by God from the abode of the dead (*šĕʿôl*), or kept from entering this abode, but the same would never be said of the heart (Ps 30:3).

This brief examination of the Psalms is very much open to augmentation and correction, but it at least outlines a good many things that are said of the soul. These are said in such a way that many of them are best understood if the soul is thought of as an entity distinct from the body, yet

---

33. The word is *beten*. "The belly stands for the body, yet with a more particular reference to the bowels as the seat of the affections, or as Delitzsch, 'the interior of the body reflecting the spiritual and physical activities and experiences.' The soul and the belly thus represent the entire man." Moll, *Psalms*, 219.

34. NIDOTTE 3:1074.

35. In the case of Psalm 63:1 the expression "my body (*bāśār*) longs for you" is literally true inasmuch as David was in the desert and lacked water.

intimately united with it. If the heart particularly relates to God morally, and the life of the soul is dependent upon the spirit (*rŭaḥ*), then the soul might be thought of as a kind of shadow-figure of the person that contains the person's life principle.[36]

Isaiah 55:3–7: that your soul may live

In Isa 55:3–7 the soul is treated as an entity that feeds on the words of Yahweh. The Lord, through his prophet, makes a strong contrast between spending money on things that do not satisfy and receiving water, wine, and milk from him without cost. Then he specifies that what he is really talking about is soul food: "Listen, listen to me, and eat what is good, and your soul will delight in the richest of fare. Give ear and come to me; hear me, that your soul may live."

Note that one's *nepeš* is said to live. Almost certainly *nepeš* does not mean "life" or "person" in this instance, but some entity within the person that truly lives only by the word of Yahweh.[37] While it is possible to translate "and *you* will delight in the richest of faire . . . and *you* will live," the contrast between things that money can buy yet are not "bread" and the life-giving words of Yahweh point to a body-soul distinction. We are reminded of Deut 8:3: "Man does not live on bread alone, but on every word that comes from the mouth of the Lord."[38]

What message do the ears of the soul need to hear in order to live? What do souls feed upon? This follows in the verses 3b–5, where the message of God's redemption in the Messiah follows, being given in the language of Davidic kingship. This redemption will give the life that the soul needs. Souls do not literally feed on water, wine, and milk, but upon words of forgiveness and grace (v. 7). The everlasting covenant that Yahweh will make (v. 5b) in connection with this living or, perhaps better, *reviving* of the soul reminds us of the promises of the new covenant in Jer 31:31–33, where

---

36. The appearance of Samuel before the witch of Endor in 1 Samuel 28 suggests some sort of bodily *appearance* for souls. In the intertestamentary period the Jews regarded persons in the intermediate state as existing in the form or shape of a body, but not in a material form. See Cooper, *Body, Soul*, 58–59, 123.

37. We would not translate as "that your person may live," or "that your life may live." The translation "that your soul may live," or "and your soul will live," is universal, going all the way back to the Septuagint.

38. Notwithstanding, Gerhardsson relates Deuteronomy 8:3 to loving God with all one's heart rather than all one's soul. Gerhardsson, *Testing of God's Son*, 51–53.

a new heart is promised. Later the Christ would make a similar promise (John 4:13–14) and extend a similar invitation (John 7:37) regarding living water.

The reading suggested here could be contested linguistically inasmuch as "your soul" can simply mean "you." However, the progress in the history of revelation, as seen in the New Testament, pushes us in the direction of the wording that has characterized the universal approach to translation since the Septuagint: "and *your soul* will live."

Ecclesiastes 12:7: the spirit returns to God

Some kind of distinction of the body and the soul or spirit is well represented in Eccl 12:7, where readers are exhorted to remember their Creator before they die, "and the dust returns to the ground it came from, and the spirit returns to God who gave it." The dichotomy is transparent: body and spirit. The text obviously is recalling Genesis 2:7, which we reviewed earlier, and identifying death as the undoing of the original creation (see Gen 3:19). Various commentators therefore assert that it is not at all an expression of hope in an afterlife, but a confirmation of the finality of death.

However, the expression "the spirit returns to God" also relates to an earlier question of Qoheleth (the Preacher/Teacher) in Eccl 3:21, where he asks, "Who knows if the spirit of man rises upward and if the spirit of the animal goes down into the earth?"[39] This question arose after Qoheleth had surmised in 3:18–20 that as things appear, the *rŭaḥ* (spirit) of humans and animals is the same. Under the sun, apart from divine revelation, no one can speak with any certainty about an afterlife, let alone a positive afterlife. All we see are dead bodies—whether human or animal. But in 12:7 he answers the question that he previously could not answer, affirming that the human spirit does actually return to God. This leads Tremper Longman to assert, "As has already been stated, Qohelet, being a confused wise man, is not above tensions and contradictions."[40]

---

39. Note that the way the question is posed—allowing the idea that the "spirit" of the animal could go "downward"—makes this use of *rŭaḥ* pretty well synonymous with *nepeš*.

40. Longman, *Ecclesiastes*, 273. Compare 32, 171. Longman's statement is tied to his view that Qoheleth is a kind of rogue wisdom teacher who is responsible only for 1:12–12:7, with another author penning an orthodox framework around Qoheleth's sayings. In contrast, Whybray sees no contradiction between 3:21 and 12:7. Whybray, *Ecclesiastes*, 168.

However, it is also quite possible to read Qoheleth's statements coherently, with 12:7 forming the answer to the problem posed at 3:21. In support of this understanding, one could argue for the more traditional view that one author penned all of the Book of Ecclesiastes;[41] distinguish carefully those comments he makes about life "under the sun" from other statements that speak from the standpoint of faith (such as 12:1–14); incorporate a much stronger emphasis on the role of Ecclesiastes in the canon, so that texts from other books of Scripture receive more weight in interpreting 12:7 (see below); and recognize the revelation-historical trajectory within the canon, so that 12:7 is understood as the adumbration of something that is more fully revealed in later eras. At the least, Eccl 12:7 offers support to the view that living humans are more than physical bodies; their life/breath/spirit is the gift of God. In fact, even the question of Eccl 3:21 presupposes this distinction.[42]

Being taken up by God and having one's spirit ascend to God ought to indicate rest. We find a beautiful expression of this rest in Isa 57:1–2: "The righteous perish, and no one ponders it in his heart; devout men are taken away, and no one understands that the righteous are taken away to be spared from evil. Those who walk uprightly enter into peace; they find rest as they lie in death." Here no fear of Sheol enters the prophet's mind— the upright enter into peace and rest: to enjoy this gift they must be living with God even while their bodies lie about dishonored by the wicked who persecuted them.

Ezekiel 37:1–14 is also instructive as a parallel to Eccl 12:7. Ezekiel must prophesy to a valley of dry bones. Having done so, he sees the bones come rattling together, develop sinews, tendons, flesh, and skin, "but there was no breath in them." Ezekiel then had to prophesy particularly to the spirit (*rŭaḥ*) to give life to these now fleshy creatures. Like Gen 2:7, a distinction is made between the flesh of humans and their life, the latter depending upon God's Spirit breathing into them.

The people of Judah, who because of exile were without hope, were to take heart from this vision, holding on to the promise that Yahweh would give them his Spirit so that they would have life and would return to the Promised Land (Ezek 37:13–14). Without doubt the prophecy refers to more than physical life, for being away from the Promised Land was

---

41. The single-author position more easily accommodates the six passages that Longman admits having difficulty accounting for. See Longman, *Ecclesiastes*, 34, 36.

42. Krüger, *Qoheleth*, 203, n. 52.

about being cut off *from God*, and being brought back meant being *in God's presence*, and, further, those in God's presence had to be holy. Thus God promised to give them a new heart and new spirit, by which he would move them to follow his decrees and laws (Ezek 36:16–32).

We may conclude that *rûaḥ* in Ezekiel 37 refers to both to the ontological life principle—what we might call the soul—as well as to the principle of new life or regeneration, the redirecting of the heart and soul/spirit to God.

This is not to say that Ezekiel's vision teaches an intermediate state—not at all—but to demonstrate that the two-fold distinction of body and spirit appears repeatedly in the Old Testament.

Psalms 27:4 etc.: dwelling with God forever

In Psalm 27 David makes a request of Yahweh that highlights the one thing he desires more than all others: "that I may dwell in the house of the Lord all the days of my life, to gaze upon the beauty of the Lord and to seek him in his temple" (Ps 27:4). Now David's palace was next to the tabernacle, but it was not *in* the tabernacle. Further, it is at least debatable whether David was referring to the existing tabernacle or perhaps thinking ahead to the temple for which he had made plans and was collecting materials so that his son Solomon could oversee its construction. Perhaps he longed to see the temple erected, so that he could seek his God there.

But lest we conclude too quickly, we need to examine a number of other similar references in others Psalms of David. For instance, Ps 61:4, "I long to dwell in your tent forever." Psalm 18:6, "From his temple he heard my cry." Psalm 29:9, "And in his temple all cry, 'Glory!'" Psalm 11:4, "The Lord is in his holy temple; the Lord is on his heavenly throne."

The reference in Psalm 11 is most intriguing, for there a connection is drawn between God's dwelling in his holy temple and his being seated on his heavenly throne. The text specifies that his throne in heaven is in view. One might argue that the earthly temple was considered to be a kind of extension of heaven, but the objection stands that the cherubim were not considered to be God's heavenly throne, but his earthly throne, if a throne at all (compare Ps 99:1 to 103:19).[43] So also, when David sings of all those in

---

43. Woudstra argues that the ark was a chest containing the key covenant documents and was thus called the "ark of the testimony" or the "ark of the covenant." Treating it as a throne emerged as an idea in the nineteenth century and is judged incorrect by Woudstra. See Woudstra, *Ark of the Covenant*, 85–103.

Yahweh's temple crying out "Glory!" (Ps 29:9), he is most likely thinking of God's heavenly dwelling place, for he begins the Psalm with an exhortation to the angelic beings: "Ascribe to Yahweh, you heavenly beings, ascribe to the Lord glory and strength" (Ps 29:1).[44]

These collected statements about Yahweh in his temple are certainly worthy of much more study than is appropriate in this context, but together they strongly suggest that David's prayer to dwell in Yahweh's house all his days, to gaze upon Yahweh's beauty, and to seek him in his temple is about dwelling with God forever in another place—in the place of which the earthly temple was but a copy (Exod 25:9, 40, etc.; and Heb 8:5).

But David was well aware that when persons die their bodies remain present on earth, lifeless. He knew the teaching, "Dust you are, and to dust you shall return" (Gen 3:19; cf. Pss 90:3; 104:29; Job 34:15). Although David did not yet distinguish between the eschatological moments of the intermediate state, resurrection, and new creation, he certainly longed to dwell with God forever even though his body might remain lifeless on earth. It is hard to escape the idea that he had some hope of his spirit or soul going to be with God.

Psalm 49:7–15: soul redeemed

The escape of the believer's soul from the place of the dead is underlined in another Psalm. Although the Hebrew of this Psalm is difficult, the lone speaker of the sons of Korah does clearly confess that God will "redeem" (*pādāh*) his "soul/life" (*nepeš*) from the place of the dead (*šě'ôl*); that "he will surely take me to himself" (Ps 49:15).[45] Delitzsch makes the point that the Psalmist is referring to the way in which God took Enoch to himself, sparing him death (Gen 5:24).[46] Virtually all commentaries by orthodox commentators take the verse to refer to a better hope, even if it was a rather shadowy idea at this point in the history of redemption. The rhymed version

---

44. This is the translation of the Holman Christian Standard Bible.

45. The semantic range of *pādāh* includes "ransom," "redeem," "deliver." See NIDOTTE 3:578–82.

46. Delitzsch, *Psalms II*, 118. More is said here about being taken up to God than in Psalm 30:3, where the rescue envisioned is clearly limited to being spared death in a time of great distress.

sung in the Canadian Reformed churches goes like this: "But God will pay my ransom and not leave me/ for he into his glory will receive me."[47]

Set in the context of earlier verses in Psalm 49, a clear contrast emerges between the wicked and the righteous. First the psalmist asserts that no man can redeem another's *nepeš* (v. 8) in such a way that it would enable a person to live on forever (v. 9). No man's riches will suffice (vv. 6, 10–12) for this. Rather, all proceed into death and will inhabit *šĕʿôl*. But the statement that no person will be enabled to live forever by having another person redeem his or her soul is followed by the confident assertion that there is indeed a way out. This becomes clear when the psalmist contends that God will provide the redemption needed to redeem his life from the place of the dead.

In verse 19 we read that the wicked man, whose splendor has "descended with him," "will never see the light." The contrast is quite obvious: even riches cannot redeem the life/soul of the man who trusts in himself and his riches, but the believer will be redeemed by God. Because God has paid the redemption, the believer becomes the possession of God, who will then take that possession to himself and will no doubt jealously guard it. It is hard to avoid the conclusion that the psalmist believed God would usher him into his presence upon death.

Once again, if we keep in mind the common-sense point that the psalmist is well aware of what happens to corpses upon death, there seems to be a strong affirmation of continued existence after death for the believer, even if the details remain vague.

Psalm 73:24–26: afterward taken into glory

In Psalm 73, a psalm of Asaph, the singer recounts how his faith had almost slipped for a time, but has now become stronger by going to the holy place of God and perceiving the truth about the ends or "final destinies" (v. 17) of human beings. He had almost become senseless in his lack of faith, but once his heart had been renewed, he recognized that God had been there all along: "Yet I am always with you; you hold me by my right hand" (v. 23). Then he proceeded to move from the present to the future in the confidence of faith: "You guide me with your counsel, and afterward you will take me into glory" (v. 24)—this in contrast to the wicked, who will be "suddenly destroyed" (v. 19).

---

47. *Book of Praise*, 121.

At the same time Asaph recognizes that while his "heart and flesh may fail" (v. 26), he has no one in heaven but his God (v. 25), who will be his "portion forever" (v. 26). What part, aspect, or form of him would be taken into glory? Not his flesh, for it may fail. He does not specify, but again, in light of further revelation in Scripture, we can be confident that we have here the adumbration of the eschatological reality of the intermediate state.

Psalm 115:17–18: praising Yahweh forevermore

I shall bring the study of these selected Old Testament texts to a close with a Psalm that contrasts the true God with the idols of the nations. The idols are dead: "They have mouths, but cannot speak, eyes, but they cannot see; they have ears, but cannot hear, noses, but cannot smell; they have hands, but cannot feel, feet, but they cannot walk" (vv. 5–7). They are like corpses. The Psalm continues, "Those who make them will be like them" (v. 8).

The ending of the Psalm is best understood in light of this contrast. We read, "It is not the dead who praise the Lord, those who go down to silence; it is we who extol the Lord, both now and forevermore. Praise the Lord" (vv. 17–18). There certainly is a theme in other Psalms of the need for the believers to remain alive and fulfill their purpose in praising the Lord (see Pss 6:5; 30:8–9; 88:5–12). That must be in view here in Psalm 115 also. Yet there is more going on in the immediate context of the Psalm itself, and it is the contrast of the dead and lifeless idol worshipers over against the true believers in Israel. One might suggest that the idolators are doubly dead—in both body and soul—due to their sin and rebellion, whereas in contrast the psalmist states, "It is we who extol the Lord, both now and forevermore."

Admittedly, the distinction in this Psalm is more between one person and another than between body and soul. The value of the text in the present discussion then simply is to point the way, for the believer, to the ongoing life that is truly life.

Dead souls in the Old Testament? Shakespeare...

Before we draw the study of these Old Testament texts to a conclusion, we need to recognize the wide semantic range of *nepeš*. Earlier we noted its flexibility. Remarkably, it can even refer to a dead person, possibly a dead "body." This occurs in Lev 21:11, where we find that the priest is forbidden to approach any dead *nepeš*, and in Lev 19:28: "Do not cut your bodies *for the dead* (literally, for a *nepeš*) or put tattoo marks on yourselves . . ." The Israelites were not to follow pagan practices wherein grieving was expressed in morbid ways and a priest was not to make himself unclean by touching a dead person.

We encounter in these usages a semantic range that appears unusual at first sight. And these are unusual usages. But their meaning is obvious from the context and does not imply a belief that a substantial "soul" dies. In these instances "soul" simply means "dead person." Meaning is determined by use, in context.

William Shakespeare used the English word "soul" with a similar range of meaning. In *Macbeth* a grieving Macduff mourns the loss of his wife and children, blaming himself: "Sinful Macduff, / They were all struck for thee! naught that I am, / Not for their own demerits, but for mine/ Fell slaughter on their souls. Heaven rest them now!"[48] Similarly, in *Henry VI* we read, "This brawl to-day/ Grown to this faction in the Temple-garden/ Shall send between the red rose and the white/ A thousand souls to death and deadly night."[49] Another example occurs, negatively expressed, in *Othello* as follows: "Well, do it, and be brief; I will walk by. / I would not kill thy unprepared spirit, / No; heaven forfend! I would not kill thy soul."[50]

In conclusion, the semantic range of *nepeš* does not create a problem for the understanding of the nature of the soul in the Old Testament.

CONCLUSION RE OLD TESTAMENT TEACHINGS

Bringing together the nine Old Testament texts studied above, together with the many parallel and elucidating texts, assembles a significant cluster of evidence for the distinction of body and soul in the Old Testament.

Beginning already in Gen 2:7, we encounter the contrast of a body from the dust and a life or soul from God's breath, and Scripture repeats this contrast in the wisdom statement of Eccl 12:7 and the prophetic parable of Ezekiel 37. The three-fold distinction of Deut 6:5 suggests that the soul is a faculty of like kind to the heart, and the frequent psalmic expression "O my soul," as referring to something "within" the singer and distinct from the body, supports this view very strongly. The world of the soul as

---

48. Shakespeare, *Macbeth*, IV, 3, lines 2108–11.
49. Shakespeare, *Henry VI*, Part I, II, 4. lines 1061–64.
50. Shakespeare, *Othello*, V, 2, lines 3334–36.

described in the Psalms—its grieving, yearning for God, clinging to him, living in hope, being satisfied with God's love, and enjoying rest—is the world of every believer. These activities do not belong to the body primarily, for the body often suffers persecution even while the soul finds peace in God. Isaiah 55 teaches us that souls were made to relate to God, indeed, to live by every word that proceeds from his mouth, particularly his words of promise. In the words of Psalm 27 and the text connected to it, who would not desire to dwell with God forever, to gaze upon his beauty and seek him in his heavenly temple, at his heavenly throne? This joy belongs exclusively to the faithful because God himself will redeem believers' souls from the place of the dead, taking them to himself (Ps 49). "Afterward you will take me into glory," sang Asaph, even though his heart and flesh might fail (Ps 73). Finally, Psalm 115 confesses the life that God shares with his children in contrast to idol worshippers, who will be as dead as the things they worship. As Henry Scougal wrote, "The worth and excellency of a soul is to be measured by the object of its love."[51]

All of these texts, treated in context and taken together, provide significant evidence pointing to an afterlife with God, immediately upon death. We may also add, briefly, a point made by Cornelis Venema about the condemnation of necromancy and communication with the dead. This practice and its condemnation in Israel confirm "at the very least a widespread conviction of continued conscious existence after death. This is particularly instructive since the Old Testament uniformly views death as the result of God's judgment curse upon humankind because of sin."[52]

We have not examined any Old Testament texts suggesting a resurrection of the body and a new creation, but these exist also (e.g., Job 19:21; Dan 12:2; Isa 26:19). This strong belief, coupled with the reality of the corpse and at the same time the promise and faith of being with God forever, has as corollary a belief in an intermediate state. After all, if a person is to be with God in glory but does not yet enjoy life in the resurrected body, that person must be present with God in some other way.

What one will not find in the Old Testament is a more detailed setting forth of the chronology of the end times. Even the prophecies are typically telescoped, the prophet being like an onlooker who observes a mountain range in the distance but is not yet able to distinguish the distances between the faraway peaks. Only with later revelation and participation in

---

51. Scougal, *Life of God*, 31.
52. Venema, *The Future*, 54.

the coming of Christ did God make clearer to his church the sequence and distinction of the various eschatological events.

My plea to readers is to embrace a canonical reading of Scripture. Take the whole book as the Book of God, ultimately penned by one divine author, God the Holy Spirit. Before relating Scripture texts to various possible ancient Near Eastern parallels—itself a science fraught with difficulty as one attempts to determine what may actually serve as a parallel—we ought to relate Scripture to Scripture. Scripture interprets itself, as the ancient rules states the matter.

Nevertheless, in order to help us appreciate the history of revelation I have avoided relating these Old Testament texts to the New Testament. God did not reveal everything in one fell swoop. The Old Testament offers but an outline of the doctrine of the intermediate state. This does not mean that what is revealed is so shadowy as to be invisible. Rather, it all fits very well with the New Testament teachings, demonstrating that the one God was governing all of this revelation, throughout history moving revelation towards a fuller description of the hope that awaits us.

INTERTESTAMENTARY PERIOD

Although no Scripture revelation was given in the intertestamentary period, God did use the developing views of the time to form and shape the thinking of early New Testament believers.

Andrew Lincoln and John Cooper have definitively demonstrated that the body-and-soul distinction was a strong belief, especially among the Pharisees in the time of Christ.[53] Deniers of this view, such as Joel Green, have not interacted with the overwhelming evidence presented by Lincoln and Cooper. Gerhardsson, who studied the interpretation of the Shema as given above, writes, "God is to be loved even when he does not *preserve the soul* of his covenant son from death, even when he demands it from him in martyrdom."[54]

The idea that the soul is the principle of life is actually quite intuitive, for when a loved one dies, we gaze upon the body. It is still present, but the life is gone. We cannot communicate any longer. Something is missing. In Scripture, and in numerous cultures, this has been understood to mean that the soul has left the body, that its life principle is gone.

53. Cooper, *Body, Soul*, 73–93; Lincoln, *Paradise Now and Not Yet*, 70, 79–83, etc.
54. Gerhardsson, *Testing of God's Son*, 75 (emphasis added).

What did our Lord Jesus and the apostles teach us about the intermediate state?

SELECTED NEW TESTAMENT SCRIPTURES

Matthew 10:28: but cannot kill the soul

When our Lord himself encouraged us not to fear persecution, he said, "Do not be afraid of those who kill the body but cannot kill the soul. Rather, be afraid of the One who can destroy both soul and body in hell" (Matt 10:28). The distinction is transparent. Note well the language of killing the soul. This is not the language of annihilation but of everlasting punishment, for Jesus himself described hell with the words of Isaiah 66:24 as the place "where their worm does not die, and the fire is not quenched" (Mark 9:48). Conversely, the comfort for believers is that when they trust in the Lord no earthly power can kill that faith, firmly established as it is in their souls. Praise the Lord for his persevering grace!

Luke 16:27–31: Lazarus in the intermediate state

Let us note next how in the story of Lazarus and the rich man the latter requests that Lazarus return to warn his brothers. Abraham says that Moses and the Prophets form a sufficient warning. But the rich man insists: "'No, father Abraham, he said, 'but if someone *from the dead* goes to them, they will repent.' He said to him, 'If they do not listen to Moses and the Prophets, they will not be convinced even if someone *rises from the dead.*'" (Luke 16:27–31, emphasis added). Jesus assumed that Lazarus was with Abraham, alive, yet not embodied. For both Abraham and the rich man agreed that if Lazarus were to return to the rich man's brothers he would have to rise from the dead, which is to say, receive back his body. Thus, in the parable he constructed, our Lord imagined Lazarus in an intermediate state, living in the soul. Jesus assumed that such was reality.

Luke 23:43: today you will be with me in Paradise

Consider what comfort it was to the thief on the cross to hear, "Today you will be with me in Paradise" (Luke 23:43). Obviously, as they both hung on the cross, they were far from Paradise. But actually not! That very literal

In Between and Intermediate

day, they would both be in Paradise. They would each remain distinct: "you" will be with "me." They would know and recognize each other. The thief, if a Jew, would have understood "Paradise" to be like a garden where souls went upon death, where the blessed dwell with God.[55]

Luke 23:46: into your hands I commit my spirit

A short time later, when Jesus said, "Father, into your hands I commit my spirit" (Luke 23:46), then obviously Jesus was not referring to his body, for it was hanging on the cross. Central to this statement is the faith of Jesus the Son in his heavenly Father. Even while his Father turned his face away and poured out his wrath, the Son turned his heart, his life, his spiritual soul, to his Father, seeking his protection. He did not "curse God and die" (cf. Job 2:9). He lived by faith. This is the faith that the Spirit of Jesus promises to cultivate in our hearts.

The evangelists Matthew and John both recorded that shortly after this, Jesus "gave up his spirit" (Matt 27:50; John 19:30). Stephen used similar language when he said, "Lord Jesus, receive my spirit" (Acts 7:59). This is not about "life in its totality," but life in the soul.[56] Both Jesus and Stephen held in common with those around them a strong belief in the survival of the soul at death and its departure from this earthly realm to go and be with God.

Interestingly, the time that Jesus spent in the intermediate state was only about forty hours, whereas many believers have spent centuries and even millennia awaiting the resurrection of their bodies. Jesus has his glorified body, and his enjoyment of this state is a seal and pledge of our own coming resurrection. The Heidelberg Catechism summarizes Scripture on this point: "Christ is true man and true God. With respect to his human nature he is no longer on earth," and "we have our flesh in heaven as a sure pledge, that he, our Head, will also take us, his members, up to himself."[57]

None of this implies a low view of the body. In fact, when the New Testament describes death as "falling asleep," it teaches us a high view of the body, for the body of the believer is not annihilated, forgotten, or alienated from God. It is the special privilege of believers to fall asleep "in Christ"

---

55. Cooper, *Body, Soul*, 87–88.
56. For the not uncommon interchange of "soul" and "spirit" in the New Testament, see the straightforward explanation in Berkhof, *Systematic Theology*, 192–95.
57. Heidelberg Catechism, Q&A 47 and 49, *Book of Praise*, 532–3.

(1 Cor 15:18) or "in Jesus (1 Thess 4:14).[58] Thus, after Stephen had asked Jesus to receive his soul and not to hold this sin against the Jewish Sanhedrin (Acts 7:59), the Scriptures record that "he fell asleep" (Acts 7:60). The Westminster Larger Catechism teaches that the members of the church, immediately upon death, enjoy communion in glory with Christ,

> in that their souls are made perfect in holiness, and received into the highest heavens, where they behold the face of God in light and glory, waiting for the full redemption of their bodies, *which even in death continue united to Christ, and rest in their graves as in their beds*, till at the last day they be again united to their souls.[59]

Philippians 1:21–24: to die is gain

No one could discuss the intermediate state without turning to the words of the apostle Paul in Phil 1:21–24, "For to me, to live is Christ and to die is gain . . . I desire to depart and be with Christ, which is better by far, but it is more necessary for you that I remain in the body." Paul's death is here a real possibility. He is in chains for Christ (Phil 1:7, 13). Identifying himself with his soul, he sounds almost Platonic: "I desire to be with Christ." Although Paul decides that he ought to remain and serve the church, his statement that he would gain, improve, get more of Christ by dying, does not sit well with the physicalist.

Physicalists charge that Christian concern for the soul has entailed a lack of care about the body, and they contend that this has bred selfishness, lack of care for the poor, endorsement of slavery, exploitation of women, capital punishment, and the ravaging and destruction of creation. Aside from the need actually to prove the case historically, their argument is opportunistic.[60] They could as easily have pointed to many texts of Scripture that admonish the church to promote justice and show love, but in their concern to make room for a "holistic," "monistic," and "physicalist" paradigm, they instead arranged tendentious arguments against the soul.

---

58. Venema, *The Future*, 51.

59. *Confession of Faith*, 223–24 (emphasis added).

60. Historically, the church has been at the forefront of helping the poor (New Testament), rescuing discarded infants (Roman Empire), setting up formal education (medieval period), establishing hospitals and more educational institutions (Reformation period), and ending slavery, child labor, and other exploitation (era of Revolutions and Victorian era).

In Between and Intermediate

If one would take to heart the deep desire that all believers should have to be holy entirely, to trust and obey God without reserve, and to be done with this body of sin, then he or she would surely agree with Paul that it is better by far to go and be with Christ. Just think what that would mean, to be done with sin! What relief! What wonder! What peace! And what a step towards glory! What an assurance of acceptance by God! To go where Jesus has prepared a place for us (John 14:2–3)! And what a flood of overwhelming and ever-increasing joy will be ours as we then "see face to face" and no longer "as in a mirror, dimly" (1 Cor 13:12–13)! Happy will be the pure in heart, for they will see God (Matt 5:8).[61]

Second Corinthians 5:1–9: we would prefer to be away from the body

When writing to the Corinthians, who themselves had a low view of the body (see 1 Cor 6:12–20), the apostle Paul again wrote in a way that on a superficial reading might appear Platonic, for he calls the human body in its present condition a "tent" which believers desire to shed in order to put on their "heavenly dwelling" (vv. 1–4). But what does he mean?

Both Ian Smith and Klaas Schilder note that the earthly tent of verse 1 refers to the present body in its suffering under the curse, while the "eternal house," also in verse 1, refers to the resurrection body in all its glory. Paul rejoices that when we lose the first we will gain the second. It is everlasting, kept safe in heaven, where Christ is. Paul would prefer not to have to die and then live, as it were, unclothed, in a bodiless state (v. 4).[62] The present body is but a temporary shelter, a tent. It belongs with a soul, but it needs to be improved or augmented, even, in a sense, replaced.[63]

But, argues Smith, as Paul grew older he realized that he likely would not remain alive until Christ's coming and so would have to enter the intermediate state. From the perspective of closeness to God, this state represents a positive gain (Phil 1:21–24), but from the perspective of the resurrection of the body, the intermediate state falls short. He will not be able to just take off the old garment (his present body, under the curse) and immediately put on the new one (the resurrection body). He will be a soul

---

61. On the *visio Dei* theme, see Van Dooren, "Foreword," in *Unity in Diversity*, ix–xiii.

62. Smith, "2 Corinthians 5:1–8," 17–18.

63. Schilder, "Letter," 27.

that longs for its body, just as the martyrs' souls do under the altar in Rev 6:9–11.[64] Paul remains assured that God made us for the very purpose of attaining to the new creation with its renewed body, and that he has given us his Holy Spirit as the assurance of this (v. 5). But this very promise, with Christ as its amen, makes him long all the more for its fulfillment. Paul's position is the very opposite of Platonism!

Since the Lord is tarrying, the apostle considers further the positive aspects of the intermediate state. He writes,

> Therefore we are always confident and know that as long as we are at home in the body we are away from the Lord. We live by faith, not by sight. We are confident, I say, and would prefer to be away from the body and at home with the Lord. So we make it our goal to please him, whether we are at home in the body or away from it. (2 Cor 5:6–9)[65]

The apostle is not confused; rather, the down payment of the Spirit within him (v. 5) has given him confidence (v. 6) to live by faith (v. 7) and even to prefer being with the Lord in the intermediate state to being here on earth in the collapsible tent of a body that suffers under the curse (vv. 1, 8). Smith rightly comments that while existing without his body is "metaphysically unattractive" to Paul, being with Christ will at the same time be "relationally attractive."[66] Paul thus lays out the benefits of dying before the return of Christ. Namely, he will be able to move from faith to sight, from being away from the Lord to being with him. As he states in Phil 1:23, there is a great gain in dying. Although the intermediate state will not yet bring believers to the goal of their salvation, it will be a blessed state in which they are enabled to see Christ their Lord.

The Heidelberg Catechism confirms these points in two different places. First, in Question and Answer 42, then in 57:

---

64. Schilder, "Letter," 27. Compare Flavel, *Pneumatologia*, 127–128.

65. Note that Paul himself knew something of the inexpressible things of the third heaven (i.e., neither the clouds and birds area [1st] nor the area of the stars in outer space [2nd], but God's dwelling [3rd]) since he had been brought there in a vision. But he was not sure whether this had happened in the body or out of the body. At any rate, he has no difficulty envisioning himself existing and experiencing things apart from his body. See 2 Corinthians 12:1–10.

66. Smith, "2 Corinthians 5:1–8," 22. The same explanation of this text, with added considerations about the possible roles of Jewish traditions and Hellenistic anthropology in Paul's teachings about the intermediate state, occurs in Lincoln, *Paradise Now and Not Yet*, 70.

42. Q. Since Christ has died for us, why do we still have to die?

A. Our death is not a payment for our sins, but it puts an end to sin and is an entrance into eternal life.

57. Q. What comfort does *the resurrection of the body* offer you?

A. Not only shall my soul after this life immediately be taken up to Christ, my Head . . .[67]

In another passage, the same catechism confirms the eschatological reality of being-in-Christ today, of already crossing over from death to life by faith and in principle having eternal life now: "58. Q. What comfort do you receive from the article about *the life everlasting*? A. Since I now already feel in my heart the beginning of eternal joy . . ."[68] Here the catechism could as well have formulated the matter this way: "Since I now already feel in my *soul* the beginning of eternal joy."

It is not entirely clear to me whether to situate the heart and soul as distinct or overlapping entities, or to posit that the heart is within the soul, or to represent the spiritual aspect of the soul as distinct from the aspects of the soul that have to do with sustaining physical life. I tend to think that the latter position best fits with Scripture, but would add that the interaction and interpenetration of the various aspects of the human inner life is beyond a comprehensive description.

WHAT IS THE SOUL AND HOW DOES IT RELATE TO THE BODY?

At any rate, on the basis of Scripture, we affirm that all human beings have souls. We are embodied souls, created to be a perfect and seamless unity of body and soul. Apart from sin, souls and bodies would never have had to separate. Thus, our characterization of human nature should emphasize wholeness more than dualism. We are made to be one unit but can, if necessary, continue to exist apart from the body.

The human soul is the instrumental cause of the body's life. The soul expresses itself through the body. We are each recognized by the unique combination of body and soul that we are, by our unique facial expressions, gaits, tones and speed of speech, laughter, etc. Our souls take in data from

---

67. *Book of Praise*, 530, 536.
68. Ibid., 536.

the senses, abstract from these data the universals,[69] and draw logical connections of many kinds. Our souls experience joy, sorrow, anger, satisfaction, and love. Within our souls we think, deliberate, and will. Our desires and affections are within the soul.

In complex ways, the brain and mind act within and perhaps alongside the soul, but do not exhaust its operations. As the soul gives life to the body, it probably is the life in every cell and part, and by it we raise our arms, dart our eyes, and twitch our ears. By way of our souls we also relate to God, and this aspect of the soul is in Scripture often called the spirit. God made us for himself, and our hearts are restless till they find rest in him.[70] This rest is found when he comes to inhabit our souls and begins to make them new. The Holy Spirit imparts truth to our minds, brings goodness and obedience to our wills, and thereby begins the renewal of our disordered affections.[71] Then our disordered loves are reorganized and our whole selves are presented as living sacrifices to the Lord (Rom 12:1–2).[72]

Scripture and the Reformed confessions of faith do not bind us to one exact theory that explains the relationship of body and soul, but theories that make more of their unity than their separation are to be preferred, for we were created whole and, when we have died, we will be whole again after the return of Christ.

If we are *not* going to espouse physicalism—and by now it should be clear that Scripture, carefully exegeted, has no room for this position—we have two main choices: either Platonic/Cartesian dualism or the more wholistic dualism of the Aristotelian/Thomistic position. There are of course variations of each, but these are mainly our choices. The charges that physicalists level against the body-and-soul distinction are usually, if not always, leveled against popular versions of the Cartesian system and almost never deal with the details of the Aristotelian and Thomistic account.

---

69. E.g., sense data shows me either an equilateral, isosceles, or scalene triangle, but the soul abstracts the idea of triangle as such.

70. Augustine, *Confessions* 1.1 (14)

71. See the Canons of Dort, ch. III/IV, 1 and 11. *Book of Praise*, 575, 577–78.

72. Augustine, *Teaching Christianity*, I:20–I:30 (114–119).

In Between and Intermediate

THE THOMISTIC AND REFORMED ACCOUNT OF BODY AND SOUL

The Cartesian system, following René Descartes (1596–1650), posits that human beings are comprised of thinking substance (soul) and extended substance (body). The problem has always been to determine how these two substances can relate. Descartes postulated that this occurred through the pineal gland in the brain. His system is rather idealist, being based entirely on his own rationalizations rather than upon observation of human nature.

John Calvin's description of the body as the prison house of the soul fit well with his approval of Plato's description of the soul.[73] However, such a description of the human body does not fit the description of God's creation as something good, nor with the longing of the soul for the body, as implied in Rev 6:9–11.

The Aristotelian account intends to describe reality as it is observed rather than in an idealistic manner. As adapted by Thomas Aquinas, this account also seeks to understand reality in a way that is consonant with the Scriptures, even if its perspective is not as such *demanded* by the Scripture. The accordance of Thomistic anthropology with Scripture, combined with its explanatory power, led the Reformed by and large to adopt it and other Aristotelian motifs. Calvin, for instance—notwithstanding the comments just made about his view of the body-soul relationship—freely makes use of four-fold causality in his account of justification and predestination,[74] and adopts a traditional view of the soul's faculties (intellect and will, though he does speak of the affections or appetites also).[75] The latter distinction regarding the soul's faculties was used even by the great Synod of Dort against the Remonstrants as key to the explanation of why conversion is not merely a matter of truth for the mind but also requires the reformation of the will—that God might maintain it as a human will that chooses, yet by regeneration might move it to embrace what is truly good.[76]

---

73. Calvin, *Institutes*, 1.15.2 and 1.15.7 (184, 195). One could plausibly argue that Calvin means that *this present body under the curse* is a prison house, for he maintains a robust doctrine of resurrection.

74. Calvin, *Institutes*, 3.14.17 (vol. 1:783–4); Calvin, *Commentary on Romans*, at 3:24 (141).

75. Calvin, *Institutes*, 1.15.3, 6–8 (vol. 1:188, 192–97). In 1.15.7 he cites Aristotle as an authority.

76. Canons of Dort, III/IV, art. 1, 11; *Book of Praise*, 575–76, 577–78.

Thomas's explanation of the relationship of body and soul states that the soul is the form of the body. His language closely follows the Aristotelian categories of form and matter (and, of course, formal and material causes). As form of the body, the soul is not merely the body's motor, but is present in the whole body, in every part. In maintaining this view, Thomas opposes Plato, for a human being is not a soul using a body, but body and soul, one substance, informed matter. A disembodied soul is not a complete person, although the soul can subsist apart from the body.

Cooper points out that Thomas abandoned Aristotle inasmuch as he held that the soul, while being "form" with respect to the body, is yet a "substance" of its own, able to continue existing. The soul, said Thomas, is an intellectual substance.[77] Cooper at first suggests—"gingerly, cautiously, and tentatively"—that "there are some striking similarities between the anthropology of Aristotle and that of the Old Testament."[78] A chapter later he concludes that the scriptural evidence of the Old Testament pushes us in the direction of some combination of Plato's and Aristotle's views, which Cooper finds exactly in Thomas. He writes, "Thomas's synthesis, not Descartes's dualism, was in the main followed by most orthodox Christian theologians, Catholic and Protestant alike. In my own Dutch Reformed tradition Abraham Kuyper, Herman Bavinck, and even Herman Dooyeweerd are heirs of this legacy..."[79]

One example of this synthesis in the Reformed tradition occurs in Peter Martyr's *Common Places* (1583), where he defends the view that because the life is in the blood, as per Gen 9:4–5, therefore one may speak of the the soul in the blood. He defends this view against the Manichaeans. Martyr adds that the soul in the blood is to be treated as a metonymy, the meaning being that the blood is a *sign* of the presence of the soul, and therefore may figuratively be called the soul itself.[80]

Another example can be found in John Flavel's *Pneumatologia* (1685). Although it is his aim to help believers live holy lives in preparation for their inevitable death and the intermediate state to follow, he also speaks eloquently of the mutual familiarity and love of body and soul, both now

---

77. Aquinas, *Summa Theologica*, 1.76.1 & 1.76.8. Cooper, *Body, Soul*, 11–13.

78. Cooper, *Body, Soul*, 49–50. On page 51 Cooper notes that in the Old Testament the soul is given to an already formed body (Gen 2:7), whereas in Aristotle the soul gives the body its structure. He also realizes that Aristotle's view would lead to annihilation at death, since a soul cannot exist apart from its body.

79. Cooper, *Body, Soul*, 72.

80. Vermigli, *Common Places*, 123.

and in the coming new creation. He finds this love described in Eph 5:29, "No one ever hated his own body, but he feeds and cares for it," and uses the following as the measure for our love of others: "You shall love your neighbor as yourself."[81] The body and soul have a "natural union . . . They are personally one; and though the soul be *what* it was, after its separation, yet to make a man the *who* he was, i.e., the same complete and perfect person, they must be re-united: hence springs its love to the body."[82] He adds these points: the body is the soul's ancient acquaintance and intimate friend, house and beloved habitation, instrument by which it does its work and business in this world, and "the soul's partner in the benefit of Christ's purchases."[83] He concludes:

> [The body] was bought with the same price, 1 Cor 6:20; sanctified by the same Spirit, 1 Thess 5:23; interested in the same promises, Matt 22:32; and designed for the same glory, 1 Thess 4:16–17. So that we may say of it, as it was said of Augustine and his friend Alippius, they are *sanguine Christi conglutinati*, glued together by the blood of Christ.[84]

When we turn to Herman Bavinck (1854–1921) we find in his account another truly wholistic description of the body-soul relation—a narrative much in line with the development of Neo-Thomism in Bavinck's own era and one that also reached back to the Reformed orthodox theologians. Bavinck delighted in the goodness of created material reality and maintained that the whole person, body and soul, was created in God's image (whereas for Calvin the soul was the principal seat of the image of God).[85] Bavinck also appreciated the extremely intricate relationship between the body and the soul.[86] He writes,

> The body is not a prison, but a marvelous piece of art from the hand of God Almighty, and just as constitutive for the essence of humanity as the soul (Job 10:8–12; Ps. 8; 139:13–17; Eccles.

---

81. Flavel, *Pneumatologia*, 121–30. Flavel recognizes the strong desire of the soul for the body, the natural fear of death, and thus tries to help readers trust in God for preservation and resurrection.

82. Ibid., 128–29.

83. Ibid., 129–30.

84. Ibid., 130. I have updated the punctuation and short forms in this quotation.

85. Bavinck, *Reformed Dogmatics*, 2:554–62. He writes, "The body is not a prison" (559), exactly the opposite statement of Calvin.

86. Ibid., 559–60.

12:2–7; Isa. 64:8). It is our earthly dwelling (2 Cor. 5:1), our organ or instrument of service, our apparatus (1 Cor. 12:18–26; 2 Cor. 4:7; 1 Thess. 4:4); and the "members" of the body are the weapons with which we fight in the cause of righteousness or unrighteousness (Rom. 6:13). It is so integrally and essentially a part of our humanity that, though violently torn from the soul by sin, it will be reunited with it in the resurrection of the dead. The nature of the union of the soul with the body, though incomprehensible, is much closer than the theories of "occasionalism" or "preestablished harmony" *(harmonia praestabilita)* or a "system of influence" *(systema influxus)* imagine. It is not ethical, but physical. It is so intimate that one nature, one person, one self is the subject of both and of all their activities. It is always the same soul that peers through the eyes, thinks through the brain, grasps with the hands, and walks with the feet . . . It is one and the same life that flows throughout the body but operates and manifests itself in every organ in a manner peculiar to that organ.[87]

These three examples make clear that a warm appreciation for the body and for the natural and everlasting unity of body and soul has been a robust part of the Reformed tradition. They also suggest that the soul should not be thought of as some, let us say, hockey-puck-sized spiritual substance in a person's chest, but rather a kind of shadow with the shape of the body, giving life to every part. Obviously we cannot be dogmatic on these points, but we can favor accounts that seem to fit the biblical data most closely.

SURVIVALISM VERSUS CORRUPTIONISM

The Thomistic and Bavinckian account given above raises a question: if body and soul are so closely united and constitute the person as a whole, do we *as persons* actually exist during the intermediate state or do only our souls exist? This is an important question that involves personal identity. Do our *persons* go out of existence at the beginning of the intermediate state and then back into existence at the resurrection?

A physicalist such as Trenton Merricks hardly pauses to consider this question, since he has no doctrine of the soul and even thinks that there are no criteria of *personal* identity over time—whether there is an intermediate

---

87. Ibid., 559. I have corrected *praestabilitia* to *praestabilita*, to reflect Bavinck's original. My thanks to William Helder for noticing this error in the English edition of Bavinck.

In Between and Intermediate

state or not.[88] But those who accept what Scripture teaches about the soul existing in the intermediate state can either hold the position of corruptionism (the soul alone exists in the intermediate state; the person is corrupted) or survivalism (the person, as such, survives via the soul).

Aside from the philosophical arguments, Scripture points to the truth of the survivalist position inasmuch as we consistently find the personal pronoun used: "I desire to depart and be with Christ" (Phil 1:23), *not* "I desire that *my soul* depart...". Again, "We... would prefer to be... at home with the Lord" (2 Cor 5:8), *not* "We prefer *our souls* to be at home with the Lord." Even the souls under the altar use the first person pronoun: "How long, Sovereign Lord, holy and true, until you judge the inhabitants of the earth and avenge *our* blood?" (Rev 6:10).[89]

THEOLOGICAL DIFFICULTIES FOR THE PHYSICALIST POSITION

Before we close I would like to present some doctrinal problems that I think Christian physicalists need to deal with.

I shall begin with the deepest problem: it is both theological and metaphysical, and has to do with perdurance of the person. Basically, in a physicalist account that includes the resurrection of the body, persons go out of existence when they die and come back into existence when they are resurrected. Philosophers such as Kevin Corcoran say that they are "reconstituted."[90] Merricks, as a Christian atomist, speaks of "reassembly."[91]

---

88. Merricks has rejuvenated ancient Epicurean atomic theory with rigor and consistency. He argues that there are no ordinary objects at all, only atoms. There are no wholes and parts, only wholes; that is, each atom is a whole. He also asserts that his physicalist position does more justice to two Scriptural doctrines in particular: the terribleness and evil of death, since it really means non-existence, and the wonder of the resurrection. See Merricks, "The Resurrection of the Body," 283–86; Merricks, "How to Live Forever," 192–95; Merricks, "Do Ordinary Objects Exist? No," [forthcoming]; Merricks, "No Criteria," 106–24.

89. The philosophical arguments in favor of survivalism are, however, valuable. See Oderberg, "Survivalism, Corruptionism, and Mereology," 1–26; Oderberg, "Persistence," 55–65; Klima, "Man=Body+Soul," 257–74.

90. Corcoran, *Christian Materialist Alternative*, 135–37.

91. Merricks, "How to Live Forever," 188–90. In Merrick's view, since there are no criteria for personal identity over time anyway, the going out of existence does not affect personal identity. Oddly, he claims that "identity can hold across a temporal gap even if there is no explanation," but then adds that "there are no criteria of personal identity over

There is no soul that keeps them existing in the intermediate state, albeit in a reduced sense. When you die, you no longer exist. You cease to be. You are not. And then, supposedly, you come back into existence. To one untrained in philosophy and metaphysics this might sound fine. But it presents a huge problem. For, once a particular person stops existing, it is impossible that this person—the very one who went out of existence—would come back into existence. Not to exist is to cease to be. To cease to be is to be gone forever. Such persons are no more and as such never will be again. Whatever is constituted afterward *cannot be* the same person.[92]

If, as most Christian physicalists argue, persons-as-bodies will be resurrected, they must admit that these new persons: never existed before and thus never committed any sin; never believed in Christ; never in fact lived on this earth; have no continuity with Adam, and thus were not condemned in him; are not united to each other specifically but will be like the angels, all created at once as unique species; thus, cannot have one man die for them in their place because he cannot stand in their place legally. The challenge for the physicalist to write an entirely new account of anthropology and soteriology that is faithful to Scripture is not a task that can be accomplished, in my opinion. It is certainly not possible without at least using some rather counter-intuitive and esoteric philosophy (not to mention minimizing the message of many Scripture texts).

When it comes to regeneration and new life, what is that, in a physicalist account? Is it, as James K. A. Smith argues in *Desiring the Kingdom*, merely the forming of habits by way of bodily repetition?[93] His arguments certainly fit the tenor of physicalism and its corollary, behavioralism. Being "transformed by the renewing of our minds" (Rom 12:2) becomes a lifelong process of behaviors-forming habits. But the scriptural message has a lot more to say about the transformation of our minds by way of the Spirit's

---

time." These two statements are incongruent.

92. Four-dimensional metaphysics, which tries to account for a thing going in and out of existence and yet being the same thing, is shown to be patently incoherent by Feser, *Scholastic Metaphysics*, 201–10. See also Moreland and Rae, *Body & Soul*, 78–85.

93. "We feel our way around our world more than we think our way through it. Our worldview is more a matter of the imagination than the intellect, and the imagination runs off the fuel of images that are channeled by our senses. So our affective, noncognitive disposition is an aspect of our animal, bodily nature. The result is a much more holistic (and less dualistic) picture of human persons as essentially embodied." He also writes, "We are not conscious minds or souls 'housed' in meaty containers; we are selves who *are* our bodies; thus the training of desire requires bodily practices in which a particular *telos* is embedded." Smith, *Desiring the Kingdom*, 57, 62 (underlining added).

In Between and Intermediate

special regenerating work, as well as about the exercise of such gifts as self-control, which imply the direction of the body by the mind rather than the other way around. Basically the physicalist position creates huge problems for our doctrines of regeneration and sanctification.

As for our Christology, Christ's human and divine natures were separated if he, in his human nature, went into non-existence between his death and resurrection. This is contra to the Creed of Chalcedon. Further, our union with Christ is broken if we go into non-existence between death and resurrection, whereas he promised to be with us *always*. Thus we could no longer confess that nothing—not even death—could separate us from the love of God in Christ Jesus our Lord (Rom 8:38–39).[94]

Finally, apart from the question of the intermediate state and the resurrection, an even more basic problem exists: If God is Spirit—substantially speaking, as we confess in the Belgic Confession, Article 1—how can humans who lack a soul, let alone a spiritual soul, relate to such a God, be considered in any way "partakers in the divine nature" (2 Pet 1:4), or worship "in spirit and in truth" (John 4:24)? Matthew Levering addresses this difficulty as follows:

> Yet how can we have intimate knowledge and supreme love of God in the kingdom without sharing more profoundly in God's spiritual nature than mere neural pathways, however, transformed, could allow us to do? Second Peter 1:4, with its promise that we shall become "partakers in the divine nature," suggests that such participation will indeed characterize the eschatological Kingdom. Other New Testament passages make a similar point, perhaps most notably Paul's assertion in 1 Corinthians 13:12 that "then I shall understand fully, even as I have been fully understood." Paul's relationship to God will then possess the supreme intimacy of 'face to face' knowledge (1 Cor 13:12).
>
> In response to Murphy's nonreductive physicalism, Terence Nichols remarks that if she were right, "then even in heaven we could not know God directly, through intuition: for that to happen, we would need a spiritual receptor, a faculty by which we could perceive the spiritual God . . . Without such a faculty, we can know God only indirectly." The vision of God, our supremely intimate sharing in the wisdom and love of the Trinity, is ruled out by nonreductive physicalism.[95]

---

94. These two points are argued by Vandenberg, "The Impact of a Gap," 248–57.
95. Levering, *Jesus and the Demise of Death*, 106. See also Carroll, "Does a Biologist

Edward Feser, having considered whether physicalism is actually able to explain all of the mind's rationality, including higher-order thinking such as abstraction, concludes, "Materialism is just a riff [variation] on Cartesianism, not its opposite."[96] His grounds for this assertion lie in the fact that materialism simply takes one side of the Cartesian mind-matter divide (matter), makes it everything, and denies the other (mind). Feser explains:

> A genuine solution requires abandoning *both* of Descartes' abstractions and rediscovering the human being as an irreducible psychophysical whole—the mental and the physical as two aspects of one thing, just as a sentence's meaning and the physical marks that make it up are two aspects of one thing. Far from being "unscientific," such a rediscovery would be a return to reality as we actually know it from experience—rather than the fallacious and ideological retreat from experience represented by Cartesianism and materialism alike.[97]

For Alvin Plantinga, the mere fact that I can envision myself apart from my body shows that I am not identical with my body and that for that reason I need not accept a purely materialist viewpoint.[98]

Secular writers also have provided strong evidence that materialism and physicalism are false—the placebo and nocebo effects, near-death experiences, and the psi effect all point to the effect of the mind on the brain and thus argue for "the spiritual brain" or the soul.[99] To these factors may be added the phenomena of memory and genius, recently convincing neuroscientists to counter the mainstream materialism in their own discipline.[100] "Mind over matter" is real.[101] Thus, the physicalist account does not, apart from what Scripture demands, even accord with reality. According to Carroll, the biologist needs to accept the reality of the human soul if he or she is at all to appreciate the difference between a human and a machine.[102] He

Have a Soul?" 24.

96. Feser, "Rediscovering Human Beings," Part 1, para. 11.
97. Ibid., Part 2, para. 8.
98. As noted in Waters, "Intermediate State," 288.
99. Beauregard, *The Spiritual Brain*, 125–80.
100. Kelly, *The Irreducible Mind*, xiii, 241–99, 423–93. The entire work covers much of the same ground as Beauregard, *The Spiritual Brain*, and is altogether a tour de force.
101. Beauregard, *The Spiritual Brain*, xiii.
102. Carroll, *Does a Biologist Need a Soul?* 25. Carroll first shows that many biologists treat all reality, including humans and animals, as machines. They dissolve the distinction between life and non-life. Carroll responds that unlike machines, living things grow,

In Between and Intermediate

also argues that Thomas's view of the body-soul relation accounts well "for the 'more' in nature that modern science recognizes."[103]

EARLY MODERN ROOTS OF PHYSICALISM

Feser was far more correct than he may have realized when connecting materialism to Cartesianism. In fact, probably the first modern after Descartes to deny the existence of the human soul was Joseph Priestley (1733–1804). His account of the thinking that led him to this position clearly demonstrates that it was a consequence of his Cartesianism. His first doubts can be traced to the concern that "matter" and "spirit" are so entirely distinct that they are unable to have any effect on each other, "insomuch that, properly speaking, my mind is no more in my body, than it is in the moon."

Priestley continues,

> I rather think that the whole man is of some *uniform composition*; and that the property of *perception*, as well as the other powers that are termed *mental*, is the result (whether necessary, or not) of such an organical structure as that of the brain: consequently, that the whole man becomes extinct at death, and that we have no hope of surviving the grave.[104]

Priestley was a Socinian with the claim to fame of having begun the first Unitarian church in England. This is the more likely place where one might expect to find physicalism—not among evangelicals who pay lip service to the inspiration and authority of Scripture!

CONCLUSION

The comfort the believer derives from belonging to Jesus Christ with body and soul, both in life and death, holds true for the intermediate state as well.

---

determine the function of their various parts, reproduce themselves, and reproduce in kind and instantaneously (that is to say, as soon as a living being reproduces, the reproduced being is another member of the species that produced it, not a transitional form in a middle state or a being-assembled conglomeration of previously-prepared parts).

103. Carroll, *Does a Biologist Need a Soul?* 27.

104. Priestley, *Disquisitions*, xiii. The quotation is his own quotation of an earlier work of his, wherein he had first expressed his doubt. The 1777 *Disquisitions* itself is the full account of his new physicalist position.. All the elect who have gone before us are enjoying these very blessings in glory, as related in Revelation 4, 5, and 6, etc.

Scripture clearly teaches that believers go to be with Christ upon death.[105] They dwell with him in heaven, but only in the soul, probably in a shadow-form similar to the shape of their bodies. Although life without the body is a reduced state, yet it also is enjoyed in the soul as a state in glory. The faithful are freed from sin. They will never again undergo persecution, suffer disease, doubt God or his promises, experience weakness of faith, undergo temptation, fear condemnation, disappoint other people, or in any way feel distant from God. Rather, they will behold the face of God in glory. While their bodies remain united to Christ and rest in their graves as in their beds, they in their souls will be surrounded by heavenly beings—angels, elders, apostles, and other creatures representing various wonderful things—and will join them in giving glory to their triune God: Creator, Savior, and Paraclete. All the elect who have gone before us are enjoying these very blessings in glory, as related in Revelation 4; 5; and 6, etc.

Although we were not originally designed to live apart from the body and though our souls rightly long to remain united with our bodies, believers should look forward to going to be with their Lord upon death. His Spirit in our hearts and he with our human nature glorified in heaven form the double pledge that all these things are true, and that in due time we will live forever with him in a new creation, body and soul, unified and whole.

BIBLIOGRAPHY

Augustine, Aurelius. *Teaching Christianity: De Doctrina Christiana*. Translated by Edmund Hill. New York: New City Press, 1996.

———. *The Confessions*. Translated by Maria Boulding. New York: New City Press, 1997.

Bavinck, Herman. *Reformed Dogmatics*. 4 vols. Translated by John Vriend. Edited by John Bolt. Grand Rapids: Baker, 2008.

Berkhof, Louis. *Systematic Theology: New Combined Edition*. Grand Rapids: Eerdmans, 1996.

Beauregard, Mario, and Denyse O'Leary. *The Spiritual Brain: A Neuroscientist's Case for the Existence of the Soul*. New York: HarperOne, 2007.

BioLogos. "Evolution and Christian Faith Grant Program." https://biologos.org/what-we-do/grant-program/.

———. "What We Believe." https://biologos.org/about-us/.

Book of Praise: Anglo-Genevan Psalter. Winnipeg: Premier Printing, 2014.

The Confession of Faith and Catechisms of the Orthodox Presbyterian Church with Proof Texts. Willow Grove, PA: Orthodox Presbyterian Church, 2008.

---

105. Having refuted physicalism in this essay, we have also refuted the lesser error of soul sleep.

Calvin, John. *Calvin's Commentaries.* Vol. 19, *Acts 14–28; Romans 1–16.* Grand Rapids: Baker, 1984.

———. *Institutes of the Christian Religion.* 2 vols. Translated by Ford Lewis Battles. Philadelphia: Westminster, 1960.

Carroll, William E. "Does a Biologist Need a Soul?" *Modern Age* 57.3 (2015) 17–31.

Cooper, John. *Body, Soul & Life Everlasting: Biblical Anthropology and the Monism-Dualism Debate.* Grand Rapids: Eerdmans, 2000.

Corcoran, Kevin. *Rethinking Human Nature: A Christian Materialist Alternative to the Soul.* Grand Rapids: Baker Academic, 2006.

Delitzsch, Franz. *Psalms,* Part 2. Translated by Francis Bolton. Grand Rapids: Eerdmans, 1968.

Devine, Daniel James. "Interpretive Dance." *World Magazine* 29.24 (2014). https://www.worldmag.com/mobile/article.php?id=32175.

Dijk, K. *Over de laatste dingen: Tussen sterven en opstanding.* Kampen: Kok, 1955.

Faber, Riemer, ed. *Unity in Diversity: Studies Presented to Prof. Dr. Jelle Faber on the Occasion of His Retirement.* Hamilton, ON: Senate of the Theological College of the Canadian Reformed Churches, 1989.

Feser, Edward. "Rediscovering Human Beings," Parts 1 & 2. BioLogos. https://biologos.org/blogs/archive/rediscovering-human-beings-part-1 and https://biologos.org/blogs/archive/rediscovering-human-beings-part-2.

———. *Scholastic Metaphysics: A Contemporary Introduction.* Heusenstamm: Editiones Scholasticae, 2014.

Flavel, John. *Pneumatologia: A Treatise of the Soul of Man.* 2nd ed. London: Parkhurst, 1698.

Genderen, J. van, and W. H. Velema. *Concise Reformed Dogmatics.* Translated by Gerrit Bilkes and Ed M. van der Maas. Phillipsburg, NJ: Presbyterian & Reformed, 2008.

Gerhardsson, Birger. *The Testing of God's Son.* Translated by John Toy. Coniectanea biblica: New Testament Series 2. 1966. Reprinted, Eugene, OR: Wipf & Stock, 2009.

Goetz, Stewart. "Is N. T. Wright Right about Substance Dualism?" *Philosophia Christi* 14.1 (2012) 183–92.

Green, Joel B. *The Gospel of Luke.* New International Commentary on the New Testament. Grand Rapids: Eerdmans, 1997.

———. *1 Peter.* Two Horizons New Testament Commentary. Grand Rapids: Eerdmans, 2007.

Hammett, John. "Southern Baptist Voices: Evolutionary Creationism and the *Imago Dei.*" BioLogos. https://biologos.org/blogs/archive/southern-baptist-voices-evolutionary-creationism-and-the-imago-dei.

Hill, Michael. "Reflections on the Soul and Cloning." *Reformed Theological Review* 56.3 (1997) 138–48.

Holman Christian Standard Bible. Nashville: Holman Bible Publishers, 2011.

Kelly, Edward F., and Emily Williams Kelly. *Irreducible Mind: Toward a Psychology for the 21st Century.* Lanham, MD: Rowman & Littlefield, 2007.

Klima, Gyula. "Man=Body+Soul: Aquinas's Arithmetic of Human Nature." In *Thomas Aquinas: Contemporary Philosophical Perspectives,* edited by Brian Davies, 257–74. Oxford: Oxford University Press, 2002.

Krüger, Thomas. *Qoheleth: A Commentary.* Hermeneia. Translated by O. C. Dean Jr. Minneapolis: Fortress, 2004.

Levering, Matthew. *Jesus and the Demise of Death: Resurrection, Afterlife, and the Fate of the Christian.* Waco, TX: Baylor University Press, 2012.

Lincoln, Andrew T. *Paradise Now and Not Yet: Studies in the Role of the Heavenly Dimension in Paul's Thought with Special Reference to His Eschatology.* Society for the Study of the New Testament Monograph Series 43. Cambridge: Cambridge University Press, 2004.

Longman, Tremper III. *Ecclesiastes.* New International Commentary on the Old Testament. Grand Rapids: Eerdmans, 1998.

Merricks, Trenton. "How to Live Forever without Saving Your Soul: Physicalism and Immortality." In *Soul, Body, and Survival: Essays on the Metaphysics of Human Persons,* edited by Kevin Corcoran, 183–200. Ithaca, NY: Cornell University Press, 2001.

———. "The Resurrection of the Body and the Life Everlasting." In *Reason for the Hope Within,* edited by Michael J. Murray, 261–86. Grand Rapids: Eerdmans, 1999.

———. "Do Ordinary Objects Exist? No." In *Current Controversies in Metaphysics,* edited by Elizabeth Barnes. London: Routledge (forthcoming, 2016). https://pages.shanti.virginia.edu/merricks/files/2014/12/Do-Ordinary-Objects-Exist_-No-WEB.pdf.

———. "There Are No Criteria for Personal Identity over Time." *Noûs* 32 (1998) 106–24.

Moll, Carl Bernhard, *Psalms.* In *A Commentary on the Holy Scriptures,* edited by John Peter Lange; translated by Philip Schaff et al. New York: Scribner, Armstrong, 1872.

Moreland, J. P., and Scott B. Rae. *Body & Soul: Human Nature & the Crisis in Ethics.* Downers Grove, IL: InterVarsity, 2000.

Moritz, Joseph. "Chosen by God: What the Image and Likeness of God (Imago Dei) IS NOT," Parts 1, 2, 3. BioLogos. https://biologos.org/blogs/archive/chosen-by-god-part-1-what-the-image-and-likeness-of-god-imago-dei-is-not, https://biologos.org/blogs/archive/chosen-by-god-part-2-what-the-image-and-likeness-of-god-imago-dei-is, and https://biologos.org/blogs/archive/chosen-by-god-part-3-election-evolution-and-imago-dei.

Murphy, Nancey. "Nonreductive Physicalism: Philosophical Challenges." In *Personal Identity in Theological Perspective,* edited by Richard Lints, Michael S. Horton, and Mark R. Talbot, 95–117. Grand Rapids: Eerdmans, 2006.

———. *Bodies and Souls, or Spirited Bodies?* Current Issues in Theology. Cambridge: Cambridge University Press, 2006.

Oderberg, David S. "Persistence." In *A Companion to Metaphysics,* edited by Jaegwon Kim, Ernest Sosa, and Gary S. Rosenkrantz, 55–65. 2nd ed. Blackwell Companions to Philosophy 7. Oxford: Wiley-Blackwell, 2009.

———. "Survivalism, Corruptionism, and Mereology." *European Journal for Philosophy of Religion* 4.4 (2012) 1–26.

Preston, Jesse Lee, Ryan S. Ritter, and Justin Hepler. "Neuroscience and the Soul: Competing Explanations for the Human Experience." *Cognition* 127 (2013) 31–37.

Priestley, Joseph. *Disquisitions Relating to Matter and Spirit.* London: Johnson, 1777.

Rickabaugh, Brandon L. "Responding to NT Wright's Rejection of the Soul: A Defense of Substance Dualism." Unpublished paper presented at the Society of Vineyard Scholars Conference, Minneapolis, MA, April 28, 2012. https://www.academia.edu/1966881/Responding_to_N._T._Wrights_Rejection_of_the_Soul_A_Defense_of_Substance_Dualism.

Schilder, Klaas. "A Letter Written in 1931 by K. Schilder about Life after Death." *Diakonia* 8.1 (1994) 26–28.

In Between and Intermediate

Scougal, Henry. *The Life of God in the Soul of Man.* 11th ed. London: Rivington, 1775.

Shakespeare, William. All works cited within this essay are available online at *OpenSource Shakespeare: An Experiment in Literary Technology.* http://www.opensourceshakespeare.org. The following pages were accessed: http://www.opensourceshakespeare.org/views/plays/play_view.php?WorkID=macbeth&Act=4&Scene=3&Scope=scene, http://www.opensourceshakespeare.org/views/plays/play_view.php?WorkID=henry6p1&Act=2&Scene=4&Scope=scene, http://www.opensourceshakespeare.org/views/plays/play_view.php?WorkID=othello&Act=5&Scene=2&Scope=scene.

Shedd, William G. T. *Dogmatic Theology.* Edited by Alan W. Gomes. 3rd ed. Phillipsburg, NJ: Presbyterian & Reformed, 2003.

Smith, Ian K. "Does 2 Corinthians 5:1–8 Refer to an Intermediate State?" *Reformed Theological Review* 55 (1996) 14–23.

Smith, James K. A. *Desiring the Kingdom: Worship, Worldview, and Cultural Formation.* Grand Rapids: Baker Academic, 2009.

Telder, Bartus. *Sterven . . . en dan? Gaan Gods kinderen, wanneer zij sterven, naar de hemel?* Kampen: Kok, 1960.

———. *Sterven . . . waarom? Over sterfelijkheid en onsterfelijkheid in bijbels licht.* Kampen: Kok, 1963.

Thomas Aquinas. *Summa Theologica.* Translated by Fathers of the Dominican Province. 1920. http://www.newadvent.org/summa/.

VanGemeren, Willem A. *New International Dictionary of Old Testament Theology & Exegesis.* 5 vols. Grand Rapids: Zondervan, 1997.

Vandenberg, Mary. "The Impact of a Gap in Existence on Christology and Soteriology: A Challenge for Physicalists." *Calvin Theological Journal* 49.2 (2014) 248–57.

Venema, Cornelis P. *The Promise of the Future.* Edinburgh: Banner of Truth, 2000.

Vermigli, Peter Martyr. *Common Places.* Translated by Anthonie Marten. London: Henrie Denham et al., 1583.

Waters, Larry. "The Believer's Intermediate State after Death." *Bibliotheca Sacra* 169 (2012) 283–303.

Whybray. R. N. *Ecclesiastes.* New Century Bible Commentary. Grand Rapids: Eerdmans, 1989.

Wiskerke, Jelier Reinier. *Léven tussen sterven en opstanding.* Goes: Oosterbaan & Le Cointre, 1963.

Woudstra, Marten H. *The Ark of the Covenant from Conquest to Kingship.* Philadelphia: Presbyterian & Reformed, 1965.

Wright, N. T. "Mind, Spirit, Soul and Body: All for One and One for All. Reflections on Paul's Anthropology in His Complex Contexts." Paper presented at the Society of Christian Philosophers, Regional Meeting, Fordham University, March 18, 2011. http://ntwrightpage.com/Wright_SCP_MindSpiritSoulBody.htm.

6

Is Hell Obsolete?
The Place of Eternal Punishment in Preaching Today

Jason Van Vliet

Hell. The lake of fire. The second death. The outer darkness. The place of weeping and gnashing of teeth. Truth be told, hell is an unimaginably horrible thing to talk about. Our visceral reaction is simply to avoid the topic altogether. Who wants to put a damper on a hope-filled topic such as eschatology by writing an essay about hell?

Still, three things convinced me that it is the right thing to do. Some years ago an elder in a congregation said to me, "We don't hear as much about hell from the pulpit today as we did thirty or forty years ago." At that point I was too young to know what the preaching had been like thirty or forty years earlier, but I had no reason to doubt that his observation was essentially correct. It made me think about my own preaching and about preaching in general. Hell *is* in the Bible.[1] So, if we are preaching the Word of God, then from time to time we should be preaching about hell. But if we are only mentioning it rarely, rapidly, and reluctantly, what is the problem?

---

1. For example, John Wenham has identified no fewer than 264 references to the final destiny of the ungodly in Scripture. See *Facing Hell*, 238.

Is Hell Obsolete?

Are we collectively embarrassed by this doctrine? Is it politically incorrect? Are we afraid we will turn off parishioners or scare off visitors? These are valid questions that deserve some honest answers; otherwise preaching about eternal punishment may well become obsolete in our churches.

The next reason for addressing this topic is the growing number of Christian authors who have called into question the church's long-standing teaching that hell is a place of eternal punishment for all those who do not truly believe in the Lord Jesus Christ. Obvious examples are Rob Bell, with his New York Times bestseller, *Love Wins,* and Brian McLaren, who wrote *The Last Word and the Word After That.* Yet there are more: Philip E. Hughes, a respected Bible commentator; John Wenham, author of the popular grammar *N.T. Elements of Greek*; Edward Fudge, whose book *The Fire That Consumes* has gone through three editions and even spawned a recent movie; and, last but not least, John Stott, who penned *A Basic Christianity,* which has sold millions and helped countless new converts.[2] These men do not all hold exactly the same view. However, they all agree on one thing: the church's traditional understanding of hell should become obsolete and be replaced with something else.[3] Are they correct? That is a question with, quite literally, eternal implications, and it deserves a response.

The final motivation behind this essay is the proverbial elephant in the room. Almost every Christian knows other people who have not embraced the Savior in faith. They are neighbors with whom we chat over the fence. They are co-workers with whom we have lunch. Sometimes these unbelievers are members of our own families. We know them very well. And when we think of the prospect of eternal punishment for them if they do not repent, it weighs heavily on our hearts. Indeed, it is hard to talk about it, but if we never do, it only becomes harder and harder.

Considering these three things, it is worthwhile to look more closely at this difficult topic. First, we will briefly survey the different views concerning what ultimately happens to the unrepentant. As we survey these views we will identify the key issues involved in each one. Next, we will

---

2. The relevant books are Bell, *Love Wins*; McLaren, *The Last Word and the Word After That*; Hughes, *True Image*; Wenham, *Facing Hell*; Fudge, *The Fire That Consumes*; Edwards and Stott, *Evangelical Essentials*. The movie is called *Hell and Mr. Fudge* and was produced in 2012.

3. "I believe that endless torment is a hideous and unscriptural doctrine which has been a terrible burden on the mind of the church for many centuries and a terrible blot on her presentation of the gospel. I should indeed be happy if, before I die, I could help in sweeping it away." See Wenham, *Facing Hell*, 256.

work through these key issues by carefully examining some pertinent passages from God's inspired Word. This will also make it possible to evaluate these different views in a responsible way. Finally, we will review what we have learned and make some suggestions about what place the topic of eternal punishment should have in preaching today. As we work through these steps, it should become obvious that our holy, just, and merciful God does teach that the unrepentant will be condemned to an eternal punishment of body and soul in hell. At the same time, we can improve our treatment of this doctrine if we connect it, more consistently and consciously, to the work and teaching of Jesus Christ, who came to save his people from the depths of hell.

THE DIFFERENT VIEWS

Broadly and historically speaking, there are three different views about what happens to unbelievers after this life. They are usually referred to as the traditional view of eternal punishment, universalism, and conditional immortality, which is also called annihilationism. Although individual theologians may nuance each of these views in various ways,[4] for our purposes we will stick to the main lines and describe each position in turn.

Eternal Punishment

In line with Christ's parable of the rich man and Lazarus (Luke 16:19–31), the church has long believed that when an unrepentant person dies his soul goes to hell, a place of spiritual anguish and torment. Then one day, when Christ returns, the bodies of both the righteous and the wicked will be raised, even as the prophet foretold in Dan 12:2 and the apostle confirms in Rev 20:11–15. All these resurrected people will appear before the glorious Christ to be judged (2 Cor 5:10). Those who have believed in God's only-begotten Son will be welcomed into eternal glory (John 3:16), but those who have refused to follow him in faith "will be convicted by the testimony of their own consciences and will become immortal, but only to

---

4. There may be a fourth view in which unbelievers are ultimately "reconciled to God in the perfection of their remorse—reconciled, but not saved." See Williams, "The Question of Hell and Salvation," 265. However, by the author's own admission this teaching could be considered a subset of the universalist view.

Is Hell Obsolete?

be tormented in the eternal fire prepare for the devil and his angels (Matt 25:41)."[5]

Paintings by various artists[6] and graphic word pictures by some preachers[7] have left people with vivid and terrifying pictures of hell in their minds. Bodies being charred by hellfire and seared by molten sulfur are among the images that understandably cause people to cringe. On the one hand, these pictures, whether visual or verbal, do find their root in God's Word where it speaks of a "lake of fire which burns with sulfur" (Rev 19:20). On the other hand, sober exegetes such as William Hendriksen caution us not to dramatize the agony of hell beyond the succinct and restrained words of Scripture itself.[8] After all, the image of fire is, in the first place, a symbol of God's holy wrath.[9] Ultimately, God's wrath involves much more than fire; it includes being forsaken by him (Jer 7:29).

The view that the unrepentant are eternally punished, in both body and soul, in hell is supported by numerous Scripture passages. A few selected examples are listed below:

> And do not fear those who kill the body but cannot kill the soul. Rather fear him who can destroy both soul and body in hell. (Matt 10:28)

> Then he will say to those on his left, "Depart from me, you cursed, into the eternal fire prepared for the devil and his angels . . . And these will go away into eternal punishment, but the righteous into eternal life." (Matt 25:41, 46)

> And another angel, a third, followed them, saying with a loud voice, "If anyone worships the beast and its image and receives a mark on his forehead or on his hand, he also will drink the wine of God's wrath, poured full strength into the cup of his anger, and he will be tormented with fire and sulfur in the presence of the holy angels and in the presence of the Lamb. And the smoke of their torment goes up forever and ever, and they have no rest, day

---

5. Belgic Confession, Art. 37. All quotations from the Three Forms of Unity, in particular the Belgic Confession and the Heidelberg Catechism, are taken from the *Book of Praise*.

6. *The Last Judgment* by Fra Angelico of Florence is such a painting. It dates from 1425–30.

7. One such sermon is the well-known *Sinners in the Hands of an Angry God* by Jonathan Edwards.

8. Hendriksen, *The Life Hereafter*, 200–201.

9. Ibid., 203.

or night, these worshipers of the beast and its image, and whoever receives the mark of its name." (Rev 14:9–11)

It is significant to note that Jesus himself defined the doctrine of eternal punishment "more specifically and in more instances than any New Testament prophet."[10] In fact, even his famous Sermon on the Mount contains no fewer than four specific references to hell or eternal punishment.[11]

Universalism

Simply put, universalism teaches that, in the end, everyone will be saved. Those who die unrepentant will still be mercifully pardoned by God, either by a sweeping sovereign decree or through some form of post-mortem evangelism.[12] Either way, all will be saved. In the early church Origen promoted universalism, in the sixteenth century various Anabaptist theologians such as Hans Denck and Hans Hut dabbled with the idea, and the recognized father of this teaching in North America is a Wesleyan preacher named John Murray, who should be carefully distinguished from the well-known Presbyterian theologian with the same name.[13] Much ink has been spilt over the question of whether the renowned theologian Karl Barth actually embraced universalism, but at a minimum he himself recognized that his teaching certainly drifted in that direction.[14]

In a similar way, it is not entirely clear what position Rob Bell finally takes in his book, *Love Wins*. In this publication he points to 1 Tim 2:4, where the apostle Paul states that God our Savior "desires all people to be saved." Immediately thereafter Bell poses the rhetorical question, "So does God get what God wants?" This query even forms the title of his fourth chapter.[15] In fact, a page later he even ramps up the rhetoric by asking, "Does this magnificent, mighty, marvelous God *fail* in the end?"[16] All this leads the reader to believe that Bell will affirm that God does ultimately

10. John Walvoord in Crockett, *Four Views on Hell*, 19–20.
11. Matt 5:22, 29, 30; 7:13.
12. For a full description of the different nuances within universalism, see Sanders, *No Other Name*.
13. "Universalism," s.v., *Encyclopedia of the Reformed Faith*, ed. McKim.
14. Barth, *Church Dogmatics*, IV/3, 477. Also see chapter 6 in Crisp, *Retrieving Doctrine*.
15. Bell, *Love Wins*, 97.
16. Ibid., 98.

Is Hell Obsolete?

get what he wants; therefore, all people will be saved. However, in the final paragraphs of his fourth chapter he says that asking whether God gets what he wants is an interesting but unanswerable question. Instead, he suggests there is "a better question, one we can answer" and that is "Do we get what we want?"[17] Bell's answer is that "if we want hell," it is ours, but "if we want heaven," it is ours. Why? Because "that's how love works . . . [and] love wins."[18]

In coming to grips with Bell's position it is important to realize that for him hell is not the lake of unquenchable fire. Instead, it refers to "the big, wide, terrible evil that comes from the secrets hidden deep within our hearts all the way to the massive, society-wide collapse and chaos that comes when we fail to live in God's world God's way."[19] In other words, it is redefined as misery in the present rather than punishment in eternity.

Thus, even if some who lean toward universalism are somewhat tentative about their stance, they are all certainly open to the possibility that those who do not believe in Jesus Christ in this life will yet, in the life to come, enjoy an eternity of blessed fellowship with God. Why do they maintain this, when Christ himself clearly states, "Whoever does not believe is condemned" (John 3:18)? Two key issues are at stake here. First, there are certain passages that speak of God desiring the salvation of all people. Rob Bell mentioned one, that is, 1 Tim 2:4. Another, similar passage is Titus 2:11, where the apostle writes, "For the grace of God has appeared, bringing salvation for all people." Second, there is the fundamental matter of God's love, which includes his tender compassion. Since God is love (1 John 4:16), how could he ever send anyone to suffer forever and ever in hell? Since God's very own name speaks of his unfailing mercy and grace (Exod 34:6), it only seems to make sense that in some way, at some point, his divine compassion would grow warm and tender (Hos 11:8), and that he would pardon unbelievers rather than subject them to an eternity of agony. A little later on we will examine these issues more carefully, but first we must outline the third view of the eternal state of the unrepentant.

---

17. Ibid., 116.
18. Ibid., 118–19.
19. Ibid., 93.

Conditional Immortality

Although the idea that all will be saved is emotionally appealing, it is hard to square with Scripture, which speaks so clearly about two exceedingly different destinies for two distinct groups of people. There are the sheep and there are the goats. The goats go to eternal punishment, while the sheep receive eternal life (Matt 25:31–46). Still, a passage like this does not fully settle the matter in everyone's mind because the question remains: since all God's ways are just and right (Deut 32:4), is it really fair for God to condemn finite human beings to an infinite punishment?

To be sure, every human being has committed many sins—more sins than he himself can count. Still, because we live for only a measurable length of time, perhaps seventy or eighty years, the number of sins that we commit must be finite. Even if we would have a hard time providing a final tally of all our offenses, certainly our omniscient God can measure the extent of our sins. And should the punishment not fit the spiritual crime? If God's own *lex talionis* is "an eye for an eye and a tooth for a tooth" (Exod 21:24; Matt 5:38), how could he ever assign an endless eternity of agony for a mere lifetime of iniquity? This is the third key issue, one for which those promoting conditional immortality have a substantial counter-proposal.

The proponents of conditional immortality state that the church has made a fundamental error in assuming that the two final destinies of human beings are equal but entirely opposite. Men such as P. E. Hughes, Edward Fudge, John Wenham, and John Stott all put forward the same basic point: yes, the destinies are opposite, but no, they are not equal. Those who embrace conditional immortality still believe that the bodies and souls of believers will be made immortal and that they will live with God, in glory, forever. By contrast, though, the bodies and souls of the unrepentant will not become immortal. Instead, they will be consumed and destroyed by the fire of hell and thus ultimately annihilated. After all, when something burns it eventually disappears, or is at least reduced to ash and smoke.

From where does this view come? The proponents of conditional immortality answer that it comes directly from the Bible. For instance, our Savior says that those who follow the broad, easy road of worldliness end up in "destruction" (Matt 7:13–14). On another occasion he warns about the wrath of God, who can "destroy both soul and body in hell" (Matt 10:28). And, according to scholars such as John Wenham, what is destroyed no longer exists. Thus, immortality is not a given for everyone. Instead, it becomes a gift reserved only for the faithful. Hence, the position is called *conditional* immortality.

It is easy to see how attractive this position is. Believers will receive all the same glorious, eternal blessings that they are accustomed to hearing about from the pulpit. Yet, at the same time, they no longer need to carry the emotional burden of concern for their acquaintances and loved ones who refuse to believe in Christ—at least, that concern is significantly reduced. In the end, unbelievers may cease to exist, but at least they will not spend an eternity in agony. The added attraction of this position is that it appears to have some solid scriptural support. The Bible speaks, even repeatedly,[20] about the wicked being destroyed. So from both an exegetical and an emotional angle, conditional immortality commends itself to sincere Christians who are vexed by the question of what happens to the ungodly in eternity. It also adds one more key issue to our list: What is the precise meaning of the words "destroy" and "destruction" in the context of God's punishment for the ungodly?

THE KEY ISSUES EVALUATED IN THE LIGHT OF SCRIPTURE

In our survey of the three common views concerning the final destiny of the unrepentant, we isolated four key issues. By way of review, they are the following:

1. How do we understand passages that seem to suggest that God wants everyone to be saved?

2. If God is perfectly compassionate, how could he condemn anyone to eternal torment?

3. If God is perfectly just, why would he give an infinite punishment to human beings who commit a finite number of sins?

4. When the Word of God speaks about the destruction of the wicked, does that mean that they will cease to exist?

    Let us look more closely at each of these important questions.

---

20. Fudge, *The Fire That Consumes*, 88.

As You See the Day Approaching
Does God want everyone to be saved?

Regardless of your doctrinal stance, it is usually possible to find some verse somewhere in the Scripture that appears to support your position. It is much more challenging, of course, to demonstrate that your position does justice to the whole counsel of God as it is revealed to us in the entire Bible. And that is certainly the case with the question at hand. If it is true that God wants to save every single human being, and if it is also true that God's power will accomplish whatever his will desires, then how do we account for the last three chapters of the Bible? Those whose names are in the book of life enter the New Jerusalem (Rev 21:27). Those whose names are not in the book are thrown into the lake of fire (Rev 20:15) and thereby cast out of the Holy City (Rev 22:15). If everyone ultimately ends up in the same place, as universalists claim, then the final chapters of the Bible are fundamentally incoherent.

Furthermore, if universalism is correct, then the doctrines of election and reprobation are clearly wrong. Yet these teachings are so clearly revealed in Eph 1 and Rom 9–11 that they must be upheld. In addition, if the universalists are in the right, then John the Baptist was in the wrong. He called people to "bear fruit in keeping with repentance," so that they might escape the wrath of God, who will burn the chaff "with unquenchable fire" (Luke 3:8, 17). Yet, according to universalists, repentance in this life is not a *sine qua non*. In their view there is always another chance after this life. Even worse, if universalism is true, then our Lord Jesus Christ, who is the Truth (John 14:6), actually promoted falsehood since he told a parable in which a rich man longed for relief from hell. However, as Abraham said to this man, "A great chasm has been fixed, in order that those who would pass from here to you may not be able, and none may cross from there to us" (Luke 16:26).

Obviously, if the teachings of the apostles, John the Baptist, and even the Lord Jesus Christ himself are all aligned against universalism, it is compulsory that we re-examine the alleged scriptural support for this teaching which is found in 1 Tim 2:3–4. Once again, these are the words that we are seeking to understand: "God our Savior . . . desires all people to be saved and to come to the knowledge of the truth." In the first place, it is obvious that "all" does not always mean "each and every person in the history of mankind." For example, a little later in this letter, in 1 Tim 4:15, the apostle Paul encourages young Timothy to give himself fully to the task at hand, and then he adds, "so that *all* may see your progress." Now, in fact, only a very small percentage of the world population at that time—let alone the people of all ages and places—could have possibly have seen Timothy's spiritual growth as a pastor. Clearly Paul is encouraging Timothy to act on his advice so that anyone, regardless of who he may be, can take note of the young man's progress. That is the sense of "all" in 1 Tim 4:15.

Turning back to 1 Tim 2:4, we need to determine what sense the word "all" has within its immediate context. Is it the absolute sense of "each and every person in the history of mankind"? Or is it the other sense of "anyone, regardless of his place and station in life"? One quick glance back to 1 Tim 2:1–2 provides the answer. There the apostle writes, "First of all, I urge that supplications, prayers, intercessions, and thanksgivings be made for *all people*, for kings and all who are in high positions."[21] The apostle is not suggesting that Timothy's congregation needs to begin praying for each and every person in the world individually. Rather, he is saying that regardless of who the person may be, also if the person is a king or high-ranking official, you should pray for such an individual. As a further motivation in these prayers, the apostle adds that God desires the salvation of all people, that is, of all kinds of different people, including kings and high-ranking officials.

A similar progression of thought is found in the letter to Titus, another co-worker of Paul. When he states that "the grace of God has appeared, bringing salvation for all people" (2:11), he has just finished writing about various different kinds of people, including older men and younger men, older women and younger women (2:1–10). The apostle even explicitly connects verse 11 and the verses 1–10 with the little, yet significant, word "for."[22] Once more, the expression "all people" refers to everyone without distinction or without regard to status or station in life.[23]

In sum, then, the "all people" whom God wants to save does not include each and every individual, as those leaning in the direction of universalism like to claim. Instead, "all people" should be identified as the "great multitude that no one could number, from every nation, from all tribes and peoples and languages, standing before the throne and before the Lamb, clothed in white robes, with palm branches in their hands" (Rev 7:9).

21. In the original Greek, the phrase for "all people" is the same as in 1 Tim 2:4.

22. Greek *gar*.

23. Also see Rom 11:32, where the apostle Paul states, "God has consigned all to disobedience, that he may have mercy on all." This "all" refers most specifically to people regardless of whether they are Jew or Gentile (Rom 11:13–14), which indeed has been a key theme in much of this letter, already from the beginning (Rom 1:16).

As You See the Day Approaching

How can a compassionate God ever cast anyone into eternal torment?

Whenever God's mercy is mentioned in connection with his punishment for sin, due caution must be exercised. The Heidelberg Catechism warns us about this in Lord's Day 4. After affirming that God will punish our sins "by a just judgment both now and eternally" (Q&A 10), the next and natural question is: "But is God not also merciful?" The Catechism wisely responds, "God is indeed merciful, but he is also just. His justice requires that sin committed against the most high majesty of God also be punished with the most severe, that is, with everlasting punishment of body and soul" (Q&A 11). In other words, we may not play one attribute of God off against another one. God's mercy never contradicts, much less cancels out, his justice. Thus, in many respects our answer to this question depends on our answer to the next question: How can a just God condemn anyone to hell? If it can be demonstrated that God is just in meting out eternal punishment, then no one should suggest that his compassion ought to neutralize his justice. Our God is justly merciful as surely as he is mercifully just. There is no tension between the attributes of our God, whom we confess to be "a *simple* and spiritual being."[24]

Yet more can be said on this topic. In fact, God has been supremely merciful in sending his Son as the one Savior who is able to redeem people from the depths of hell. Indeed, both the justice and mercy of God are simultaneously displayed in no greater way than in Christ's "most bitter passion and death."[25] However, if someone steadfastly refuses to accept God's own mercy in faith, must God yet extend alternative mercy to such an individual and save him outside of faith in Christ? May it never be! "Or do you presume on the riches of his kindness and forbearance and patience, not knowing that God's kindness is meant to lead you to repentance?" (Rom 2:4) God's mercy was never meant to provide people with an escape route to flee from repentance in this present age.

Even more important, universalism's appeal to God's tender mercy ultimately negates God's sovereignty, and in so doing even robs God of his very own deity. The point is this: once we *require* God to exercise his mercy

---

24. Belgic Confession, Art. 2. In this article the word "simple" is not the antonym of "difficult" but, rather, of the term "composite." In other words, God's simplicity means that his essence cannot be subdivided into various parts; neither can his attributes be considered in isolation from each other.

25. Ibid., Art. 20.

toward all, then he is beholden to our wishes rather than to his own will. Then there is no longer any room for the voice of God to say, "I will have mercy on whom I have mercy" and "I will harden whom I will harden" (Rom 9:15, 18). Instead, we open our brash mouths and lay down the stipulation that God simply *must* have mercy on everyone. Such a God is neither supreme nor sovereign, for he is subject to a humanly engineered law of compassion that is higher than he is. Worse yet, such a God is no longer the true God who reveals himself in Scripture. The God of the Bible is "over all and through all and in all" (Eph 4:6; cf. Rom 9:5), but the god of universalism is no longer over all. On the contrary, he is under at least one thing, the Law of Universal Mercy.[26]

How can a just God punish finite human beings for an infinite length of time?

In many ways this issue is the crux of the whole matter. We do well to consider it carefully. In the first place, there are those who question whether everlasting punishment is indeed eternal or whether it simply lasts for a long time. Now it is true that especially in the Old Testament the Hebrew word 'ôlām, which is used for eternity, can mean "a very long time." For example, the mountains mentioned in Habakkuk's prayer are certainly very old (3:6), but they are not eternal, since God was there before the mountains were brought forth, and he alone is from everlasting to everlasting (Ps 90:2).[27] Similarly, the Greek word, aiōn, which often refers to eternity in the New Testament, can also describe a long time. In Rom 16:25–26 the apostle speaks about the revelation of the mystery "that was kept secret *for long ages* but has now been disclosed." Indeed, the fact that the mystery, which is Christ (Eph 3:4–6), is now disclosed indicates that its former state of secrecy cannot possibly be eternal.

Still, even if the scriptural words for eternity can refer to long periods of time, the question remains whether this is the case in connection with the punishment of the unrepentant. And that question must be answered in the negative. The book of Revelation makes this clear. In Rev 14:11 the worshippers of the beast suffer the full strength of God's wrath, and "the smoke of their torment goes up forever and ever." This specific phrase, "forever

---

26. Jonathan Edwards uses a similar argument, as described in Davidson, "Reasonable Damnation," 49–50.

27. The Hebrew word, 'ôlām, is used here also.

and ever" (*eis tous aiōnas tōn aiōnon*), is used twelve other times in Revelation: once for God's punishment upon the city of Babylon (19:3); once for God's punishment of the devil, the beast, and the false prophet (20:1); once for the reign of God's people (22:5); and nine other times for God himself or his glory (1:6; 1:18; 4:9, 10; 5:13; 7:12; 10:6; 11:15; 15:7; 22:5).[28] In particular, the nine occurrences referring to God's essence and glory seal the case. God does not exist for a long time; he exists forever and ever, that is, eternally. Thus, when the apostle John speaks of torment "forever and ever," he is referring to eternal, not long-lasting, punishment.

This only brings us back to our pressing question: how can God justly punish finite transgressors with an infinite punishment? One of the better places to begin is the teaching of Christ himself in the Sermon on the Mount. Shortly after announcing that he has come to fulfill the law, Jesus clarifies how he calls for a righteousness that far exceeds anything even the strictest Pharisee would dare to require (Matt 5:17–20). Two examples drive home the point. Anyone who calls his brother a fool "will be liable to the hell of fire" (Matt 5:22). Similarly, anyone who even looks lustfully at a woman had better act decisively to resist that temptation lest his "whole body be thrown into hell" (Matt 5:29–30). Both times punishment in hell is threatened for seemingly minor offenses. How easy it is to toss out a hasty insult or steal a quick, lustful glance. Yet Jesus teaches that these offenses are worthy of eternal punishment. This type of straightforward language radically readjusts our understanding of the gravity and enormity of our transgressions.

Why does Jesus speak of such a severe punishment for such seemingly small sins? This only begins to make sense when we consider the full majesty of the One who is ultimately offended by our sins. King David understood this well when he committed his sin of adultery. When Nathan the prophet confronted him with his wrongdoing, he prayed to God, "Against you, you only, have I sinned" (Ps 51:4). Did David not transgress the seventh commandment with Bathsheba and thus against his first wife, Michal? To be sure, he did. Nonetheless, during this confession his mind was overwhelmed with the guilt of how he had offended his Lord: *against you only*, O God, have I sinned. This also means that the enormity of sin is measured not merely by *what* we do but also by *against whom* we do it.

---

28. This phrase "forever and ever" is also found elsewhere in the New Testament: Gal 1:5; Phil 4:20; 1 Tim 1:17; 2 Tim 4:18; Heb 13:21; 1 Pet 4:11. Each time it is clear, also from the context, that it refers to eternity, not merely to a long time.

Is Hell Obsolete?

This is already true on a human level. According to Canadian law, someone who is convicted of killing a police officer or the queen is subject to a more severe punishment than one who kills an ordinary citizen.[29] From one perspective, murder is murder and the result is the same: a human being is killed, whoever that person may be. Looking at it from another angle, though, the law of the land acknowledges that when the offense is committed against someone who holds a weighty office, the punishment should be correspondingly more severe. If that is so, how much more true this must be for offenses committed against God, who is the Most High, infinitely more majestic and honorable than any earthly king or queen. Herman Bavinck says it well when he writes:

> Sin is not a weakness, a lack, a temporary and gradually vanishing imperfection, but in origin and essence it is lawlessness (*anomia*), a violation of the law, rebellion and hostility against God, and the negation of his justice, his authority, even his existence. Granted, sin is finite in the sense that it is committed by a finite creature in a finite period of time, but as Augustine already correctly noted, not the duration of time over which the sin was committed but its own intrinsic nature is the standard for its punishment.[30]

In short, sin committed against an infinite Majesty is worthy of an infinite punishment.[31]

Yet, can we say more in defense of God's justice? Perhaps we can. In hell the ungodly undoubtedly agonize over how foolish they were to reject the Christ during their life on earth. Yet Scripture also indicates that in hell the unrepentant are as full of aggression as they are overcome with agony. Christ repeatedly describes hell as the place of weeping and gnashing of teeth (Matt 8:12; 13:42, 50; 22:13; 24:51; 25:30; Luke 13:28). It is easy to assume that the weeping and the gnashing of teeth refer to one and the same form of suffering: anguish from the torments of hell. However, a comparison between the Old and New Testaments suggests that gnashing of teeth is an expression of anger and aggression, not a result of agony. Precisely the same phrase, "gnashing of teeth," occurs in four Old Testament passages

---

29. An online reference to these laws can be found here: http://laws-lois.justice.gc.ca/eng/acts/C-46/section-231.html.
30. Bavinck, *Reformed Dogmatics*, 4.711.
31. Heidelberg Catechism, Lord's Day 4.

and one other New Testament passage, beyond the seven New Testament passages that refer to hell.[32] For easy reference, they are cited below:

> Like profane mockers at a feast, they gnash at me with their teeth. (Ps 35:16)

> The wicked plots against the righteous and gnashes his teeth at him. (Ps 37:12)

> The wicked man sees it and is angry; he gnashes his teeth and melts away; the desire of the wicked will perish!" (Ps 112:10)

> All your enemies rail against you; they hiss, they gnash their teeth, they cry: "We have swallowed her! Ah, this is the day we longed for; now we have it; we see it!" (Lam 2:16)

> Now when they [the Jewish leaders] heard these things they were enraged, and they ground their teeth at him [Stephen]. (Acts 7:54)

Especially when they are considered in their immediate context, all of these passages have one thing in common: some enemy is filled with such a burning rage against someone else that he is single-mindedly determined to harm, or even kill, his opponent. The point of the idiom is not that he clenches his teeth in pain, as one might do at a doctor's office when receiving a needle, but rather that he grits his teeth in malicious determination as he vents his anger on his adversary.[33]

Accordingly, if hell is the place where the ungodly gnash their teeth, against whom are they venting their fury? During their present life those controlled by the sinful nature hate God's people (John 15:9), each other (Titus 3:3), and even God (Rom 1:30). Sadly, their triple anger does not stop in the afterlife. Without ceasing, they continue to gnash their teeth against the redeemed saints, against their fellow rebels, and against the God who created them. And if their raging against God is eternal, is he not just in punishing them eternally? Eternal punishment for eternal, hate-filled aggression: God's just judgment is far closer to "an eye for an eye" than we might have first thought.

---

32. There is one more reference to the gnashing of teeth in Job 16:9, also in the context of anger; however, it has been left out of consideration here because it is a poetic description of God's wrath.

33. Some commentators affirm that the gnashing of teeth is a sign of vexation. See Nolland, *The Gospel of Matthew*, 357–58. However, on the basis of the Old Testament evidence it is better to connect it to aggression, as is done by Davies and Allison, *Commentary on Matthew VIII–XVIII*, 31.

Is Hell Obsolete?

Will the unrepentant be destroyed?

Those who embrace conditional immortality have repeatedly complained that no one responds in earnest concerning the passages they bring up about the ungodly being destroyed.[34] Lest that charge be leveled once more, we will attempt to interact, albeit briefly, with four key passages that Edward Fudge brings forward, two from the Old Testament and two from the New Testament.[35]

The first passage is Isa 66:22–24, which is clearly eschatological, for it speaks of the new heavens and the new earth. It also mentions that all shall "look on the dead bodies of the men who have rebelled against [the Lord]." Working out the implications of this, Fudge comments, "They look at corpses, not living people. They view their destruction, not their misery."[36] However, the prophet immediately continues by saying, "For their worm shall not die, their fire shall not be quenched, and they shall be an abhorrence to all flesh." The death described here by Isaiah is clearly not death as we know it today. If a body is buried today, worms will infest the corpse and speed its decomposition until all the flesh is consumed. At that point the worms will die off. Surprisingly, such is not the case here in Isaiah's prophecy. Similarly, if a corpse is burned, the fire will eventually die out when the body is fully reduced to ash. Once more, such is not the case here in Isaiah's prophecy. Those who rebel against the Lord will suffer death in the *eschaton*; however, stating that fact does not resolve the matter. We still need to determine precisely what kind of death is meant in passages like this.

A second Old Testament passage to which Fudge draws our attention is Mal 4:1–3, in which all evildoers are like stubble on the day of the Lord's judgement. The Lord's wrath sets them ablaze "so that it will leave neither root nor branch" (v. 1); in fact, all that will be left is ashes, which the righteous will tread under their feet (v. 3). Fudge admits that the language used by Malachi is symbolic, but he also asserts that "the symbol corresponds to fulfillment . . . The picture does not include perpetual torment, though it does include a total consumption by destroying fire."[37] So, for Fudge the

---

34. For example, Wenham, *Facing Hell*, 230–34.

35. Here I have intentionally selected four passages that Fudge brings forward as significant ones.

36. Fudge, *The Fire That Consumes*, 111.

37. Ibid., 116.

consuming fire is symbolic, but it is also real and literal. If that is the case, though, then the treading of the righteous upon the ashes of the wicked must also be real and literal in some way. Yet how could this be possible if there is great chasm fixed between heaven and hell so that no one can cross over to the other side (Luke 16:26)? Fudge cannot require a literal fulfillment of Mal 4:1 but then avoid such a fulfillment two verses later in Mal 4:3.

This leads us to the third and fourth passages, both from the New Testament. Matthew 7:13, 14 and Matt 10:28 can be taken together, for they both refer to the destruction of those who refuse to follow the ways of the Lord. In these passages our Savior uses the Greek verb *apollumi* or its cognate noun *apōleia*. This word can refer to reducing things, or even people, to ash, as the Lord did when he destroyed the population of Sodom and Gomorrah (Luke 17:29), but it does not always denote such a complete obliteration. For example, the same word is used to describe wineskins that burst but are still there, albeit in a ruined state (Matt 9:17). It can also refer to sheep that are lost but obviously still exist (Matt 10:6). In fact, this particular term is commonly used to describe death or the process of dying, as when the disciples in the boat cry out to Jesus, "Save us, Lord; we are perishing" (Matt 8:25; see also Matt 2:13; 12:14; 27:20 and many other occurrences). Moreover, destruction *in the sense of dying* is the most appropriate meaning for Matt 7:13–14 because the broad way that leads to destruction is contrasted with the difficult path that leads to life. It goes without saying that life and death are the expected antonyms in this case.

Now we have come full circle, back to Isa 66:24. To be sure, the ultimate destiny of the unrepentant in hell is the destruction by death. The apostle John explicitly says, even twice, that the lake of fire is the second death (Rev 20:14; 21:8). Up to this point, we can agree with those who promote conditional immortality. Where we must part ways, however, is in our understanding of what this second death entails. For those embracing conditional immortality, the second death is virtually the same as the first death. In both deaths the bodies of the unrepentant are reduced to almost nothing, the first time by decomposition in the grave, the second time by the fire of God's wrath. The only significant difference in the second death is that the soul, along with the body, will be reduced to nothing by the same hellfire.

Yet is this the picture that Scripture gives of the second death? Already from Isa 66:24 we learn that there is something fundamentally and qualitatively different about the second death. *Unlike in the first death*, the worm does not die and the fire is not quenched. These words are picked up by Christ himself when he describes hell as the place "where their worm does not die and the fire is not quenched" (Mark 9:48). This also corresponds with the description of those who worship the beast and his image. As the apostle says, "the smoke of their torment rises forever and ever" (Rev 14:11). In short, whereas the process of destruction in the first death is completed after a finite amount of time, in the second death this process is never-ending. Moreover, the second death is not characterized in the first place by a cessation of breathing, but rather by an ultimate and eternal separation from God. The second death is the state of being utterly forsaken by God (Matt 7:23, 25:41), not utterly removed from existence. Those opting for conditional immortality need to reckon with these fundamental differences between the first and second deaths.

Truth be told, it is hard to confess this truth. Our understandable emotions urge us to find some other solution, even any other solution. Yet sound doctrine involves confessing God's revealed truth, even when it is heart-wrenching to do so.

IMPLICATIONS FOR PREACHING ABOUT ETERNAL PUNISHMENT

Now that we have addressed various key issues concerning eternal punishment, it is good to pull things together and describe how this should be applied, first of all in preaching but secondly in pastoral situations. In order to keep matters as concise as possible, this will be done by presenting four theses accompanied by brief explanations. It should be clear that each thesis will have Christ as a focal point.

1. *Preachers should preach about eternal punishment as Christ himself did—occasionally but not dominantly, directly but not dramatically.*

    The topic of hell is neither pleasant nor politically correct. Nevertheless, preachers are ambassadors of Christ, not messengers of the current *Zeitgeist*. Both in parables and in his other teaching, Jesus Christ, the good and compassionate Shepherd, did not shy away from speaking about hell, even though his main theme was repentance and the coming of the kingdom (Matt 4:17). Furthermore, his descriptions of hell were direct and unsettling. It is from Christ that we hear about hell as the place of "weeping and gnashing of teeth" (Matt 8:12) and the place where "their worm does not die and the fire is not quenched" (Mark 9:48). At the same time, our Chief Prophet and Teacher did not carry on at length, graphically describing people's sufferings in hell. If servants of Christ are trying to find the right balance in their preaching, also concerning eternal punishment, a good place to start is by following the example of the Master himself, Jesus. Another helpful guide in this matter is the Heidelberg Catechism, which explicitly mentions eternal punishment in Lord's Days 4, 15, 16, 19. If this Catechism is used as a regular, annual guide in preaching, a minister will teach his congregation about eternal punishment at least four times every year.

2. *Preaching about eternal punishment is meant in the first place to sanctify saints, not scare off the unconverted.*

Jesus spoke about hell in the Sermon on the Mount, which was delivered in the first place to "his disciples" (Matt 5:1–2). Likewise, Christ gave the stern warning about fearing him who can destroy both soul and body in hell to the twelve apostles (Matt 10:1–5, 28). In a similar fashion, the apostles who spoke about eternal punishment did so in their letters to Christian congregations. Even some of the most graphic language about hell, found in the Book of Revelation, is given to the servants of Jesus Christ (Rev 1:1). The point is simply this: stark warnings about hell should be directed in the first place toward believers so that they do not fall asleep in their sins nor give in to the perennial temptation of hypocrisy. By contrast, preaching to the unconverted nations focuses on announcing Christ crucified in our place (1 Cor 2:2), not on sinners suffering in the hands of an angry God. Of course, the topic of hell may well come up in evangelistic settings, and it need not be avoided. In line with our Savior's own approach, however, the primary focus of this doctrine is to sanctify saints, not to win souls for Christ.

3. *Preaching about eternal punishment is emotionally difficult but doctrinally beneficial.*

It is hard to preach about hell. How do you factor in the presence of children whose imaginations can easily run wild? What consideration do you give to adults who may have family members who have completely turned their backs on the Lord? What if there are guests in the worship service? These questions should not determine the message, but the preacher certainly ought to keep them in mind as he crafts his sermon. All of this can be mentally draining at times. Yet the blessings outweigh the sacrifices. How will God's people even begin to properly understand the enormity of their sins unless preachers tell them that even a careless verbal jab is enough to make them liable to "the fire of hell" (Matt 5:22)? Such a truth is so far removed from commonplace thinking that if a preacher never proclaims it, his congregation can hardly be expected to grasp it.

Furthermore, how will God's people ever appreciate the full extent of Christ's work for them unless they know something about the hell he went through on the cross for their sake?[38] Beyond that, how will God's people rightly confess their God unless they realize that he is sufficiently holy and just to condemn the ungodly to hell? Without the doctrine of hell, it is entirely possible that we begin to embrace a skewed, if not idolatrous, conception of who our God really is. In short, many different teachings of grace are brought into razor-sharp focus against the pitch-black background of the outer darkness, which is eternal punishment. Why would we ever want to deprive God's people of that kind of doctrinal clarity?

4. *Thinking about the eternal destiny of unbelieving acquaintances really requires the godly to focus all the more intensely on Christ.*

It would not be right to end this study without speaking plainly about the most emotional and pastorally sensitive aspect of this topic. How should children of God work, in their own hearts, with the reality that they know persons who refuse to repent and who appear to be on the broad road that leads to destruction? We say, "Pray for them, especially for their repentance. So long as they are still alive, there is still time to repent." Yes, that is correct. And we say, "Speak to them wisely yet earnestly. Lovingly and understandingly call them to repentance." Yes, that is also good counsel.

Yet, can we say more? After all, the suffering of godly souls over unrepentant acquaintances is so great—far greater than we often realize. Thankfully, there is more to say. As Jesus himself explained, God the Father has given Christ "authority to execute judgment, because he is the Son of Man" (John 5:27). Thus, on Judgment Day the living

---

38. Heidelberg Catechism, Lord's Day 16, Q&A 44.

and the dead will appear, to be precise and specific, before "the judgment seat of Christ," not the judgment seat of God in some generic sense (2 Cor 5:10). That truth changes our perspectives. Whereas we are naturally preoccupied with the fact that someone we know may be eternally condemned, Scripture encourages us to focus on Christ, the one who will ultimately be responsible for doing the condemning.

To speak plainly, the One who will say to the unrepentant person, "Depart from me, you cursed, into the eternal fire prepared for the devil and his angels," is the very same One who said, "Blessed are the poor in spirit" (Matt 5:2), and who also said, "Come to me, all who labor and are heavy laden, and I will give you rest" (Matt 11:28). In other words, he who is Abounding Compassion personified, Jesus Christ, is also the one who will personally cast all the ungodly into eternal punishment.[39]

Moreover, lest we forget, this Christ is true God and *true man*, having the same full range of human emotions that we have. In the present frailty of our minds and faith, we may wonder, "How will Christ, the most compassionate man who ever lived, be able to cast his and my enemies into hell? After all, he knows each and every unrepentant sinner more intimately and fully than I do. How will he be able to do that?" At present we cannot answer the *how*; we can only confess, on the basis of God's Word, the truth that it will be so.

Still, there is consolation and hope. On the final day of our Savior's return, our frail hearts and minds will be fully and completely transformed into the likeness of Christ's heart and mind (1 Cor 2:16; 2 Cor 3:18). And then, somehow, we will be able to work with this truth, intellectually and emotionally. Right now, it is simply too much for us. At present "we know in part . . . but when the perfect comes, the partial will pass away" (1 Cor 13:10). And when the partial passes away, we will be able to understand how Christ, who is true God and true man, can condemn the ungodly, each one of whom he knows full well. And when the partial passes away, we, too, will be able to work this difficult matter through in our own hearts and minds. Let us constantly pray for greater Christ-likeness, also when we need to deal with this most difficult doctrine of everlasting punishment.

---

39. Heidelberg Catechism, Lord's Day 19, Q&A 52.

Is Hell Obsolete?

BIBLIOGRAPHY

Barth, Karl. *Church Dogmatics*. Edited by G. W. Bromiley and T. F. Torrance. Translated by A. T. Mackay and T. H. L. Parker. 2nd ed. Peabody, MA: Hendrickson, 2010.

Bavinck, Herman. *Reformed Dogmatics*. Grand Rapids: Baker Academic, 2003.

Bell, Rob. *Love Wins: A Book about Heaven, Hell, and the Fate of Every Person Who Ever Lived*. New York: HarperOne, 2012.

Book of Praise: Anglo-Genevan Psalter. Winnipeg: Premier Printing, 2014.

Crisp, Oliver. *Retrieving Doctrine: Essays in Reformed Theology*. Downers Grove, IL: IVP Academic, 2010.

Crockett, William V., ed. *Four Views on Hell*. Grand Rapids: Zondervan, 1992.

Davidson, Bruce W. "Reasonable Damnation: How Jonathan Edwards Argued for the Rationality of Hell." *Journal of the Evangelical Theological Society* 38 (1995) 45–56.

Davies, W. D., and Dale C. Allison. *Commentary on Matthew VIII–XVIII: A Critical and Exegetical Commentary on the Gospel according to Saint Matthew*. International Critical Commentary. Edinburgh: Bloomsbury T&T Clark, 2000.

Edwards, David L., and John Stott. *Evangelical Essentials: A Liberal Evangelical Dialogue*. Downers Grove, IL: InterVarsity, 1989.

Fudge, Edward. *The Fire That Consumes: A Biblical and Historical Study of Final Punishment*. Fallbrook, CA: Verdict, 1982. (3rd ed., Eugene, OR: Cascade Books, 2011.)

Hendriksen, William. *The Bible on the Life Hereafter*. Grand Rapids: Baker, 1959.

Hughes, Philip E. *The True Image*. Leicester, UK: InterVarsity, 1989.

McKim, Donald, ed. *Encyclopedia of the Reformed Faith*. Louisville: Westminster John Knox, 1992.

McLaren, Brian D. *The Last Word and the Word after That: A Tale of Faith, Doubt, and a New Kind of Christianity*. San Francisco: Jossey-Bass, 2008.

Nolland, John. *The Gospel of Matthew: A Commentary on the Greek Text*. New International Greek Testament Commentary. Grand Rapids: Eerdmans, 2005.

Sanders, John. *No Other Name: An Investigation into the Destiny of the Unevangelized*. Grand Rapids: Eerdmans, 1992.

Wenham, John. *Facing Hell: The Story of a Nobody, An Autobiography 1913–1996*. Carlisle, UK: Paternoster, 1998.

Williams, Stephen. "The Question of Hell and Salvation: Is There a Fourth View?" *Tyndale Bulletin* 57 (2006) 263–83.

7

A New Earth?

Gerhard H. Visscher

To what degree do we expect the new world that is coming to be a physical, new earth? And if we believe it will be a physical world with such things as plants, trees, and mountains, do we expect it to be an entirely new world, or do we expect this present world to be renewed, renovated, and so better than it is now? I have noticed, both in preaching and in teaching, that the predominant focus regarding the believer's future is on heaven and that heaven is understood predominantly as a non-physical kind of place. It is as if the "intermediate state" has become eternalized, and the return of a new earth is minimized or ignored. Thus, I would like to present some strong biblical arguments for the position that after the return of our Lord we will dwell upon a renewed physical new earth that has been united with the heavens.

THE RESURRECTION OF THE BODY

It is good to note, first of all, that the position that the new earth will be a physical one is but the logical conclusion of the resurrection of the body.

A New Earth?

While it may be true that our Three Forms of Unity[1] say little about a "new earth," the earthiness of this place, in my judgment, goes hand in hand with the doctrine of the resurrection of the body. Of what benefit will the physical resurrection be if we have no place on which to plant the feet of our resurrected bodies? We need to be aware of a tendency to spiritualize the eternal state. Seeing how our resurrection is linked up with the resurrection of our Lord Jesus Christ (Phil 3:21; Lord's Day 22), would such a spiritualizing not actually lead to a denial also of the physical resurrection of the Lord Jesus Christ?

SECOND PETER 3

There are many texts of Scripture that *seem* to support a less than physical eternal space. Think, for instance of 2 Peter 3, a passage that probably contributes in a major way to the prevalent "less than physical new earth" view. After all, the apostle Peter writes: "The heavens will *disappear* . . . Since everything will be *destroyed* in this way . . . That day will bring about the *destruction* of the heavens by fire . . ." (2 Pet 3:10–12).[2] Despite initial appearances, however, there are a number of good arguments to demonstrate that Peter is not speaking about the absolute destruction of everything.

First of all, what does Peter mean when he says that when the Great Day comes, the world will be *destroyed*? Does he mean it will be eliminated? Does he mean that God will start all over with a brand new world?

Notice that he uses the same words about the Flood in 3:6: "by these waters also the world of that time was deluged and *destroyed*." But the world after the Flood was not a completely different world, was it? It was a renewed world. Cleansed by water, and made new. If the "destruction" wrought by the water of the Flood did not cause the world to vanish, is it unreasonable to suggest that the "destruction" which will be wrought by fire will not cause the world to vanish either? Just as the world after the Flood is the first one washed clean by water, so the final world could be the present one even more radically purged by fire.

Secondly, back in Peter's first letter he also talked about something becoming new—namely, us, the people of God. A renewal is happening

---

1. That is, the Belgic Confession, the Heidelberg Catechism, and the Canons of Dort.

2. Scripture quotations in this essay are taken from the New International Version of 1984.

through the resurrection of Jesus Christ, says Peter (1:3). And by "new" he did not mean "absolutely new," did he? We are not annihilated and then brought back into existence. We are still the same people; we look the same, but through the Spirit of God and the power of God's Word we have been renewed, born again, and are better than ever before (1:3, 23). At one point, in 1 Pet 1:7, he even speaks about our faith being tested by trials. But notice what the trials do: they test us, purify us, even as gold is tested by fire and found to be genuine. Chapter 1:7 states, "These [trials] have come so that your faith—of greater worth than gold, which perishes even though refined by fire—may be proved genuine."

It seems that what happens to the persons in 1 Peter 1 happens to the world in 2 Peter 3. The world as we know it is going to be tested, refined, purified by fire. There is a parallel to this in Paul's writing; he often writes about a "new creation" and "new life" (2 Cor. 5:17; Rom 6:4; Gal. 6:15). In 2 Cor 5:17 he cries out, "If anyone is in Christ, he is a new creation," and even though he appends to this "the old has gone, the new has come," we know that we are not just spiritual after we are in Christ, and we do not cease to be physical. The newness is elsewhere.

Thirdly, something of this is also obvious from the Greek words that are used there. Greek has two words that mean "new." The one refers to something new and young in time or origin, whereas the other means "new in nature or in quality."[3] It is the latter word that is consistently used here and in the Book of Revelation. The Bible is not talking about a world totally other than the present one, but about this universe gloriously renewed. One can think of what happens over a period of time to a forest through the process of a forest fire. Some would reference here Mount St. Helens and the process of renewal and new life that happened there.[4]

Fourthly, and somewhat more theologically, destruction in the sense of annihilation would represent a victory for Satan. The late Anthony A. Hoekema put this well when he wrote:

> If God would have to annihilate the present cosmos, Satan would have won a great victory. For then Satan would have succeeded in so devastatingly corrupting the present cosmos and the present

---

3. See note in Bauer-Danker re καινός: "in the sense that what is old has become obsolete, and should be replaced by what is new." *A Greek-English Lexicon*, 497(3b).

4. Alcorn, *Heaven*, 148. On the general point regarding the renewal of creation, see also Venema, *Promise of the Future*, 467; Piper, *Future Grace*, 371, 376; Beale, "The Eschatological Conception," 44; Dumbrell, *End of the Beginning*, 191.

earth that God could do nothing with it but to blot it totally out of existence. But Satan did not win such a victory. On the contrary, Satan has been decisively defeated. God will reveal the full dimensions of that defeat when he shall renew this very earth on which Satan deceived mankind and finally banish from it all the results of Satan's evil machinations.[5]

Lastly, but certainly not least, there is another point to note at the end of 2 Pet 3:10, where we have a textual variant. Significant scholars have acknowledged that the best manuscripts read "and the earth and the works in it will be found" (*kai gē kai ta en autē erga heurethēsetai*).[6] Throughout history scribes and scholars have been uncertain what to make of this reading and have therefore proposed translations based on either a less preferable reading of the original Greek or an emendation of the Greek. As a result we end up with translations such as "the earth and everything in it will be *laid bare*" (NIV84, NIV) or "will be *burned up*" (NASB, RSV, KJV). The debate seems to be continuing because the latest New Testament text to appear has rendered it "the earth and the works in it will *not* be found." This, however, has no manuscript support in the Greek, and is supported only by two ancient translations, namely, a Syriac version and one in the Sahidic dialect of Coptic. The best translation and textual support, in my judgment, we find in the NRSV, which reads: "the earth and everything that is done on it will be *disclosed*."

The point is that if you take the view that this world will be entirely burned up and eliminated, then the best reading of chapter 3, verse 10, makes no sense indeed. But my question is: do the Scriptures ever really give warrant for such a view? The fire is not the fire of total destruction. The fire is the fire of renewal. What happened to the world after the Flood, happens to the world after the fire. After forty days and forty nights, Noah found land again. Earth. It was there. And, no doubt, when the Lord comes again, there will be destruction, and that aspect of his return will certainly be horrible. And the consequences for all of creation will be phenomenal. Who will be able to stand? But the point is: after the fire has done its purifying work, "the earth and the works in it *will be found*." We will find

---

5. *The Bible and the Future*, 281.
6. Metzger, *A Textual Commentary*, 768; Omanson, *A Textual Guide*, 500. There is a very significant article on this textual variant by Wolters, "Worldview and Textual Criticism," 405–13. Wolters advocates the view presented above. N.T. Wright also defends this view in *The Resurrection of the Son of God*, 463.

land again—earth, a new one; *this* one, renewed. And works—the works of people will be found on it.

REVELATION

If an exegetical approach seems a little tenuous, the best hermeneutical test is to assess whether it resonates elsewhere in Scripture. We do indeed find some similar indications of this world being renewed in the Book of Revelation. We need to turn to the end of Revelation 21, where John is speaking about a new heaven and a new earth, the New Jerusalem—specifically to Rev 21:24, 26, where we read the following: "The kings of the earth will bring their splendor into it . . . The glory and honor of the nations will be brought into it." What does this mean? I believe that John is working here with a theme from Isa 60:6 about the future glory of Zion.[7] Isaiah says there about Israel: "Nations will come to your light and kings to the brightness of your dawn." John sees this fulfilled in the vision. In the east, kings of the nations were often seen as the *bearers*, the *representatives* of their respective cultures. To assemble kings together, then, was in an important sense to assemble their national cultures together. They came as authorities; here they appear to be representing the captains of industry, educational leaders, craftsmen, and tradesmen, etcetera.

What does it mean when John tells us that the kings come marching into the New Jerusalem, "bringing the glory and honor of the nations"? The best explanation is not that this is a bold statement of the personal salvation of these men. Rather, this is a beautiful statement about the continuity between this life and the life to come. It is saying that there, in the new Jerusalem, God will also include something of the cultural and industrial and technical achievements of mankind. Just as kings came from all kinds of nations and all kinds of loyalties and brought their treasures to the Jerusalem on this earth, so kings of all kinds of nations and loyalties will in some way bring their treasures to the new Jerusalem in the new heaven and the new earth. To be sure, if they are not Christian kings, their stay will be very temporary. Again, the imagery is symbolic here. They will not remain, but their glory and their honor—that will be brought in and remain.

What is more, these texts should be seen in a context which is much more "earthy" than we have generally been led to think. Whereas some people's expectations, I suspect, are more akin to an eternal space ride, it is

---

7. Particularly recommended here is Mouw, *When the Kings Come Marching In*.

A New Earth?

very striking that the new Jerusalem comes down out of heaven and God himself comes and makes his eternal home with us in this restored creation.

We tend to spiritualize the images of "garden" and "city," but are they not meant to make us think also of some very earthy realities such as dirt and concrete and buildings? Even the fact that according to the early verses of Revelation 21 the holy city is said to "come down" from heaven—is that not in one line with the motifs about God coming down in the garden, the tabernacle, the temple, and the incarnation of our Lord Jesus? It is the city that has become a perfect cube (21:16), resembling the holy of holies in this new world where God and man dwell together forever. It is the gardenlike city of Revelation 22 from which the curse has been removed. Even "the throne of God and of the Lamb" is found in this gardenlike city (22:3). The biblical final picture is not one of only heaven restored, or only earth restored, but it is heaven and earth restored together in the wondrous recreation based on the blood of Christ. In an interesting publication, J. Richard Middleton nudges us in these directions. For example, he writes:

> [W]e should not identify "paradise" in the New Testament with "heaven" . . . ; rather, "paradise" more correctly refers to God's original intent for human earthly flourishing . . . which now comes to fruition in a garden-city, on a renewed (even grander) Mount Zion, as the focused center of God's presence in the new heaven and new earth.[8]

We really need to accept the "how much more" of New Testament Scripture regarding the life to come. There will be a physicality of sorts in the life to come.

MORE SCRIPTURE

We find such notes in more of the New Testament than we might expect. First Corinthians 15—that long and delightful chapter about the great benefits of the resurrection—ends with the thought that "our labor in the Lord is not in vain." Why? Surely it is because, also in Paul's view, in the world of the final resurrection there is going to be not only a spiritual but also a material realm. We are going to need resurrected bodies because we are going to live on that which is not only a new heaven but also a new earth, in which somehow even some of the consequences of our labors will be evident. I

---

8. Middleton, *A New Heaven and Earth*, 172.

As You See the Day Approaching

believe not only that the souls of believers go to heaven. I believe also the resurrection of the body. "We look forward to the resurrection of the dead and the life of the world to come" (Nicene Creed). That is our confession, is it not? I believe Jesus Christ, through whom God created all things, and also reconciles all things to himself, "whether things on earth or things in heaven, by making peace through his blood, shed on the cross" (Col 1:20). The cosmic significance of the work of Christ is wonderfully proclaimed in that text. It is not just some of this world, but "the whole creation" that "has been groaning as in the pains of childbirth" and is awaiting the restoration of all things (Rom 8:22).

Even the question of our purpose in that future world is cast in this light. Will we really be living in an eternal worship service? Revelation 22:5 recalls Genesis language about Adam having dominion when it says that God's people "will reign for ever and ever."

Again, contrary to expectations, the Bible is not teaching us that you and so many more millions are laboring in this life all for nothing. God does not bring man into this world with the mandate to cultivate and develop all of creation for thousands and thousands of years, only to destroy in the end everything that man brings about. God does not give you and me an office and calling to fulfill every day, and then in the last day considers everything that we ever did to be worth nothing at all. It is not so that the only things that have eternal consequences are the things we do for the church, and that everything else will perish forever. Christ is Lord of everything. He died not just to bring souls to heaven, but also so that the same people would set their feet on a new earth. The Scriptures present the relationship between now and later as that of sowing and reaping, ripening and harvest, kernel and ear. There is even an "earthiness" about many of the terms our Lord Jesus used; for example, "Well done, my good servant! . . . Because you have been trustworthy in a very small matter, take charge of ten cities" (Luke 19:17). Notice the reference to "cities," not "clouds."

The Kings of the earth will bring the splendor of the nations into Zion. The earth and the works in it will be found. Eduard Thurneysen has been quoted as saying:

> [T]he world into which we shall enter . . . is therefore not another world; it is this world, this heaven, this earth; both, however passed away and renewed. It is . . . these fields, these cities, these streets, these people, that will be the scene of redemption. At present they are battlefields, full of the strife and sorrow of the not yet

A New Earth?

accomplished consummation; then they will be fields of victory, fields of harvest, where out of seed that was sown with tears the everlasting sheaves will be reaped and brought home.[9]

Did this Barthian scholar overstate the matter? Perhaps, but how many have not understated the matter? To this question we will have to take a "wait and see" posture. One thing is evident: it is a tremendous comfort to the people of God. The brokenness of this world is seen and felt in sickness, cancer, tragedy, war, and more.

But what will the new world be like? Imagine: Take this world. Strip it of sin and all of sin's consequences: unkind words, thoughts, actions, deeds without love, alienation from God and fellow humans. Remove all the diseases, the hospitals, the funeral parlors, the cemeteries. Remove the handicaps and the disabilities. Introduce perfect fellowship with God. And there you have it: a renewed world, a world in which you and all God's people can live with God forever. Just "wait and see."

Is our body disposable, lowered into the grave? Yes, said the Corinthians, and they went to the prostitutes. No, says Paul, "The body is . . . for the Lord, and the Lord for the body . . . Therefore honor God with your body"(1 Cor 6:13, 20). Is the world really disposable? No, says Peter. Yes, it will be purified, and that process will be deep and it will be drastic and it will be dreadful. But then, "the earth and the works on it will be found."

It will be a real new world for real people, entirely new in Christ.

Under the power of the Holy Spirit, Peter, John, and Paul all build on the Old Testament promises. Whereas the meek will inherit the land in Ps 37:11, in Jesus' words of Matt 5:5, the meek will receive the earth. Whereas Abraham is promised the land of Canaan in Gen 17:8, the children of Abraham are promised the earth in Rom 4:13. In the new age of the Spirit, Peter too speaks about the day when "the time comes for God to restore everything, as he promised long ago through the prophets" (Acts 3:21).

In the same vein, Peter works with the words of Isaiah: "in keeping with his promise, we are looking forward to a new heaven and a new earth, the home of righteousness" (2 Pet 3:13). What promise? The promise of God in Isa 65:17–19:

> Behold, I will create
> new heavens and a new earth.
> The former things will not be remembered,

---

9. As quoted by Hoekema, *The Bible and the Future*, 281.

nor will they come to mind.
But be glad and rejoice forever in what I will create,
For I will create Jerusalem to be a delight and its people a joy.
I will rejoice over Jerusalem and take delight in my people;
the sound of weeping and of crying will be heard in it no more.

BIBLIOGRAPHY

Alcorn, Randy. *Heaven*. Wheaton, IL: Tyndale, 2004.

Beale, Gregory K. "The Eschatological Conception of New Testament Theology." *Eschatology in Bible and Theology: Evangelical Essays at the Dawn of a New Millennium*. Downers Grove, IL: InterVarsity, 1999.

———. *A New Testament Biblical Theology*. Grand Rapids: Baker Academic, 2011.

Comfort, Philip W. *New Testament Text and Translation Commentary*. Carol Stream, IL: Tyndale, 2008.

Danker, Frederik William, ed. *A Greek–English Lexicon of the New Testament and Other Early Christian Literature*. 3rd ed. Chicago: University of Chicago Press, 2000.

Dumbrell, William J. *The End of the Beginning: Revelation 21–22 and the Old Testament*. Homebush West, NSW: Lancer, 1985.

Gilmore, John. *Probing Heaven: Key Questions on the Hereafter*. Grand Rapids: Baker, 1989.

Hoekema, Anthony A. *The Bible and the Future*. Grand Rapids: Eerdmans, 1979.

Middleton, Richard J. *A New Heaven and a New Earth: Reclaiming Biblical Eschatology*. Grand Rapids: Baker Academic, 2014.

Metzger, Bruce M. *A Textual Commentary on the Greek New Testament*. 2nd. ed. New York: United Bible Societies, 2001.

Mouw, Richard J. *When the Kings Come Marching In: Isaiah and the New Jerusalem*. Grand Rapids: Eerdmans, 1983.

Omanson, Roger L. *A Textual Guide to the Greek New Testament*. Stuttgart: Deutsche Bibelgesellschaft, 2006.

Piper, John. *Future Grace*. Sisters, OR: Multnomah, 1995.

Venema, Cornelis P. *The Promise of the Future*. Carlisle, PA: Banner of Truth, 2009.

Wolters, Al. "Worldview and Textual Criticism." *Westminster Theological Journal* 49 (1987) 405–13.

Wright, N. T. *The Resurrection of the Son of God*. Christian Origins and the Question of God 3. Minneapolis: Fortress, 2003.

8

"Until He Comes"
Eschatological Aspects of the Reformed Worship Service

Arjan de Visser

INTRODUCTION

WHAT BETTER WAY TO conclude a series of studies on eschatology than by reflecting on the topic of worship. To use Pauline terminology, prophecies will pass away and tongues will cease, but worship abides. John Piper said something similar when he compared missions and worship: "When this age is over, and the countless millions of the redeemed fall on their faces before the throne of God, missions will be no more. It is a temporary necessity. But worship abides forever!"[1]

"Eschatology and worship" is a topic too broad to handle in one essay; hence we will focus on the question to what extent the Reformed worship tradition has an eschatological flavor. Are Reformed people, as they gather

---

1. John Piper, *Let the Nations Be Glad*, 17.

for worship on a Sunday morning, stimulated to look forward to the Day that is approaching?

This contribution has four parts: first, biblical foundations for our topic; second, eschatological aspects of preaching; third, eschatological aspects of the rest of the worship service; fourth, some concluding suggestions.

BIBLICAL FOUNDATIONS

First of all, we need to determine whether we are on solid biblical ground if we say that there should be an eschatological quality to Christian worship. Thanks to Dr. Smith's contribution we have already seen that there is much eschatology in the Psalms. That is a connection between eschatology and worship right there.

If we go to the New Testament, it will be helpful to focus on the letter to the Hebrews. There is a strong connection between eschatology and worship in Hebrews. "Do not neglect to meet together," it says in Heb 10:25, "but encourage one another, and all the more as you see the Day approaching" (NIV84).[2] The exhortation to gather for worship regularly is conveyed with an urgency that is rooted in an eschatological perspective.

Eschatology is an important aspect throughout the letter to the Hebrews. Time and again attention is drawn to the things that are "to come." In Heb 2:5 the author refers to "the world to come," in 6:5 he mentions the "powers of the age to come," and in 10:3 he refers to "the coming one who will come and not delay." The Christian believers who received this letter are reminded that a glorious inheritance is waiting for them. In 4:9 the author speaks about a Sabbath rest that remains for the people of God, and he exhorts his readers to strive to enter that rest. In chapter 11 he mentions the examples of Abraham, Moses, and other believers in the old covenant who lived and died in faith, trusting that they would inherit "a better country, that is, a heavenly one" (11:16, NIV84). At the end of the letter, believers are reminded that we have no lasting city in this world, but that "we seek the city that is to come" (13:14).

Whatever their situation may have been, the first recipients of the letter seemed to be in danger of losing this future perspective. They are exhorted to pay close attention to the promises of salvation. They are exhorted not to drift away from it (2:1) and not to "neglect such a great salvation" (2:3).

---

2. Scripture quotations are taken from the English Standard Version unless otherwise indicated.

"Until He Comes"

They are warned not to follow the example of the Israelites, who failed to enter the promised land because of disobedience (4:11). In other words, as Christian believers we are called to pursue a life of holiness as we look forward to the Great Day of the return of the Lord.

A recurring theme in Hebrews is the centrality of the person and work of Christ for our salvation. Jesus Christ, the Son of God, was made lower than the angels for a little while (2:9). He suffered and tasted death in order to bring many sons to glory (2:10). Because he did this, he was raised from the dead and crowned with glory and honor (2:7, 9). What happened next had enormous implications for our Christian life and future: Christ ascended into heaven. "Christ has entered, not into holy places made with hands, which are copies of the true things, but into heaven itself, now to appear in the presence of God on our behalf" (9:24). The ascension of Christ was a highly significant event. It changed worship both in heaven and on earth.[3]

We live during the time between the ascension of Christ and the return of Christ. The letter to the Hebrews describes this time from the perspective of Christ's being "seated at the right hand of the throne of the Majesty in heaven" (8:1). He is interceding for believers on earth who put their hope in him. Because he is a perfect and eternal High Priest he is able to save "those who draw near to God through him, since he always lives to make intercession for them" (7:25).

This reality affects the life and worship of believers on earth. Access to God in worship is possible *now*. On various occasions in the letter, believers are exhorted to "draw near to the throne of grace" and to do so with confidence (4:16, 7:25). By the blood of Jesus "we have confidence to enter" (10:19). And since they have "a great priest over the house of God," Christian believers are encouraged "to draw near with a true heart in full assurance of faith" (10:21, 22). The phrase "drawing near," it should be noted, is a worship-related term that alludes to the old covenant custom of drawing near to the Lord in the temple. Christian believers are strongly encouraged to do so together. The author warns against "neglecting to meet together" (10:25). He exhorts them to "continually offer up a sacrifice of praise to God, that is, the fruit of lips that acknowledge his name," and adds, "Do not neglect to do good and to share what you have, for such sacrifices are pleasing to God" (13:15–16). In other words, while the entire life of Christian believers is meant to be a priestly service to God, the highlight is the

---

3. The connection between worship in heaven and on earth is a major theme in Van Rongen, *Met al de heiligen*. See, e.g., vol. 1, 18.

worship service, when they meet together to offer up a sacrifice of praise to God.

The close connection between the church on earth and the heavenly throne room is described in an impressive way in Hebrews 12: "But you have come to Mount Zion and to the city of the living God, the heavenly Jerusalem . . ." (12:22). A comparison is made between the people of Israel (who came to Mount Sinai) and the Christian congregation that has come to the heavenly Jerusalem. What the people of Israel experienced at Mount Sinai was impressive: a blazing fire, darkness and gloom, the sound of a trumpet, and a voice that was so terrifying that the people begged God no longer to speak to them. Even Moses himself trembled with fear. But now, thanks to Jesus Christ, we have come to the city of the living God, the heavenly Jerusalem. This is to be understood realistically, not metaphorically. Just as the people of Israel "came to" Mount Sinai, so the Christian congregation "comes to" the festive gathering of angels in heaven, to the assembly of the firstborn who are enrolled in heaven, to God, the judge of all, to Jesus, the mediator of a new covenant, and to the sprinkled blood that speaks a message of forgiveness and reconciliation.

In many ways, therefore, the Christian church enjoys the privileges of a better covenant (8:6). Because we have Christ in heaven, our worship today is more glorious than the temple worship of the old covenant. At the same time, we realize that Christian worship has a preliminary character.[4] To mention one aspect, our worship has its deficiencies. It is not always as inspiring as we would like it to be. Much of this is our own problem. We do not always come to church with the right attitude. The minister does not always have a first-class sermon. The singing and music is not always well done. Even at the best of times, a beautiful worship service gives us only a foretaste of heavenly worship.

If I may use a somewhat risky analogy, the relationship of the Lord Jesus in heaven and his church on earth may be compared to the long-distance relationship of a young man and young woman (for example, one living in Canada, the other in Australia). They maintain contact by various ways and means: emails and texting every day, and a Skype session once a week. It works to a certain extent, and the relationship can even grow over time, but nothing is better than being together in the same space, and being able to touch one another physically. The young couple long for the day when they will be reunited. In the same way, the Christian

---

4. Barnard, *Die Erediens*, 468.

church maintains the relationship with the Lord through reading the Word of God and prayer, and the contact is intensified during the weekly worship service. It works and it is beautiful. Thanks to the work of the Holy Spirit, the relationship between Christ and his church grows stronger over time. But both the Bridegroom and the Bride look forward to that big event in the future, the marriage feast of the Lamb (Rev 19:6–9). It is only then that worship will be perfectly glorious.

In conclusion: biblical worship has (or should have) a strong eschatological character. As we are connected to the worshiping assembly in heaven, we see the Day of the Lord approaching. This implies three things. First, we look up and we look forward. We lift up our hearts (*sursum corda*) to the Lord and we look forward to the Day that is approaching. Second, we think of Christ in heaven, seated at God's right hand, interceding for us, and we remember his promise: "Behold, I am coming soon" (Rev 22:7). Third, we rejoice in the fact that through Christ we already have access to the throne room of God, and we look forward to the day when we will join Christ, who will be singing God's praise "in the midst of the congregation" (Ps 22:22; Heb 2:12).

PREACHING AND ESCHATOLOGY

As we move on to examine eschatological aspects of Reformed worship, it will be beneficial first to reflect on the sermon. After all, the proclamation of God's Word is an important part of the Reformed worship service, and if anything, one would expect preaching to have an eschatological flavor.

Perhaps the word *flavor* is not strong enough. It would be better to speak of eschatological *urgency*. The apostle Paul displays this urgency when he writes to Timothy: "I charge you in the presence of God and of Christ Jesus, who is to judge the living and the dead, and by his appearing and his kingdom: preach the word; be ready in season and out of season; reprove, rebuke, and exhort, with complete patience and teaching" (2 Tim 4:1, 2). Faithful preachers proclaim the gospel knowing that Christ Jesus is coming to judge the living and the dead. This gives their preaching a real urgency.

Faithful preaching does not just talk about eschatology. Preaching itself also fulfills an eschatological function. The Lord Jesus referred to this when he said that the gospel of the kingdom would be proclaimed throughout the whole world as a testimony to all nations, and that then the end would come (Matt 24:14). The preaching of the gospel is the instrument by which the Holy Spirit works faith and repentance in the hearts of people, thus saving them from the rule of the devil and giving them a place in the kingdom of God. In order for the last day to come, the gospel needs to be preached.

In the history of the Christian church this eschatological aspect of preaching has gone through highs and lows. A man whose preaching had a strong eschatological quality was Martin Luther. It was not just that Luther preached on eschatological passages, but also that there was an eschatological framework to his preaching. It had everything to do with his understanding of justification. Luther's so-called "Tower Experience" (when he began to understand the gospel message of Rom 1:16–17) occurred precisely in relation to the last judgment. Carter Lindberg observes: "His discovery of the gospel basically changed his view of Christ's return and the last judgment. He now understood Christ's return and judgment as the joyous redemption of Christ's believing community."[5] In Luther's understanding, justification was never just a psychological experience of feeling accepted by God. It always had an eschatological dimension. Because we have been justified by faith through Christ, we can joyfully expect the return of Christ. "Justification is received here and now, but will receive its full realization in the moment of judgment before the eternal God."[6] For those who believe in Christ, there is no need to fear the Day of Judgment.

This Biblical understanding of justification and eschatology gave Luther's preaching a real intensity. He believed that preaching is a matter of life and death because it is the medium through which salvation is bestowed.[7] This is also the reason Luther felt obliged to preach as often as he could. During his life he developed his own style of preaching, which has been characterized as popular and conversational, using direct address, dialogue, and dramatic form. He addressed his sermons not to the educated in the church but especially to the young people in attendance. Luther always felt that he was engaged in an eschatological struggle for their souls and that the outcome was eternal in its effect.[8]

How many preachers have been able to follow the great Reformer's example in this respect? In the Lutheran tradition the eschatological

---

5. Lindberg, "Eschatology and Fanaticism," 265–66.
6. Ibid. 266–67.
7. Edwards, *A History of Preaching*, 287.
8. Ibid., 296.

framework that gave urgency and intensity to Luther's preaching was lost over time. Jane E. Strohl offers a sobering assessment of Lutheran preaching today: "In the more than five hundred years since the Reformation, the intense eschatological framework, in which all of Luther's central doctrines took shape, has been lost."[9]

John Calvin's preaching style was different from Luther's, but his understanding of eschatology was basically the same. It is striking that in his *Institutes* Calvin devotes a full chapter to the meditation of the future life (Book 3, Chapter 9).

What about the followers of Calvin? Does preaching from Reformed pulpits, generally speaking, display the urgency and intensity and joy that come from having a biblical grasp of eschatology? Or has our preaching lost its sense of intensity too? It is hard to make a judgment in this regard, but we should be aware of several factors that can weaken the eschatological quality of contemporary Reformed preaching.

First, there is the influence of the society around us, with its focus on instant gratification in the here and now. In the context of the church this can easily translate into expectations that the preacher's message must be relevant *now*, and have something to offer for the current life of the hearers, never mind what will happen in the future.

Second, in Christian theology at large the return of Christ has become a neglected theme. Liberal theologians do not like the idea of a Judgment Day. They prefer to focus on the Kingdom of God, an idea that is more palatable to the modern mind. In much contemporary theology, even evangelical theology, the return of Christ to judge the living and the dead is ignored. Instead, the focus is on the idea that God is "a missionary God," a God who is on a mission to establish his kingdom in the world (the *Missio Dei* concept).[10]

Reformed preachers will have to stand firm and not give in to the temptation to ignore the Day of Judgment in their preaching. It may be much more palatable in our days to suggest that the Kingdom of God will be established in an evolutionary way, but the Word of God teaches us that man is appointed to die once, and after that comes judgment (Heb 9:27). Therefore, faithful preachers need to speak with intensity and urgency as

---

9. Strohl, "Luther's Eschatology," 361.

10. To mention an example, in the highly acclaimed book by evangelical author Chris Wright, *The Mission of God*, the concept of the coming judgment does not function at all.

they call on their hearers "to wait for [God's] Son from heaven, whom he raised from the dead, Jesus who delivers us from the wrath to come" (1 Thess 1:10).

Let me end this section by offering a few suggestions for preachers of the gospel. First, make sure that your own understanding of the gospel includes a robust understanding of eschatology. You do not have to always preach on eschatological passages, but you need to make sure that your message fits within the eschatological framework. This will give your preaching intensity and urgency.

Second, do indeed preach on eschatological passages from time to time. In the Old Testament there is so much already, ranging from expectations about life after death (Pss 16:19; 49:15; Job 19:21–27) to prophecies regarding the Day of the Lord (Joel 2:28—3:21), Ezekiel's visions of restoration (Ezekiel 40–48), and Isaiah's prophecies regarding the new creation (Isaiah 65, 66).[11] In the New Testament we have the teaching of our Lord in various parables and, more specifically, in Matthew 24 and 25. There are many passages in various New Testament epistles and, of course, the Book of Revelation. In addition, the Christian days of commemoration (Christmas, Good Friday, Easter, Ascension, Pentecost) provide good opportunities for eschatological preaching.

ESCHATOLOGY AND LITURGY

The Reformed order of liturgy as followed on the Christian feast days and, indeed, each Sunday, is not only replete with eschatological themes, but is even set within an eschatological framework. It is important to set the right tone even before the worship service formally begins. A standard way of helping the congregation get into the right frame of mind is the traditional *sursum corda* exhortation, spoken by the minister: "Lift up your hearts!" This beautiful expression goes back to Calvin's custom in Geneva.[12] With these words the congregation is reminded that in worship we "draw near" to God (Heb 10:21, 22) and "come to" the heavenly Jerusalem, where Jesus is, our mediator (Heb 12:22–24).

The worship service typically starts with the votum and salutation. With the votum the congregation expresses its trust and faith in God: "Our help is in the name of the Lord, who made heaven and earth" (Ps 124:8).

---

11. See Kaiser, *Preaching and Teaching the Last Things*.
12. Calvin used to say: "Lève le coeur!"

"Until He Comes"

By referring back to God's work of creation, the congregation expresses its faith that this great God will also be powerful to help in the present and in the future. The eschatological aspect is implicit here.

After this, the congregation receives God's greeting. One of the Scripture passages used for this purpose is Rev 1:4-5: "Grace to you and peace from him who is and who was and who is to come, and from the seven spirits who are before his throne, and from Jesus Christ the faithful witness, the firstborn of the dead, and the ruler of kings on earth." Much could be said about the rich Trinitarian content of this greeting, but for our purpose we will focus on the way God introduces himself to his people: "From him who is and who was and who is to come . . ." There is an obvious allusion here to the covenant name with which God revealed himself to Moses in the old covenant: "I am who I am" (Exod 3:14). That name contains the promise that the love of the Lord is steadfast, that it endures forever, and that he will not forsake the work of his hands (Ps 138:8).

It is interesting to note that in the greeting we find the formulation "the one who is and who was *and who is to come.*" Instead of "and who is to come," one might have expected "and who will be." The phrase "who is to come" proclaims that the Lord is not just eternal but that he will also come to visit his people, set them free, and make them share in his covenantal blessings. From a New Testament perspective we see in this blessing an allusion to the return of the Lord Jesus. In the Book of Revelation this promise is repeated in the letter to the church in Philadelphia (3:11) and again, three times, at the end of the book: "Behold, I am coming soon" (Rev 22:7, 12, 20). We may conclude that every time the greeting from Revelation 1 is used at the beginning of the worship service, the congregation is drawn into the eschatological perspective that the Lord Jesus, the one who "is the same yesterday and today and forever" (Heb 13:8), is coming back.

One of the first items in the usual order or worship is the reading of the Ten Commandments, the Decalogue. While eschatology is not prominent here, there are nevertheless aspects that point to the future of God's covenant people. There is a warning that the Lord will visit the iniquity of those who hate him, but that he will show steadfast love to thousands of those who love him and keep his commandments. The fifth commandment comes with a clear promise: ". . . that your days may be long in the land that the Lord your God is giving you" (Exod 20:12). The prophetic value of these promises has not been exhausted yet!

Prayers

What about the prayers in the worship service? The Word of God encourages the Christian church, as the Bride of Christ, to pray for the return of the Bridegroom. The Spirit and the Bride say, "Come." And the one who hears is exhorted to say, "Come," as well (Rev 22:17). What is the situation with respect to the prayers that we hear from our pulpits every Sunday? Again, this is hard to answer. Let me simply raise the question: Do our ministers lead the congregation, as Bride of Christ, in praying for the return of the Bridegroom? In this regard a comment by T. Brienen is worth contemplating. He remarks that much depends on the faith of the minister himself. If his own faith is "tuned-in eschatologically," it will come through in the way he leads the worship service, and the congregation will be drawn into the eschatological perspective.[13] This will certainly come out in the ministry of prayer.

Psalms and Hymns

An important part of the worship service is the ministry of praise. Ever since John Calvin initiated the Genevan Psalter, there has been a strong emphasis on Psalm singing in the Reformed tradition. There is no need to say much about the eschatological content of the Psalms as Dr. J. Smith has already discussed this topic in his contribution. Suffice it to say that those churches who sing the Psalms in the worship service have much opportunity to include eschatological content in their singing.[14]

As for the hymn repertoire of the Reformed tradition, there are hymns with eschatological content that are shared within the broader Protestant tradition; for example, John Newton's "Day of Judgment! Day of Wonders!" and Isaac Watts's "Behold the Amazing Gift of Love." Other hymns are not expressly eschatological but do contain eschatological aspects nonetheless; for example, the ancient *Te Deum* and the hymn "Christ Shall Have Dominion."

---

13. Brienen, "Liturgie en Prediking," 619.

14. A few examples: the Canadian Reformed Churches use the *Book of Praise*, which contains the Anglo-Genevan Psalter (with versifications of the Psalms on the Genevan melodies); the United Reformed Churches use the *Psalter Hymnal* (with versifications of the Psalms on other melodies).

"Until He Comes"

Interestingly, there are some eschatological hymns in current Reformed hymnals that have not gained much acceptance outside of Reformed circles yet. An example is the hymn "Come, Lord Jesus! Maranatha!" which is based on a Dutch hymn by Tom Naastepad.[15] Another example is "By the Sea of Crystal," by William Kuipers.[16]

Overall, looking at the Psalms and hymns sections of various Reformed church books, we may be thankful that there is a sizeable collection of Psalms and hymns with eschatological content.

Baptism

Let us move on and examine the sacraments, paying special attention to the liturgical forms that are being used in Reformed churches. With respect to baptism, many churches still use the classic form for the baptism of infants.[17] As the form explains the meaning of being baptized in the name of the triune God, Father, Son, and Holy Spirit, it becomes clear that there are eschatological implications in each case. When we are baptized into the name of the Father, it means that the Father established an eternal covenant of grace with us. He adopts us for his children and heirs. When we are baptized into the name of the Son, it means that we are united with him in his death and resurrection. When we are baptized into the name of the Spirit, it means that we shall be cleansed from our sins and renewed, "till we shall finally be present without blemish among the assembly of God's elect in life eternal."[18]

In the prayer before baptism the congregation prays: "We pray that he (she), following him day by day, may joyfully bear his (her) cross and cleave to him in true faith, firm hope, and ardent love. Grant that he (she), comforted in you, may leave this life, which is no more than a constant death, and at the last day may appear without terror before the judgment seat of Christ your Son." Similarly, after the administration of baptism: "May he (she) live in all righteousness under our only Teacher, King, and High Priest, Jesus Christ, and valiantly fight against and overcome sins, the

---

15. Hymn 67 in the Canadian Reformed *Book of Praise* (2014 edition); translated and adapted from the Dutch hymn "Eens als de bazuinen klinken."

16. Hymn 469 in the blue *Psalter Hymnal* (CRC, 1959), hymn 620 in the grey *Psalter Hymnal* (CRC Publications, 1987).

17. For example, *Book of Praise*, 597–99.

18. Forms for Baptism, *Book of Praise*, 597, 600.

devil, and his whole dominion. May he (she) forever praise and magnify you and your Son Jesus Christ, together with the Holy Spirit, the one only true God." When we reflect on all this, it is clear that baptism is placed in an eschatological perspective.

Lord's Supper

The same applies to the other sacrament which the Lord instituted for his church, the Lord's Supper. In fact, with the Lord's Supper the eschatological character is even more prominent. Two aspects may be mentioned in this respect. First, according to the command of the Lord Jesus, believers "proclaim the Lord's death *until he comes*" (1 Cor 11:26). What this means is explained well by the classic form for the celebration of the Lord's Supper: "Let us in all tribulation await our Lord Jesus Christ, who will come from heaven to change our mortal body to be like his glorious body and take us to himself forever."[19]

The second aspect is observed in the fact that the Lord's Supper is intended to be *a meal*. It has to do with food and drink, bread and wine. The meaning of this meal is rich: (a) It is a pledge that the Lord Jesus has given his body and shed his blood for the forgiveness of our sins. (b) It is a symbol of the fellowship that Christian believers experience as members of one body. (c) It is a foretaste of the marriage feast of the Lamb. This last aspect was highlighted by the Lord himself when he instituted the Lord's Supper: "I tell you I will not drink again of this fruit of the vine until that day when I drink it new with you in my Father's kingdom" (Matt 26:29). This is confirmed in the Book of Revelation, when the Lord shows the apostle John the vision of the marriage feast of the Lamb, and when the angel says to him, "Write this: Blessed are those who are invited to the marriage supper of the Lamb" (Rev 19:9).

There is much to contemplate here. The Lord's Supper is the culmination of a tradition of covenantal meals found throughout the history of God's people in the old covenant. Think of that impressive event at Mount Horeb when Moses and Aaron, Nadab and Abihu, and seventy of the elders of Israel went up the mountain and saw the God of Israel. "They beheld God," it says, "and they ate and drank" (Exod 24:11). It was a wonderful experience for the leaders of Israel. It told them that their covenant God

---

19. Prayer before the Lord's Supper, *Book of Praise*, 606

"Until He Comes"

wanted to have fellowship with them, and it was a foretaste of greater things to come.

When the Son of God came down to earth to dwell among God's people, it is striking that meals were very important in his ministry. He ate with his disciples, he ate with tax collectors and sinners, and he fed multitudes of people. He also described the future kingdom of heaven in terms of eating and drinking: "I tell you, many will come from east and west and recline at table with Abraham, Isaac, and Jacob in the kingdom of heaven" (Matt 8:11). When the Lord instituted the Lord's Supper, he was initiating the next stage in the history of redemption. From that point on, followers of Christ would eat bread and drink wine knowing that he was in their midst. But they would also realize that a more beautiful future was awaiting them: The time will come when Christian believers will eat and drink with all the believers of the old and the new covenant in the presence of their Lord and Savior.

From this perspective it is regrettable that more and more congregations are giving up on the tradition of celebrating the Lord's Supper around a table, and replacing it with celebrating it in the pews. Admittedly, there are practical reasons for moving from the table to the pews, but at the same time something profoundly symbolic is lost, namely, that the Lord's Supper is intended to be a meal. Celebrating the Lord's Supper while being seated around a large table is a beautiful foreshadowing of the marriage feast of the Lamb.

Have Reformed churches always recognized the eschatological aspects of the Lord's Supper? Critics have argued that the Reformed tradition has been so preoccupied with theological discussions regarding the Lord's Supper (for example, with the Roman Catholic Church about transubstantiation; with the Lutherans about the real presence of Christ), that other aspects have been eclipsed.[20] Whether this is true or not, some self-examination would be beneficial.

In this connection it will be helpful to reflect on an element of the form for the celebration of the Lord's Supper that we have not discussed yet: the *sursum corda* (the section of the form that is often called "exhortation"). These are the words spoken by the minister just before the communion as such: "In order that we may now be nourished with Christ, the true heavenly bread, we must not cling with our hearts to the outward symbols of bread and wine, but *lift our hearts* on high in heaven, where Christ, our

---

20. Wainwright, *Eucharist and Eschatology*, 159–76.

advocate, is, at the right hand of his heavenly Father." This formula was born out of the struggle during the Reformation. The Roman Catholic Church encourages its members to cling to the elements of bread and wine. The Reformed church exhorts its members to lift their hearts on high in heaven, where Christ is seated at the right hand of his Father. It is important for the minister, as he reads the form, to give due attention to the *sursum corda*. If our minds are with Christ in heaven as we celebrate the Lord's Supper, our eschatological awareness and our longing for his return will be strengthened.

Conclusion

Now that we have walked through the Reformed worship service, it will be clear that there is a distinctly eschatological quality to the Reformed liturgy. In various elements of the worship service, especially in the sacraments, the eschatological hope of the Christian faith comes through clearly. The question, of course, is whether these aspects do indeed form part of the *active* faith of the believers. At the deepest level, it is a question of love. The more the Bride loves the Bridegroom, the more she will long for his return. If the love grows cold, however, that longing will disappear.

CONCLUDING SUGGESTIONS

Let me end with some concluding suggestions. First, given the worldview of the society around us and the sinful inclinations of our own heart, we will have to make a consistent effort to keep the eschatological expectation alive in our day-to-day Christian faith. Only then will our worship have an eschatological quality. This is especially true for those who lead in worship. To repeat the comment made by Dr. Brienen, if our ministers are "tuned-in eschatologically" it will come out in their preaching and in the way they lead the congregation in worship.

Second, as Bride of Christ the Christian church is expected to pray for the return of the Bridegroom; therefore let ministers and elders who lead the congregation in the ministry of prayer make it a point to pray at least once a month for the return of Christ. "Come, Lord Jesus, Maranatha!"

Third, we should as much as possible safeguard the Lord's Supper's character as a meal because it helps the congregation look forward to the marriage feast of the Lamb. Celebrating around a large table is a beautiful way to do this. For those congregations who celebrate in the pews, let them think of ways to maintain the meal character of the Lord's Supper. One way to do this is to read eschatological passages from Scripture and sing hymns with eschatological content during the celebration of the Lord's Supper.

Fourth, our hope for the future is based on the fact that we have the Lord Jesus in heaven, seated at the right hand of God the Father. For this reason I agree with Rev. G. van Rongen that Ascension Day deserves to be celebrated with more enthusiasm than is generally done.[21]

We started by asking the question whether the Reformed worship tradition has an eschatological flavor. We have seen that there are many elements in the Reformed worship service that have the potential to stimulate God's people to look forward to the Day that is approaching. If these elements function only formally, they will have little impact. In order for the worship service to have a truly eschatological flavor, our expectations regarding the return of Christ need to be part of our living and active faith. Ultimately, eschatology is rooted in love. The more we love the Lord, the more we will look forward to his return. We do have the Lord's promise: "Surely I am coming soon" (Rev 22:20). May we learn to say and to sing more and more: "Amen. Come, Lord Jesus!"

BIBLIOGRAPHY

Barnard, A.C. *Die Erediens*. Pretoria: N.G. Kerkboekhandel, 1981.
Book of Praise: Anglo-Geneva Psalter. Winnipeg: Premier, 2014.
Brienen, T. "Liturgie en prediking in eschatologische kaders." In *Eschatologie: Handboek over de christelijke toekomstverwachting*, edited by W. van 't Spijker, 615–26. Kampen: De Groot Goudriaan, 1999.
Edwards, O. C. Jr. *A History of Preaching*. Nashville: Abingdon, 2004.
Kaiser, Walter C. Jr. *Preaching and Teaching the Last Things: Old Testament Eschatology for the Life of the Church*. Grand Rapids: Baker Academic, 2011.
Lindberg, Carter. "Eschatology and Fanaticism in the Reformation Era: Luther and the Anabaptists." *Concordia Theological Quarterly* 64 (2000) 259–78.
Piper, John. *Let the Nations Be Glad!: The Supremacy of God in Missions*. 2nd ed. Grand Rapids: Baker Academic, 2003.
Rongen, G. van. *Met al de heiligen: Liturgie in hemel en op aarde*. 2 vols. Barneveld: De Vuurbaak, 1990.
Strohl, Jane E. "Luther's Eschatology." In *The Oxford Handbook of Martin Luther's Theology*, edited by Robert Kolb et al., 353–62. Oxford: Oxford University Press, 2014.
Wainwright, Geoffrey. *Eucharist and Eschatology*. 3rd ed. Akron, OH: OSL Publications, 2002.

---

21. Van Rongen, *Met al de heiligen*, vol. 1, 18.

As You See the Day Approaching

Wright, Christopher J. H. *The Mission of God: Unlocking the Bible's Grand Narrative.* Downers Grove, IL: InterVarsity, 2006.

Subject and Name Index

Adam
   Chart of contrasts with Christ, 33
   Creation of Adam, body and soul, 22–23, 77–79
   First Adam and Last/Second Adam, 9, 13, 24, 25–26, 49
   Having dominion, 140
   Humanity's unity with Adam, 104
   And image of God, 73
   In the covenant of works, 23
   Life in the garden "death-like," 21, 32
   Pre-fall Adam without sin but not glorified, 14–15, 23, 32
   Pre-fall body of Adam, 22
   Relation to the animals, 73, 76
Adamic epoch correlated with death, 21, 28n8, 32, 33
Age, aeon, present age, age to come, 8, 9, 21n2, 34, 51, 63, 66, 122, 123, 144
Anabaptist, 55, 57, 116
Animals, 22, 58, 72, 73–74, 76, 77n24, 78, 83, 106n102
Annihilation, Annihilationism, 16, 92, 93, 100n78, 114, 136
Aristotle, Aristotelian, 17, 71n4, 77n24, 98, 99–100
Association for Reformed Political Action, 58

Barth, Karl, 4–5, 116
Bavinck, Herman, 14–15, 61, 100, 101, 125
Belgic Confession, 105, 115, 122
Bell, Rob, 113, 116–117

Biologos, 73–75
Braaten, Carl, 2–3

Calvin, John, 71n5, 99, 101, 149, 150, 152
Canons of Dort, 98
Cartesian, Cartesianism, see Descartes, René
Change, political/social/cultural, 63–5
Childs, Brevard, 45
Christ, see God—Son.
Christian home, 67
Cooper, John, 6, 70n1, 75n19, 82n36, 91, 100
Conditional immortality, 118–119
Corcoran, Kevin, 72, 103
Covenant
   Covenant of works, 14, 23
   Covenant of grace, 21, 27, 28, 153
Creeds (of Nicea, Chalcedon), 26, 105, 140
Creation order anticipates Spiritual order, 23
Culture, cultural engagement, 13, 56, 57, 59, 67, 94, 138, 140

De Visser, Arjan, 17–18, 143–158
Democracy, 58, 64
Descartes, René, 17, 77, 98–100, 106, 107
Dooyeweerd, Herman, 100

Ecology, 76, 94
Eden, Garden of, 21, 25, 27, 28, 32, 92–93, 139

Subject and Name Index

Edwards, Jonathan, 115n7, 123n26
Eschatology, eschatological, eschaton
   Advance from physical to spiritual, 23
   Already-not yet tension, 8, 14, 15, 17, 54, 63, 64, 140–141
   Contrast of sub-eschatological and eschatological, 21, 23
   "Day of the Lord," 43
   Distinct uses of term, 1–2, 15, 18, 37
   Etymology and origins of term, 1–2
   Eschaton, 1–2, 4, 7, 11, 36–37, 127
   Eschatological fulness in Christ by the Spirit, 20–21, 27–28, 32, 34
   Eschatological vs. protological life, 25–26, 28n8
   The "last days," 8, 9, 11, 17, 54, 65
   Limits of application, 49–51
   And Reformed liturgy, 150–156
   Longing for Christ's return, 156, 157
   Preaching of eschatology, 147–150
   Reformed vs. Lutheran views of eschatology, 14
   Synonym for redemptive-historical, 2, 8
Evolution, Theistic evolution, 16–17, 72–75
Exile, exiles, exile and citizenship, 55, 59, 63, 64

Fergusson, David, 2
Feser, Edward, 104n92, 106, 107
Flavel, John, 100–101
Flood, 17, 61, 135, 137
Forgive, forgiveness, 21, 29–30, 33, 80, 82, 146, 154
Fudge, Edward, 113, 118–119, 127–128

Gaffin, Richard, 8, 11–12, 26n6, 27n7
Gerhardsson, Berger, 79n31, 82n38, 91
Green, Joel, 72, 75, 91
God
   Attributes of God, 6, 43, 105, 117, 122, 124–125
   Father, 25n5, 67, 93, 153, 156
   Son, 20–35, 93, 105, 140, 153, 156
   Holy Spirit, 20–35, 96, 98, 147, 148
   Trinity, 6, 25n5, 105, 108, 153

Hauerwas, Stanley, 55
Heart (*lēv* and *kardia*), 62–63, 79–82, 85, 87–88, 89–90, 97, 98, 117, 132, 147, 150, 155–156
Heaven, heavenly realms, heavenly country, 7, 9, 16, 17, 63, 64, 67, 71, 85–86, 90, 94, 96, 108, 117, 134–135, 138–142, 144–147, 150, 154–156
Heidelberg Catechism, 45, 66, 71, 76, 93, 96–97, 122, 125, 130, 131, 132, 135
Hell, 7, 16, 42, 70, 71, 92, 112–132
   Differing views on hell, 114–119
   First death and second death, 128–129
   Four key issues, 119
   Helps us appreciate Christ's work, 131
   Jesus speaks of hell, 116
   Pictures of hell, 115
   Preaching about hell, 129–131
   Reasons to study hell, 112–113
   Weeping and gnashing of teeth, 125–126
Hendriksen, William, 65n25&27, 67n31, 115
Hermeneutics, 34, 39, 91, 138
   Application, 40, 49–51
   Explication, 37–44
   Implication, 37, 44–49
   Meditation, 40–41
   Poetry, 40
   Setting, 40
   Translation, 40, 50–51, 56
   Redemptive-historical, 2, 3, 10, 12, 38, 51
   Typology, 38, 45, 49
Historia salutis and *ordo salutis*, 10, 27–28
Hoekema, Anthony, 54n1, 136–137, 141n9
Holy Spirit, see God—Holy Spirit
Hughes, Philip E., 113, 118

Intermediate State, 16, 70, 90–97, 102, 107–108, 134

Subject and Name Index

Jenson, Robert, 2–3
Jerusalem, New Jerusalem, Jerusalem that is above, 34, 46, 49, 55–56, 120, 138
John the Baptist, 16, 59–60, 120
Judgment, Final judgment, 43

Kingdom of God, Two Kingdoms, 3, 10, 11, 16, 44, 61–67, 64, 105, 148, 149, 155
Kline, Meredith, 25n5
Kuyper, Abraham, 16, 60, 63, 100

Law, biblical and natural, 60
Lincoln, Andrew, 91, 96n66
Lindberg, Carter, 148
Liturgy, Reformed, and eschatology, 150–156
  Ascension Day service, 157
  Baptism, 153–154
  Lord's Supper, 154–156
  Prayers, 152
  Psalms and Hymns, 152–3
Longman, Tremper, 83, 84n41
Luther, Martin; Lutherans, 14–15, 148–149

Merricks, Trenton, 72, 103–104
Middleton, J. Richard, 139
Millennial views, 12–13
Mitchell, David, 46–47
Moritz, Joseph, 74
Mosaic epoch correlated with death, 21, 32, 33
Moses, 28–33
  Chart of contrasts with Christ, 33
Mostert, Christiaan, 5
Murphy, Nancey, 72, 78

New creation, 17, 78, 86, 134–143

Origen, 116

Pannenberg, Wolfhart, 2n5, 5–7
Paradise (see Eden, Garden of)
Pentecost, 12, 20–21, 27–28, 49, 150
Physicalism, 71–76, 98, 104–108
Pilgrims, 16, 55, 63

Placebo effect, 106
Plantinga, Alvin, 106
Plato, Platonic, Platonism, 17, 77, 94, 95–96, 98, 99, 100
Priestley, Joseph, 107
Psalms, Psalter
  Books 1–5, 46–47
  Christology, 48–49
  Didactic and eschatological, 47, 51
  Editors of the Psalms collection, 45–47
  Interconnectedness of, 47–48
  Interpretation of, 40, 47
  Structure of, 46, 47–48,
  Timeless, catholic character, 51
Political activity of Christians, 16, 54–67
Redemptive-historical, see Eschatology and Hermeneutics

Renewal
  Of the world, 54, 136–137
  Of the believer, 98, 135
Resurrection of Christ, 4, 8, 9, 11, 21, 24–27, 32–33, 105
Resurrection body of Christians (see also Soul, relation to body), 11, 21–22, 42n10, 70, 75, 90, 93, 95, 97, 102, 103, 134–135, 139–140, 153
  Contrasted to Adam's body, 23–4
  Contrasted to present "dead" body, 23–4
  Christ inaugurates genus of, 25
  Spiritual body, 25
Ridderbos, Herman, 10–11, 64n24, 66n29
Runia, Klaas, 5n12

Schilder, Klaas, 7, 14, 45n21, 95
Schweitzer, Albert, 3
Sin, 4, 124–126, 156
Scougal, Henry, 90
Sheol (*Šĕ'ôl*), 41–43, 81, 86, 87
Shakespeare, William, 89
Shalom, 56
Smith, James K. A., 13
Smith, Jannes (John), vii, ix, 36–53, 104

161

Subject and Name Index

Soul, self, etc. (*nepeš* and *psychē*)
  Activities and experiences of the soul, 81, 82
  Animal soul, 77n24, 83, 89–90
  Dead souls, 88–89
  In second death, 128
  Nature of the soul, 82, 85, 91, 100, 102, 108
  Relation to the body, 77, 81, 83, 91, 97–98, 99, 101–102
  Relation to spirit, heart, mind, 79–80, 81, 82, 97–98, 106
  Righteous and wicked souls, 71
  Soul sleep, 71n4&5, 72, 108n105
  Survivalism versus corruptionism, 102–103
  Uses of Hebrew for "soul," 40, 42, 77–78, 83n39, 87–88
Spirit (*rūaḥ* and *pneuma*)
  Human spirit, 81, 82–83, 86–87, 88–89
  Divine Spirit (see also Holy Spirit), 81
Stott, John, 113, 118
Strohl, Jane E., 149
Suffering as a Christian, 66
Sursum corda, 147, 150

Telder, Bartus, 41n8, 71n4&5
Temple, tabernacle, 58, 85–86, 90, 139, 145, 146
Templeton Foundation, 73
Three Forms of Unity, Confessions of Faith, 98, 135
  See also Belgic Confession, Heidelberg Catechism, Canons of Dort
Thomas, Thomas Aquinas, Thomism, 17, 77, 98–100, 102, 107
Thurneysen, Eduard, 140–141
Tigger, 49
Tipton, Lane, ix, 13–14, 20–35
Translation, see Hermeneutics

Universalism, 16, 116–117, 120–123

Van Dam, Cornelis, 15–16, 54–69
VanDrunen, David, 16, 61–62
Van Raalte, Theodore G. (Ted), vii, ix, 16–17, 1–19, 70–111
Van Vliet, Jason, 16, 112–133
Venema, Cornelis, 62, 65n28, 90, 94n58
Vermigli, Peter Martyr, 100
Visscher, Gerhard, 16, 134–142
Vos, Geerhardus, 7–10, 20, 40n5, 43n15, 45n22, 47n28

Wenham, John, 112n1, 113, 118, 127n34
Westminster Confession of Faith, 15, 71
Westminster Larger Catechism, 94
Wilson, Gerald, 45–46
Wiskerke, J. R., 41n8, 71n5
Witness, witnesses, witnessing, 65, 66–67
Worship, 17, 145–147
Wright, N. T., 75, 137n6

Scripture Index

OLD TESTAMENT

Genesis

1:26	74
2:7	22, 23, 24, 77–79, 81, 83, 84, 89
2:19	78
3:19	83, 86
5:24	86
12:2–3	56
17:8	141

Exodus

3:14	151
20:12	151
21:24	118
24:11	154
25:9, 40	86
32–34	29–32
32:30	29
32:32	29
33:3	29
33:14	29
34:6	117

Leviticus

12:11	88
19:28	89

Deuteronomy

4:6	56
6:5	79, 89
32:4	118

Job

2:9	93
19:21–27	150
19:21	90
32:18	81
33:4	81
34:15	86

Psalms

1–150	36–51
1	47
1:5–6	43
2	48
2:9–12	44
4:7	44
5:5, 6	43
6	81
6:5	42, 88
7:6	44
7:8	43
8	49
9:8	43
9:16–18	43
9:17	42

Psalms *(continued)*

Reference	Page
11:4	43, 85
12:5	43
16	49
16:10	42
16:11	43
16:19	150
17:3	81
17:15	43
18:5	42
18:6	85
19:14	81
22:22	147
26:2	81
27:4	85–86
29:1	86
29:9	85, 86
30:3	81
30:8–9	88
30:9	44
31:9	80
31:17	42
34:2	44
34:20	42
34:22	42
35:9, 10	42
35:16	126
35:23	44
37:11	141
37:12	126
38:3	80
42–43	76, 81
44:23	44
48:14, 15	43
49	90
49:7–15	86–87
49:14	42
49:15	150
49:19	87
50	46
50:4	43
51:4	43, 124
51:10	81
55:15	42
56:8	44
57:1	81
57:7	81
61:4	85
62:1	81
62:5	81
63:1	81
63:2–5	81
63:8	81
65:6	79
67	56
73–83	46
73	90
73:17	87
73:24–26	87–88
73:24	43
82:8	43
84:2	81
85:10–13	44
86:2	81
86:13	42
88:3	42
88:5–12	88
88:10–12	42, 44
88:11	41
89	46
90–106	46
90:2	79, 123
90:3	86
90:8–12	44
93:1	44
94:2	43
95:5	79
96:10–13	44
96:10	43
96:13	43
98:4–9	44
98:9	43
99:1	85
101:5–8	44
102:25	44
103:1–5	80
103:1	80
103:19	85
104:29	86
107:23	43
108:1	81
109:24	80
110	46
110:6	43, 44
111–118	47

Scripture Index

112	49
112:9–10	43
115	90
115:5–8	88
115:17–18	42, 88
116:3	41, 42
116:7	81
121:4	44
124:8	150
133:3	43
137	56
138:8	151
139:16	44
140:10–13	43
145	44
145:20	43
146:7–9	43
147:2–3	43
149:6–9	44

Ecclesiastes

3:18–20	83
3:21	83, 84
12:1–14	84
12:7	83–85, 89

Isaiah

26:19	90
31:3	81
42:6	56
55:3–7	82–83
57:1–2	84
60:6	138
65–66	150
65:17–19	141–142
66:22–24	127
66:24	92, 128–129

Jeremiah

7:29	115
29:5–7	55–56
29:6	56
29:10	56
33:31–33	82–83

Lamentations

2:16	126

Ezekiel

36:16–32	85
37	24, 26, 85, 89
37:1–14	84
37:13–14	84
40–48	150

Daniel

1	58
3	58
4:27	58
4:34–37	58
6	58
6:25–27	58
12:2	90, 114

Hosea

11:8	117

Joel

2:28—3:21	150

Habakkuk

3:6	123

Scripture Index

Zechariah

9–14	46
12:1	78

Malachi

4:1–3	127–128

NEW TESTAMENT

Matthew

2:13	128
4:17	129
5:1–2	130
5:2	132
5:5	141
5:8	95
5:10	66
5:11	44
5:13–16	67
5:17–20	124
5:22	124, 131
5:29–30	124
5:38	118
6:13	64
7:13–14	118, 128
7:23	129
8:11	155
8:12	125, 130
8:25	128
9:17	128
10:1–5	130
10:6	128
10:28	92, 115, 118, 128, 130
11:28	132
12:14	128
12:28	64
13:31–32	67
13:33	64
13:42	125
13:50	125
14:3–4	59
22:13	125
24–25	150
24:14	148
24:51	125
25:21, 23	67
25:30	125
25:31–46	118
25:41	115, 129
25:46	115
26:29	154
27:20	128
27:50	93

Mark

2:1–12	64
9:48	92, 129, 130
10:15	64

Luke

3:8	120
3:17	120
3:19	59
6:22	44
13:11–16	64
13:28	125
16:19–31	75, 114
16:27–31	92
17:29	128
19:17	140
23:43	75, 92–93
23:46	75, 93
24:44	45

John

3:16	114
3:18	117
4:13–14	83
4:24	76, 105
5:27	131
5:39	45
6:15	65
6:39	54

Scripture Index

7:37	83
10:35	49
12:48	54
14:2–3	95
14:6	120
15:9	126
16:26	120
18:36	65
19:30	93

Acts

2:17	54
2:25–35	49
2:25, 31	45
3:21	141
5:41	44, 66
7:54	126
7:59	93
7:60	94
9:4	66
13:6–12	59
14:22	66
21:7	54
22:22–30	59
22:24–26	59
23:11	60
24:25	59
27:24	60

Romans

1:16–17	148
1:30	126
4:13	141
6:4	136
6:23	23
8:16	76
8:17	66
8:22	140
8:38–39	105
9–11	120
9:5	123
9:15	123
9:18	123
12:1–2	98
12:2	104
13:1–5	57
14:11	64
16:25–26	123
16:26	128

1 Corinthians

2:2	130
2:9	67
2:16	132
3:14	67
6:12–20	95
6:13, 20	141
10:20–31	58
11:26	154
13:10	132
13:12–13	95
13:12	105
15	139
15:18	94
15:42–49	21–28
15:58	67

2 Corinthians

3:6–18	21, 28–32
3:18	66, 132
5:1–9	95–97
5:8	103
5:10	114, 132
5:17	76, 136
9:6–11	49

Galatians

1:4	34
3:4–29	34
3:14	34
4:3	34
4:6	34
6:15	136

Scripture Index

Ephesians

1	120
2:18	33
2:22	33
3:4–6	123
4:6	123
5:8	67

Philippians

1:7	94
1:13	94
1:21–24	94–95
1:21	44
1:23	45, 76, 96, 103
2:10–11	64
3:20	55
3:21	135

Colossians

1:20	140

1 Thessalonians

1:10	150
4:14	94

2 Thessalonians

1:7–10	64
2:8	64

1 Timothy

2:1–2	57, 121
2:3–4	120
2:4	116, 117, 121
4:15	120–121

2 Timothy

3:1	54
4:1,2	147

Titus

2:1–10	121
2:11	117, 121
3:3	126

Hebrews

2:1	144
2:3	144
2:5	144
2:7	145
2:8	64
2:9	145
2:10	145
2:12	147
4:9	144
4:11	145
4:16	145
6:5	144
7:25	145
8:1	145
8:5	86
8:6	146
9:24	145
9:27	149
10:19	145
10:21, 22	150
10:25	144
11:16	144
12:22–24	150
12:22	146
13:8	151
13:14	144
13:15–16	145

James

1:2	44

1 Peter

1:3	136
1:7	136
1:23	136
2:11	55
4:12–13	66

2 Peter

1:4	105
3:6	135
3:10–12	135–138
3:10	17
3:13	141

1 John

4:16	117

Revelation

1:1	130
1:4–5	151
1:7	54
3:11	151
4–6	108
6:9–11	96, 99
6:10	103
7:9	121
9:11	41
11:3–10	65
11:11–19	64
12:12	64
14:9–11	115–116
14:11	123, 129
14:13	67
19:3	124
19:6–9	147
19:9	154
19:20	115
20:1	124
20:11–15	114
20:14	128
20:15	120
21	138, 139
21:8	128
21:24, 26	138
21:16	139
21:27	120
22:3	139
22:5	124, 140
22:7	54, 147, 151
22:12	151
22:15	120
22:17	152
22:20	151, 157

www.ingramcontent.com/pod-product-compliance
Lightning Source LLC
Chambersburg PA
CBHW071458150426
43191CB00008B/1384